Published by Straight Talk Books
P.O. Box 301, Milwaukee, WI 53201
800.661.3311 • timeofgrace.org

Cover image: © Stephen Strathdee/Thinkstock

Printed in the United States of America

ISBN: 978-0615831541

grace
for today

Dedication

I would like to dedicate this book to two amazing people, Daryl and Nancy Raabe. It is difficult to imagine how Time of Grace could have survived its birth without their leadership and sacrifice. They were among the four initial donors who helped us raise our start-up capital to hire a producer and install television equipment in St. Marcus Church. Nancy served without pay as our first staff person and worked for years to build the business office. Daryl has been the chairman of the board of directors for Time of Grace's entire history. Thank you, my friends, for your vision, determination, multitude of talents, and generous spirit.

Introduction

"Grace and peace to you from God our Father and the Lord Jesus Christ," Paul wrote (Galatians 1:3).

Grace belongs to you too, but I'm not sure that people know what a treasure they have. In ordinary English usage, *grace* means elegance and beauty in movement and style.

But in the Bible, *grace* has a hugely important additional meaning: the undeserved, unconditional, universal love that God has for all people, past, present, and future. In the Bible, *grace* means that God chooses to love the unlovable, forgive sinners, and pardon criminals. It encompasses the Father's willingness to sacrifice his own Son on a cross, the Son's willingness to humble himself to the point of death in order to lift us up, and the Spirit's determination to work within us to believe and live the gospel.

We've decided to call these daily devotions *Grace for Today*, because everything important in our lives is built on God's grace to us. By grace God now views us as his children; we can stop beating ourselves up and rejoice in our new identity. By grace God pours his favor on us; we can now assume that we have divine help in our thinking and talking. By grace God chooses to listen compassionately to our every prayer; we can assume that we can count on him to be with us wherever we go. By grace we can show other people the same mercy and kindness that God first showed us.

If your life is as crazy busy as mine, you know how easy it is to skip a touch with God's wonderful Word. These little daily devotions are Bible studies for busy people. Each one has a story, an application, but most important of all, a nugget of God's Word to encourage you in your faith and in the certainty that you live in grace. God's grace.

Pastor Mark Jeske

January

"Do not fear, for I am with you; do not be dismayed, for I am your God. I will strengthen you and help you; I will uphold you with my righteous right hand."

(Isaiah 41:10)

January 1

a fresh start

Don't you wish you could be more selective about your memory?

My computer's hard drive remembers only what I want it to remember. Pictures that are fuzzy or taken by mistake when I bumped the camera trigger? Delete! Drafts of letters I never sent? Delete! Piles of spam e-mails? Delete! But why oh why do I continue to remember things that still bring me pain years after they first happened? Why do old sins come back to haunt me? Why do little irritations refuse to go away? Why am I still angry with people whom I thought I had forgiven?

New Year's Day is a great time for fresh starts, and one of my goals this year is to take out the trash in my brain. Starting today, I am not going to let the debris of the past clutter up my service to the Lord or rob me of my joy at being his child. No more grudges; no more guilt; no more revenge fantasies; no more self-pity. St. Paul is my mentor: **"One thing I do: Forgetting what is behind and straining toward what is ahead, I press on toward the goal to win the prize for which God has called me heavenward in Christ Jesus"** (Philippians 3:13,14).

Care to join me?

_____

_____

_____

_____

_____

Jesus went first; I will be okay

St. Paul wrote in 1 Corinthians that the true sting of death is the sin that caused it. Human mortality is not beautiful. It is part of the divine curse on human evil. We do well to respect it and understand it.

But we do not have to fear it. The reason for that confidence? Our divine and human Savior, Jesus Christ, took on our humanity in order to experience fully every aspect of human life, including the experience of dying. He already went through the process of watching his life ebb away.

By bearing our death for us in that way, he took all the sting out of it. **"Surely he took up our infirmities and carried our sorrows. . . . He was pierced for our transgressions, he was crushed for our iniquities; the punishment that brought us peace was upon him, and by his wounds we are healed"** (Isaiah 53:4,5).

This means that dying is not the beginning of the end of everything; it is the beginning of the beginning of everything. It doesn't signify the loss of everything but rather the gaining of everything. Through Jesus' dying, you are guaranteed forgiveness of your sins, a "not guilty" verdict in God's court, and peace with God forever.

_____

_____

_____

_____

_____

January 3

show patience at home

It is one of the sad consequences of our competitive, media-driven, consumerist culture that we expect perfection in others but excuse mediocrity in ourselves. Restaurants and hotels live on the edge, knowing that all it takes is one bad experience and a customer will never be back.

When you first get married, you are marrying a rookie, someone who will make rookie mistakes. That's why God tells husbands and wives to let go of Mommy and Daddy and stick like glue to their spouses—never, ever comparing a husband to Daddy or a wife to Mom. It's an inherently unfair comparison, since you are remembering mature veterans. Cut your spouse some slack.

"As God's chosen people, holy and dearly loved, clothe yourselves with . . . patience. Bear with each other and forgive whatever grievances you may have against one another" (Colossians 3:12,13).

Think of how often God has had to be patient with you. Think of how he has nurtured you and put up with stuff and invested energy and resources in you. Think of how you learned from your failures and thrived on encouragement and praise. Well, hello! How about extending some of that same patience to your spouse?

Lord, forgive us our sins as we forgive our spouses who sin against us.

---

be an optimist

We live in an age of cynicism.

If you listen to today's hipsters and pundits and comedians, the dominant theme is sarcasm. The baby boomers were doubters, but their children don't believe in much of anything anymore. They mock it all. All social institutions are viewed as inherently flawed and passé— government is assumed to be abusive; businesses all just organized rip-offs; the church corrupt and lying; and monogamous, lifelong marriage just slavery.

Our world needs Christians and the Christian message more than ever. We can be bringers and explainers of hope to a world that is desperate for something noble and big and good to believe in again. We can spread a message that our God is still powerful and wise and loving and that he is already living in the future to make it better for his believers.

Who could be more of an idealist than a biblical Christian? **"Wait for the Lord; be strong and take heart and wait for the Lord"** (Psalm 27:14). For believers the future is always better than the past. Christ makes optimists of us all, for he is already writing the ending chapters of the book of our lives *and they contain a happy ending.*

Do you believe this? Do you know someone who needs to hear this?

_____

_____

_____

_____

_____

you have backup

By now you've watched enough TV cop shows to know that an officer should never go into a dangerous building alone. Always call for backup.

How can a parent ever fully relax? When your kids are little, they are vulnerable to a thousand dangers and risks, from SIDS to choking to falling down the stairs. But the risks are just as big when they are high schoolers and go out on the streets by themselves. What parent of teenagers hasn't worried about automobile accidents, alcohol, and drugs?

Once Jesus scolded his disciples for brushing off the importance of children. In that rebuke is a marvelous comfort for every Christian parent: **"See that you do not look down on one of these little ones. For I tell you that their angels in heaven always see the face of my Father in heaven"** (Matthew 18:10).

Did you catch the significance? You have backup! God's powerful angels have specific personal assignments, and they know the names and whereabouts of the little ones at all times. They must report to the Father and have all of his authority and power behind them.

Someday, when we're in heaven, God may choose to tell us how many hair-raising disasters his invisible agents averted. Maybe we'll get to meet the angels who watched over our kids. I hope so—I've got a big load of thanks to deliver.

_____

_____

_____

_____

_____

exalt your God

I'm pretty sure you haven't heard the word *exalt* this week. It's one of those Bible words that most people don't use regularly.

But you can probably figure out what it means. "Alt" is from the same word as "altitude." Altitude is your elevation, i.e., how high you are. Now you might think that God is already way up in the skies and he doesn't need any more altitude. As the Most High God, he's as far up there as he can get, right?

Well, I'll tell you one place where he's not at the highest possible point—and that's in your heart. That's where he needs some hoisting and mud jacking. When you exalt God, you lift him up where he belongs—above you!

You exalt him when you look up and say, **"Yours, O Lord, is the greatness and the power and the glory and the majesty and the splendor, for everything in heaven and earth is yours. Yours, O Lord, is the kingdom; you are exalted as head over all"** (1 Chronicles 29:11).

So today, let him know, "God, you are big and great and amazing! Today I'm going to treat you the way you deserve. I'm proud of you. Today I'm going to *exalt* you."

_____

_____

_____

_____

_____

January 7

I am with you

Of all the losses that the human race sustained when Adam and Eve were driven out of the Garden of Eden, one of the most grievous was the loss of direct and immediate contact with God. Now that relationship would have to be built and nourished "at a distance," as it were. Because our minds are clouded with sin and weakness, we tend not to believe in things we can't see or touch. We are all doubting Thomases at times.

Sometimes God may seem very remote or not there at all. Pink Floyd has a line in one of its songs, "Is there anybody out there?" In your darker moments of weakness and despair, have you ever feared that nobody was listening to your cries for help?

God no longer physically walks the earth as he did in the person of Jesus Christ, but he is always present in many ways. **"Never will I leave you; never will I forsake you"** (Hebrews 13:5). His Spirit fills the universe. His Word reveals his mind and purpose and mighty acts. The splash of baptismal water is your adoption ceremony and the seal of his ownership claims. The Supper merges his divine body and blood with yours.

He is near to you right now.

_____

_____

_____

_____

_____

real wealth

Are you a wealthy person? You'd probably say no. You've probably fantasized a thousand times about what you'd do if you had some real money. There's always a better car, a better house, a better paycheck dangling in front of you.

But you really are wealthy, you know. Jesus Christ has made you a spiritual millionaire. Everything on this earth is fading; only what is in heaven will last. Possessing cash is like playing a temporary board game—you have a little fun and then it's over. The Bible tells us the marvelous story of how God's Son, Lord of the universe, impoverished himself on this planet so that he could give us access to the eternal joy of heaven.

"You know the grace of our Lord Jesus Christ, that though he was rich, yet for your sakes he became poor, so that you through his poverty might become rich" (2 Corinthians 8:9). Your greatest treasure is the forgiveness of sins that you enjoy through the shed blood of Jesus. For it is that forgiveness which guarantees that you may call yourself Jesus' brother or sister and claim heaven as your real home.

Heaven eternally is better than cash right now. Do you believe that?

_____

_____

_____

_____

_____

January 9

our living Redeemer

There are times in our lives when we feel strong, smart, invincible, immortal, and totally in control. And then there are those times when we know we are broken, miserable, weak, lost, and trapped. The apostle Paul didn't mind those times. God had told him, **"My grace is sufficient for you, for my power is made perfect in weakness"** (2 Corinthians 12:9).

That's why Paul could conclude, **"Therefore I will boast all the more gladly about my weaknesses, so that Christ's power may rest on me. That is why, for Christ's sake, I delight in weaknesses, in insults, in hardships, in persecutions, in difficulties. For when I am weak, then I am strong"** (verses 9,10).

One of the most precious names for our God is "Redeemer." A redeemer is a mighty rescuer—often a relative—who bails you out of a tough situation at great personal cost.

You have a living Redeemer in Jesus, who willingly gave his life so that you could live with him forever. He doesn't mind it at all when you feel weak. When you are full of yourself and proud, you don't feel like you need God. It is only when you cry out your need to him that he can fill it with himself.

will she encourage your faith?

Do strong dating relationships just happen, more or less by accident, or are they carefully chosen? I guess the answer is both. Sometimes you plan the relationship. And sometimes you are startled to realize that you have fallen in love with someone you thought was just a friend. A key question is what to do when you realize that you are getting deeper and deeper into a relationship with someone who is not a Christian.

It's just not a good idea for a Christian to marry a non-Christian. **"Do not be yoked together with unbelievers. For what do righteousness and wickedness have in common?"** (2 Corinthians 6:14). Granted—that is a principle, not a law. It is possible, of course, that you may help an unbeliever come to faith in Christ. But it is just as likely that the nonbeliever will become a boat anchor in your spiritual life and drag you under.

What will married life be like if your faith in Christ is just tolerated? mocked? sabotaged? resented?

Wouldn't you rather go through life with someone who will pray for you? pray with you? go to church with you? read the Scriptures with you? sing hymns with you? receive Holy Communion with you? be a true partner in raising your children as Christians?

_____

_____

_____

_____

_____

I'm in prison

Some chains are visible. St. Paul's certainly were. Imprisoned first in Jerusalem, then Caesarea, then in Rome, he died a captive, a victim of the first wave of official persecution of Christians by the Roman Empire. Joseph spent time in an Egyptian prison, falsely accused of sexual assault on his employer's wife.

Shadrach, Meshach, and Abednego were bound and sentenced to die by King Nebuchadnezzar of Babylon. Their courageous testimony in front of a blazing furnace is a masterpiece of courage, trust, and serene resignation: **"If we are thrown into the blazing furnace, the God we serve is able to save us from it, and he will rescue us from your hand, O king. But even if he does not, we want you to know, O king, that we will not serve your gods or worship the image of gold you have set up"** (Daniel 3:17,18).

God can use even imprisonment of his children to advance his saving agenda. Through his guidance, faith is planted and strengthened in human hearts and he is given glory. The prophet Isaiah said that **"freedom for the captives and release . . . for the prisoners"** (61:1) is a thrilling part of Christ's gospel work. Sometimes he brought about truly miraculous releases—Shadrach and friends and Joseph were not only released but promoted to high governmental positions. Corrie ten Boom survived the Nazi concentration camp at Ravensbrück through a miraculous "clerical error."

Some, like St. Paul and Dietrich Bonhoeffer, bring glory to God by suffering martyrdom. Their release from prison coincided with release from all earthly suffering.

you're not on your own

A repeated human tragedy that always hurts my heart is to hear about a child who was abandoned by both parents. The kid later says, "I've been on my own since I was _____" (fill in the blank here with some terribly young age).

Satan seeks to destroy you spiritually, and so he lies to you. He wants you to fear that you've been abandoned by your God, that you're on your own in life, that God only watches from above but is not actually engaged in making anything happen for you personally.

This is rot. God does indeed watch over you personally and individually, all the time. But he also acts on your behalf, giving you the things you need and arranging things to make your life better. Read Psalm 121 for its intensely personal comfort: **"The LORD watches over you. . . . [He] will neither slumber nor sleep. . . . The LORD will keep you from all harm—he will watch over your life . . . both now and forevermore"** (verses 5,4,7,8).

You never walk alone.

_____

_____

_____

_____

_____

God in my senior years

An elderly saint always had the same complaint when I came to visit him: "Ah, I'm no good no more." Physical pain, dim eyesight, and loneliness had ground away his sense of being worth something.

He was so focused on what he didn't have that he missed the joy of using what he did have. The more we realize that we are actors in God's play, in which he provides the script and tells us the roles he needs us to play, the happier we will be. The Bible tells amazing stories of the great things that God accomplished through people in their 70s, 80s, and 90s, people like Abraham, Moses, and the apostle John.

Not only will God show us how we can be useful to his agenda; he promises to help us along as our bodies grow weaker. **"Even to your old age and gray hairs I am he, I am he who will sustain you. I have made you and I will carry you; I will sustain you and I will rescue you"** (Isaiah 46:4).

Seniors are just as valuable to God as people of any other age. You don't have to be afraid of your final years—your God will fill them and help you home with confidence and joy. Call on him for what you need. Let him use you where he needs you.

_____

_____

_____

_____

_____

I'm afraid of losing my job

The 21st century has been a hard ride so far, hasn't it? As the economy changes, positions change. Jobs disappear. New positions arise for which few are prepared. Old companies go under. Marketing overseas is no longer an option for many firms—it is life or death. More and more American products go abroad, but so do more and more jobs.

How many people do you know who have lost their jobs? Are you fearful for yours? Have you had hours reduced? a pay freeze? benefits cut? pressure for early retirement? regular corporate layoffs? Have you had to burn up savings to survive? Do you know people who fear losing their homes?

Constant money anxiety erodes the soul, doesn't it? Money fear and money arguments damage marriages. Parents feel like failures because they can't invest in their children's education the way they would like.

Only God could dare to promise us that he blesses us even when we are weak and broken. In his most painful and miserable moments, Paul heard God's voice: **"He said to me, 'My grace is sufficient for you, for my power is made perfect in weakness.' Therefore I will boast all the more gladly about my weaknesses, so that Christ's power may rest on me"** (2 Corinthians 12:9).

_____

_____

_____

_____

_____

let go of anger

Emperor Palpatine spoke for Satan himself, and spoke also for the unconverted beast inside each of us, when he tried to goad Luke Skywalker into violence: "Give in to your anger. . . . Make yourself more my servant. . . . I can feel your anger. . . . Let the hate flow through you."

People generally like being angry. It makes them feel righteous and aggrieved. We love it when movie characters burst out of their passivity and good manners: "I'm mad as h---, and I'm not going to take it anymore." We admire gangsters who bypass the (slow) criminal justice system and simply carry out their own revenge.

Anger usually destroys. It rarely builds. **"My dear brothers, take note of this: Everyone should be quick to listen, slow to speak and slow to become angry, for man's anger does not bring about the righteous life that God desires"** (James 1:19,20).

Let go. Let God take care of retribution and vengeance. Pray for the Spirit's brakes on your mouth. Forgive your enemies . . . and your friends.

God is full of compassion

Do you put off thinking about God because you are so ashamed of certain features of your life? Do you find it hard to pray because you would feel like such a hypocrite? Have you sinned often, not out of ignorance but in spite of knowing better?

Are you possibly afraid of God himself? Are you afraid that judgment day will be terrifying because you are so unworthy? Are you afraid to die? Well, guess what—your Savior Jesus knew that you needed his help. He died and rose again to take away your guilt. All of it. He did it, not to give a reward to the perfect but to be able to forgive sinful fools like you and me.

In repentance and faith, throw your guilt at the foot of his cross. In Luke chapter 15, Jesus tells us that when the prodigal son returned home in sorrow, he humbled himself before his father: **"His father saw him and was filled with compassion for him; he ran to his son, threw his arms around him and kissed him"** (verse 20).

That's the kind of hug from God that is waiting for you.

_____

_____

_____

_____

_____

mutual submission

I read somewhere that China's leaders are finding out that their "one child" policy is producing a whole generation of spoiled and self-centered only children. I guess I'd have to agree that siblings sure can keep you humble.

At our family's last holiday gathering, the pictures and movie clips that brought most shrieks of laughter and mockery were those that portrayed family members in an embarrassing way. I hope my relatives were laughing with me and not at me.

It's not such a bad thing to be taken down a few pegs. Satan is always trying to get us to self-inflate with the flatus of ego. It is a good thing to make oneself small and others big. St. Paul wrote, **"Submit to one another out of reverence for Christ"** (Ephesians 5:21).

Home is a great place to practice complimenting, comforting, and cleaning up after other people. Home is a great place to practice treating other people as more important than you, of extending yourself and expending yourself to make somebody else's life better. If you can't love your parents, siblings, and kids unconditionally, you probably won't be able to do it for anyone.

Why put yourself through this? Out of reverence for Christ, of course.

_____

_____

_____

_____

_____

pray with confidence

Here's a prayer misconception that God would like to correct. You would think that an appropriate attitude for needy, often foolish, often backsliding Christians when they approach the throne would be absolute humility. You would think that we would offer up our requests timidly, not daring to think that the Great One would think our little problems as worth his time. You would think that we would tiptoe around him, walking on eggshells of fear, murmuring our needs quickly, and then backing away toward the door.

Nonsense, says the apostle James. You are God's beloved child, a royal prince or princess of heaven, a royal priest of the heavenly temple. God wants you to believe in the importance of your requests and believe him when he says he eagerly receives information about the parts of your life in which you need help. **"When he asks, he must believe and not doubt, because he who doubts is like a wave of the sea, blown and tossed by the wind. That man should not think he will receive anything from the Lord; he is a double-minded man, unstable in all he does"** (James 1:6-8).

Doubt comes from Satan. If he can plant doubts in your brain and lead you to suspect that God is laughing at you, has contempt for you, is ignoring you, or is blowing off your troubles, your prayer voice will be timid indeed and soon stop. But believe his Word! Claim your new identity! Speak up! No fear! No doubts! He smiles when he sees you approach.

forgive them

How do they do it? How do kids figure out so early how to push parents' buttons? And why? Do they enjoy driving us crazy? Are they deaf? brain-dead? I mean, they don't pick up their clothes, they leave dirty dishes lying around, they hit their brother and then deny it, and then give us lip and eye rolls when we try to explain acceptable household behaviors. In our weaker moments, fatigue and self-pity can lead us to nurse an ongoing resentment toward our own children. What to do?

One of Jesus' disciples, Simon Peter, thought that forgiving another person seven times was the absolute ultimate limit. **"How many times shall I forgive my brother . . . seven times?"** Listen to Jesus' reply: **"I tell you, not seven times, but seventy-seven times"** (Matthew 18:21,22).

You know, if we just step back a little, our kids aren't driving us any crazier than we made our own parents. And if we start limiting our patience and forgiveness with the other people in our lives, especially our kids, we are forgetting how often God still forgives us. In fact, I think one of the reasons God made childhood last so long is to teach parents how he feels about us.

Our Lord Jesus nailed all our sins to his cross, and we can bask in daily mercy and forgiveness. We honor him not only by believing his gospel promise for us but by sharing it with the young sinners around us.

---

submit to authority

It might seem as though Christians would be subversive citizens. After all, we acknowledge a monarch who is superior to our president, and our first allegiance is to Christ. The Bible to us has authoritative force greater than the U.S. Constitution.

And yet our heavenly Sovereign commands us to show respect, even submission, to our earthly government. **"*Submit* yourselves for the Lord's sake to every authority instituted among men: whether to the king, as the supreme authority, or to governors, who are sent by him to punish those who do wrong and to commend those who do right. For it is God's will that by doing good you should silence the ignorant talk of foolish men"** (1 Peter 2:13-15).

Think of Shadrach, Meshach, and Abednego again, who willingly worked in service to the Babylonian government that had destroyed their own country. Today many Christians throughout the world live in countries whose Communist or Muslim leadership is outwardly hostile to the Christian faith. An attitude of loyalty and cooperation *even to a government with which they have some strenuous disagreements* will make Christ look good and bring God's blessings.

Christians have a mandate not to be social revolutionaries but to spread the love and forgiveness of Christ. That process goes better if the ignorant talk of foolish men is silenced.

January 21

one in Christ

One of my most precious possessions is my Hank Aaron baseball card from the 1950s. When I was a kid, he was one of my heroes. I found out much later as I got older that his life as a Brave was often very difficult. When he would travel, the team, most of which were white, would stay in a regular hotel, but the colored players had to stay in a colored hotel. Hank had some painful stories to tell.

Even though the civil rights movement brought about legal equality, racism still exists. Laws can punish racist behaviors, but laws can't change people's hearts. Only the gospel can. The gospel of Jesus changes your heart and the way you think. It changes the way you feel. It takes away your fear that somebody who is different from you is going to hurt you. It helps you see the world through God's eyes.

What do God's eyes see? **"There is neither Jew nor Greek, slave nor free, male nor female, for you are *all one in Christ Jesus*"** (Galatians 3:28). God loves us all—in fact, he created diversity to make your life richer. Diversity gives you the opportunity to reach out to those who aren't a part of your tribe. To serve others who aren't like you. To join together as unique individuals who are loved by God to share a common purpose—spreading his Word.

Look around you. See someone different? Go say hi.

_____

_____

_____

_____

_____

God acts because you asked

Have you ever watched children with a piñata at a birthday party? A hollow animal has been created out of thin plaster. The blindfolded children swing a stick until someone hits the animal. As it breaks, a shower of candy and gifts pours out. When you pray, you may feel blindfolded and feel as though you are flailing about in the dark. But a prayer to God's throne in the name of Jesus always connects with a heavenly piñata, and blessings rain down *because you were swinging your stick!*

C. S. Lewis calls this the dignity of causality. God gives you and me the honor of influencing what happens tomorrow. The reason? When God hears the prayers of his children, he not only cares; he acts. **"'Because of the oppression of the weak and the groaning of the needy, I will now arise,' says the Lord"** (Psalm 12:5). Did you catch that? God loves you enough to let your thoughts and ideas and needs lead him to change his governance of the world.

Your prayers make a difference. Every prayer you say changes something somewhere. The future is not hardened and unmovable. Your prayers can alter the future.

---

your income is a blessing

It's hard to keep life in balance, isn't it? Work and play, spouse and kids, me and others.

Here's where some balanced thought is especially needed—what is the source of my income? Isn't it me? I need to get a job. I need to show up and work. The payroll checks have my name on them, don't they?

Of course they do. A problem arises, however, when we overdo that self-reliance to the point where we forget that God is the ultimate cause behind it all.

"You may say to yourself, 'My power and the strength of my hands have produced this wealth for me.' But remember the Lord your God, for it is he who gives you the ability to produce wealth, and so confirms his covenant" (Deuteronomy 8:17,18). God is certainly capable of direct miraculous intervention in our lives, and you may have some sweet stories of miracles in your life. Generally, though, he prefers to work with and through people wherever possible.

But remember that behind all the people are his busy hands, his kindly eyes, and his loving smile.

_____

_____

_____

_____

_____

one God

It's okay to have diversity of food tastes. Frankly, I have my own opinions on broccoli and Brussels sprouts. If you like them, I hope you eat them all.

I have no interest in trying to dictate your food intake. But I care intensely about what you believe in, more specifically *whom* you believe in. Because if you're off worshiping a false god, you will not only have a life that's harder and sadder than it could be, but I will be cheated of your company in heaven.

There are not many gods. There are not many equally true religious philosophies. There are not many equally valid paths to heaven. There are not many equally valid truths.

The God of the Bible is jealous about his identity and message. **"There is one body and one Spirit—just as you were called to one hope when you were called—one Lord, one faith, one baptism; one God and Father of all"** (Ephesians 4:4-6).

I hope you cultivate a very tolerant and accepting worldview when it comes to food, music, art, and tattoos. I hope you will never be ashamed to urge people to faith in the one God, the God of the Bible.

_____

_____

_____

_____

_____

talking and listening

Walt Disney knew that children wished animals could talk. So he gave them a talking mouse, duck, and dog, plus an entire chatty menagerie of other animals. Even after decades of Disney, however, animals still don't talk. People alone can do that.

God talks. It was his marvelous decision to share that ability with his children. But with that ability comes serious responsibility. When your mother was comforting you about playground bullies, she encouraged you to shrug off mean words, since "names will never hurt me." Nice try, Mom, but you know that's not true.

Words have enormous power. In fact, **"The tongue has the power of life and death"** (Proverbs 18:21). Words can crush the life and hope out of a person. Words can help a broken heart start beating again. Words are God's chosen vehicle for sharing the good news of our Savior Jesus Christ.

We could all stand a tongue overhaul in God's shop. Listen first.

_____

_____

_____

_____

_____

January 26

no fear

There is a line of BMX clothing called No Fear. I suppose the hook is to make the wearers think that they are as cool as the motocross guys who fearlessly swoop around the dirt track. Is it good to have no fear at all?

Fear in the sense of *respect* is good. We should all fear and respect Satan's vow to destroy us. We should all respect God's words and will. But sometimes our peace of mind and cheerful spirit are ruined by fears that God thinks are small. Do you dread bad things that might happen? Does your mind always go to the worst possible outcome? Does a cold make you think of pneumonia? Does a stock market dip make you dread bankruptcy?

"As for me, I watch in hope for the Lord, I wait for God my Savior; my God will hear me" (Micah 7:7). The One who is listening when you pray commands ten thousand times ten thousand angels. There is no limit to his power, to his love for you, or to his willingness to help you.

Happy life rule #1: Don't sweat the small stuff. Happy life rule #2: Relax. God thinks your troubles are mostly small stuff. No fear. Really.

_____

_____

_____

_____

_____

free from hell

As bad as aging, dying, and burial are, eternity in hell is far worse. It is living death. It is dying without ending. It is suffering without relief. It is despair without hope. Its terror is the ultimate terror and lurks behind every other thing on earth that we dread.

Does your imagination need a little help to visualize it? Have you watched any modern horror movies lately?

Better yet, do you remember what the crucifixion of Jesus looked like? **"About the ninth hour Jesus cried out in a loud voice, . . . 'My God, my God, why have you forsaken me?'"** (Matthew 27:46). As bad as the physical torment must have been—torn flesh, screaming muscles, dehydration, shock, and exhaustion from loss of blood—the spiritual torment was far worse.

On the cross, as his Father turned his back on him in righteous contempt, Jesus experienced the full weight of the world's condemnation. At that moment he was alone, all alone, to bear his misery. That is what hell will be like.

And because God's pure and innocent Son endured it for you, you won't have to. You are free.

_____

_____

_____

_____

_____

glorified bodies

I've occasionally heard people say, "I don't need money, fancy vacations, fame, or a huge home as long as I have my health." Well, what if you don't have your health anymore? Most baby boomers will remember a famous line from The Who song "My Generation" that talked about hoping to die before getting old. Are you afraid of the aging process? Do you feel sick or weak or old right now?

If you're a believer in Christ, you can enjoy the wisdom and serenity that come with age, knowing that shaky hands and bad knees are only temporary. Soon we will all enjoy glorified bodies. Isaiah says in chapter 35, **"Strengthen the feeble hands, steady the knees that give way; say to those with fearful hearts . . . your God will come . . . to save you"** (verses 3,4).

Complete physical restoration of bone, tissue, cartilage, blood, hair, and skin is a piece of cake to the Lord of the universe. We're going to look so good in heaven that we will probably need name tags to recognize one another.

_____

_____

_____

_____

_____

I worry all the time

Lord, I know you want us to pay attention. I know it's good to be concerned, to be well-organized, to avoid being careless and heedless and thoughtless. But as you well know, I go way beyond all that. Lord, we both know that I am a worrier.

I'm not proud of that. In my better moments I trust you. In my better moments I am willing to wait for clarity and deliverance. But in my lesser moments I am afraid, jittery, snappish, pessimistic, and self-pitying. I feel alone, I am terribly aware of Satan's evil intent, and I am too quick to assume the worst.

Here are the thoughts I want to have in my mind. Lord, please help me think like this: **"My heart is not proud, O Lord, my eyes are not haughty; I do not concern myself with great matters or things too wonderful for me. But I have stilled and quieted my soul; like a weaned child with its mother, like a weaned child is my soul within me"** (Psalm 131:1,2).

Please remind me about your steadfast purpose, your unlimited power, your matchless mercy, your watchful eyes, and your great wisdom, because sometimes I forget. I want to feel like a weaned child with you—satisfied, relaxed, tummy full, content, and serene. Can we start now?

_____

_____

_____

_____

_____

I feel used

Some days I am certain that there is no justice. Yesterday I received a parking ticket even though I had paid to park. And I keep getting incorrectly billed exorbitant amounts by a certain local company whose retail manager admits that the billing is incorrect.

How about you? Do you have tire tracks on your shoulder blades right now? Does it grieve you that people who have taken advantage of you seem to be getting away with it? **"They say, 'The Lord does not see; the God of Jacob pays no heed'"** (Psalm 94:7). It's hard to stay cheerful when it sure looks like crime *does* pay.

Here's the truth: **"Does he who implanted the ear not hear? Does he who formed the eye not see?"** (Psalm 94:9). Back in my student days I always tried to sit way in the back so that the teacher couldn't see when I was fooling around or doing homework for a different class. After I became a teacher myself, I had to laugh when I realized that you could see everything from up in front. My old professors knew what was going on.

From his lofty vantage point, God sees and remembers everything. At just the right time he will compensate people who have done what is right and bring judgment upon those who have done evil. Relax. Let go. Sleep well.

_____

_____

_____

_____

_____

all good is from God

How could you have been an apostle of St. Paul's caliber and not gotten a big head? How could you not be arrogant after receiving personal revelations from the Lord Jesus Christ, given apostolic authority to proclaim God's very words directly, given the ability to perform amazing miracles, authorized to write 13 books of the New Testament, and even given power to raise a young man from the dead?

Here's how: **"Here is a trustworthy saying that deserves full acceptance: Christ Jesus came into the world to save sinners—of whom I am the worst. But for that very reason I was shown mercy"** (1 Timothy 1:15,16).

Paul had painful memories of his early life. As a young man he had viciously persecuted believers in Christ. He had watched approvingly as the first martyr, Stephen, was stoned to death. He had personally seen to the arrest and imprisonment of many Christians.

Thus he was always aware that everything good in his life was worked in him by God's mercy. Can you say with me, "Everything good in *my* life was worked by God's mercy"?

_____

_____

_____

_____

_____

February

"I will instruct you and teach you in the
way you should go: I will counsel you
and watch over you."
(Psalm 32:8)

the path to eternity

How blessed you are! How favored of the Lord! You've been given the secret of the path to eternal life!

Nobody knows it by nature. Nobody can reason it out. Scientific inquiry will never find it. Neither NASA nor the National Geographic Society will discover it. No non-Christian religion can get you there. But the Lord has led you to the Bible, and the Bible has led you to Christ. In Scripture alone is the revealed knowledge that "whoever lives and believes in me will never die" (as Jesus told Martha in John 11:26). **"You have made known to me the path of life; you will fill me with joy in your presence, with eternal pleasures at your right hand"** (Psalm 16:11).

Though your life right now may be dogged with frustrations and brokenness, when you stand before a smiling Savior, you will be filled to the brim with joy. Though now your body may ache and the struggle for survival may be hard, in heaven you will be filled with pure pleasure in God's new world. You will beam at your triumphant companions in faith, "This was *so* worth the wait!"

In your circle of influence, are there any people who as yet don't know about the path of life?

_____

_____

_____

_____

_____

till death us do part

There's an old joke about a classroom blooper: the teacher asks, "What is the word to describe one man staying married to one woman?" A kid responds, "Monotony."

Ha, ha. He meant the word *monogamy*, of course. But that inadvertent, youthful marriage pessimism describes a sad human reality. A beautiful ceremony, two expensive rings, and a wedding license are not sufficient to keep people committed to each other. Even the great King David could not keep his eyes (and hands) off Bathsheba, another man's wife. God had the sordid details of David's theft, adultery, lying, and murder written down so that we could learn from it. The momentary flash of excitement gave way to months and years of misery and damaged many other people's lives as well.

Jesus himself taught that it was God's original (and current) marriage intent that what he had joined together no one should separate. One man/one woman till death us do part is still his promise for a happy life. Proverbs 5:15 puts it like this: **"Drink water from your own cistern, running water from your own well."**

Do you believe this?

Jesus feels your pain

Have you ever gone through a long stretch of physical pain? Does your body hurt right now? If you do any reading in the Bible, you will notice that you have a lot of company. The men and women whom you meet on Scripture's pages share the full measure of the brokenness of human life with you and people of all ages.

You will meet people wounded by swords and arrows; people with leprosy and chronic hemorrhaging; people with withered limbs and paralysis, fevers and epilepsy, and broken bones. It's bad enough to suffer pain. Worse is when it's chronic, when it just won't stop. Sometimes God provides quick and miraculous healing.

And sometimes he doesn't. Are you waiting for relief right now? **"I wait for the Lord, my soul waits, and in his word I put my hope. My soul waits for the Lord more than watchmen wait for the morning, more than watchmen wait for the morning"** (Psalm 130:5,6).

Here is your hope: Jesus sees your pain. Jesus feels your pain with you, because he was and is human just like you. He sets limits to your suffering. He has already planned your rescue. It won't last a minute longer than he has decreed. And he always makes it work for you, for the benefit of his kingdom, and for his greater glory. Always.

_____

_____

_____

_____

_____

February 4

build a spiritual environment

A characteristic of a healthy congregation is that it feels like a family—people feel a sense of belonging, care about each other, and feel valued. The reverse is equally true—a characteristic of a healthy home is that it feels like a church.

I don't mean that your house needs an organ or that the seating should be hard wooden pews. But your home does need a spiritual environment. Your family needs to connect with God each day, not just on Sundays. Your home can be a temple of worship, Bible study, prayer, and Christian songs. Paul writes, **"Let the word of Christ dwell in you richly as you teach and admonish one another with all wisdom, and as you sing psalms, hymns and spiritual songs with gratitude in your hearts to God"** (Colossians 3:16).

Here's another truth—it will never happen by itself. Our lives are hectic. Parenting is exhausting, and if you wait until you have extra time and feel peppy, that day will never come. Just as it is important for husbands and wives to make time for each other, your family's relationship with God will flourish if the mother and father decide to make God welcome in their home.

Would morning, afternoon, or evening work best in your home? Do you have a Bible, prayer book, and hymnal or songbook handy?

February 5
arrogance gets in the way

Is it good to be self-reliant? Of course. If you are a parent, you have spent years and huge amounts of energy teaching and training your kids to take care of themselves. Self-reliance is good. Self-absorption is not.

I know one reason why people don't pray much and why God doesn't hear from me more: arrogance. When you're pretty full of yourself and think you can do it all, praying seems like begging, or worse, a waste of time.

Jesus told a story about a farmer who thought his huge profits were realized because he was such a genius: **"'What shall I do? I have no place to store my crops.' Then he said, 'This is what I'll do. I will tear down my barns and build bigger ones, and there I will store all my grain and my goods. And I'll say to myself, "You have plenty of good things laid up for many years. Take life easy; eat, drink and be merry."' But God said to him, 'You fool!'"** (Luke 12:17-20).

I think that's one major reason why God lets people, including his believers, suffer. It is vital that we see our limitations, our sin, our mortality. We utterly depend on God's providing and forgiveness every day.

Practice with me: "Lord, I need you. Help me today."

_____

_____

_____

_____

_____

a sacred trust

It is a hard lesson to learn that all my money isn't mine and that even my wage-earning skills are a gift from someone else. We all need repeated training in that radical concept. Wait—there's more. The Giver of all seems to think that the resources he gives should be used for his agenda.

Jesus told a parable in which he was the star. **"A man of noble birth went to a distant country to have himself appointed king and then to return. So he called ten of his servants and gave them ten minas** [a gold Persian coin worth at least $4,000]. **'Put this money to work,' he said"** (Luke 19:12,13).

The Savior has set us free from the guilt of our sins, from the dread of death, and from an eternal death sentence in hell. Wait—there's more. He also has set us free from the bottomless pit of self-absorption and self-seeking. It is liberating and exhilarating to use our God-given resources in service to our King.

There is nothing like the sweet feeling of being a channel for God to use his money for his purposes. This is why we were made. This is joy.

_____

_____

_____

_____

_____

talk their language

Simple question: What's the difference between the church and a country club? Sarcastic answer: There isn't any. Country clubs thrive on being seen as exclusive. They are hard and expensive to get into, and they sure aren't for everybody.

Jesus' gift of salvation is for everybody though, and he wants his church to be that way too. He wants his church to serve people, not vice versa. In all the church's blessed work of spiritual reclamation, it is Jesus' intent that the tellers adapt to the hearers, speaking their language, telling the great stories of divine rescue in terms that the hearers will understand and appreciate.

"Though I am free and belong to no man, I make myself a slave to everyone, to win as many as possible. . . . I have become all things to all men so that by all possible means I might save some. I do all this for the sake of the gospel, that I may share in its blessings" (1 Corinthians 9:19,22,23).

Does your congregation try to speak the language of unchurched and lost people? Do you?

_____

_____

_____

_____

_____

February 8

trophy wife

Donald Trump wasn't the first, and he assuredly won't be the last to trade in an older wife for a newer model. It seems to be a status thing for some men who have "made it" in life to put in for a spouse upgrade.

Guys, who are the husbands that you think are the luckiest? What's your definition of a trophy wife? *Sports Illustrated* swimsuit-model figure? *Vogue* magazine face? Here's a concept: **"A wife of noble character is her husband's crown"** (Proverbs 12:4). Or this: **"Charm is deceptive and beauty is fleeting; but a woman who fears the Lord is to be praised. Give her the reward that she has earned"** (Proverbs 31:30,31).

Husbands, are you blessed to be married to a woman with courage, integrity, and work ethic? Are you proud of her? Is she the dearest human treasure of your life, the crown you wear with pride? Have you told her lately? Have you thanked God for her today?

_____

_____

_____

_____

_____

I lost my temper again

I don't mean to do it. Really, I don't. Lord, I know what you say in your Word: **"Refrain from anger and turn from wrath; do not fret—it leads only to evil"** (Psalm 37:8). But I have a boiling point, and it seems as if the people in my life just keep provoking me.

Don't they see how hard I'm trying to keep everything together? Can't they see the points I'm trying to make? Don't they realize I can't stand being laughed at?

I guess I'm just making excuses. I know I hurt people when I get angry. I feel so righteous at first. I love the surge of adrenaline, the wildness of letting go. I think that if I let the anger come out of me, then it won't stay bottled up inside. But I hurt people, and I know I hurt you too.

I'm sorry, Lord; please forgive me. Help me have the humbleness and grace also to ask for forgiveness from the people who had to bear the brunt of my tirade. Please send a special measure of your Spirit and replace my anger with inner peace. Help me listen more and shout less. Help me trust other people more and get over some of my terrible insecurities. Help me trust that you will make all things right in the end. You are good to me, and your mercy endures forever.

_____

_____

_____

_____

_____

it'll be all right

How are you feeling right now? How are your insides doing? Are you calm and peaceful, or are your feelings all churned up?

All of us live with a lot of stress. The people you walk past on the street—yeah, the ones who look so normal—are dealing with debts, gambling addictions, family breakups, job layoffs, health crises, STDs, and huge auto repair bills. But the worst kind of stress is to live with a permanent fear that God is angry with us and is going to punish us sooner or later. But get this—one of the Holy Spirit's main goals for your life, one of his *fruits*, is to give you peace inside.

The Bible says in Romans 5:1, **"Since we have been justified through faith, we have peace with God through our Lord Jesus Christ."** Whenever you let the Spirit speak to you through his Word, he gives you the calm assurance that you are God's child, that your sins have been forgiven, and that God actually likes you.

Everything will be all right.

_____

_____

_____

_____

_____

February 11

I'm injured

In 1866, the year after the Civil War ended, one half of the budget of the state of Mississippi was used to purchase artificial limbs for returning veterans who had suffered battlefield amputations.

Children also can suffer injuries that steal their freedom of movement. **"Jonathan son of Saul had a son who was lame in both feet. He was five years old when the news about Saul and Jonathan** [i.e., their deaths] **came from Jezreel. His nurse picked him up and fled, but as she hurried to leave, he fell and became crippled. His name was Mephibosheth"** (2 Samuel 4:4).

Do you know someone who is the prisoner of a major injury? car crash? workplace accident? One of God's temporary liberating strategies is to use a disaster to bond people together. We all grow when we help and are helped. Another is his gift of the growing science of prosthetics. What a thrill it is to see how people with artificial legs can dance and even run.

Best of all is the total restoration that God promises in heaven. Isaiah chapter 35 promises that in heaven the lame will leap like deer. I can't wait.

_____

_____

_____

_____

February 12
nobody likes me

Isn't it amazing how long our memories of rejection persist? Last to be chosen for sports . . . no one to dance with at the prom . . . years of struggle to get hired . . . 40 years old and still single. What's even worse than not having anyone close is to be rejected by the one person you thought you could count on.

When memories of rejection dominate our thoughts, it's because we are putting human relationships in first place. The way out of that gloom is to let God take his throne back in our lives. Sometimes God allows us to be rejected and burned by other people so that his steadfast love will shine all the brighter. **"Though my father and mother forsake me, the Lord will receive me"** (Psalm 27:10).

When you read the stories of the books of Joshua and Judges, you get the sense that God will do absolutely anything—even breaking the very laws of the universe he created—to make the lives of his people better. If God's faithful love and promises are the first thing we trust in and depend on, everything else will fall into place in its time. When you know that you can absolutely depend on the Lord's affection for you, you can face anything. **"In the day of trouble he will keep me safe in his dwelling; he will hide me in the shelter of his tabernacle and set me high upon a rock"** (Psalm 27:5).

_____

_____

_____

_____

_____

it's my fault

Why does God allow us to suffer?

There are many answers to that vexing question. Here's an important one: because not all suffering is bad. Sometimes pain is therapeutic. Sometimes pain helps improve our hearing and memory. Sometimes pain helps us see our aching need for God.

"When he [the prodigal son] came to his senses, he said, 'How many of my father's hired men have food to spare, and here I am starving to death! I will set out and go back to my father and say to him, "Father, I have sinned against heaven and against you. I am no longer worthy to be called your son; make me like one of your hired men."' So he got up and went to his father" (Luke 15:17-20).

Counselors know that often you have to let alcoholics bottom out before they decide that they are ready to seek help. The pain and loneliness experienced by the prodigal son in Jesus' parable broke his pride and led him to confess his miserable sins. His empty belly assisted him in realizing how badly he had hurt his father and his God. He had only one asset left—he was still his father's son, and he humbly decided to ask for mercy.

The Bible promises you, **"If we confess our sins, he is faithful and just and will forgive us our sins and purify us from all unrighteousness"** (1 John 1:9). Today would be a good day for your confession.

_____

_____

_____

_____

express your love and thanks

Well, the Day is here (I mean February 14, of course). Have you bought your stuff? Over 190 million love-themed greeting cards change hands in the U.S. in mid-February each year, not to mention the tons of chocolate, acres of flowers, and heaps of jewelry. Why do we all go crazy at the same time?

You may have heard that the real name for February 14 is St. Valentine's Day. Indeed, the Catholic Church's calendar of saints lists St. Valentine's feast day as 2/14, but details of the original person are very sketchy. It could have been a Roman priest who was martyred in A.D. 269, but there are other Valentines listed as saints. There appears to be no connection between martyred Christians and Hallmark.

The love associations go back at least as far as Chaucer, who wrote that birds were known to mate on "seynt Volantynys" day. Regardless of how we got here, our culture demands that people pay attention to those they love on this day. What a good idea! Just as birthdays are handy annual reminders to make people feel important, 2/14 is a helpful nudge for all of us to express our love.

St. Paul wrote to his friends in the congregation at Philippi: **"I thank my God every time I remember you"** (Philippians 1:3). This would be a great time for me to thank every one of you who prays for Time of Grace, supports us, or uses our materials to help connect people with their Savior Jesus. I thank my God every time I remember all of you. I love you.

_____

_____

_____

_____

free from guilt

Guilt is a tremendous short-term motivator, isn't it? You can get your husband and children moving through nagging and guilt trips. You can even rouse yourself to quite a bit of energy at first through shame and self-scolding.

But it wears off, leaving you worse off. Consistently using guilt as a motivator eventually leaves you (and your spouse and children) with a strongly negative self-image: "I never do anything right." Sadly, negative motivation gets addictive, and we instinctively reach for the stick instead of the carrot.

You can't stop the negativity toward other people until you first stop it in your own heart. The primary message of the Bible is that God unconditionally and freely decided to love you. He pre-forgave you all your sins, hoping to inspire you in that way to embrace his love and choose to change your sinful life. **"'Come now, let us reason together,' says the LORD. 'Though your sins are like scarlet, they shall be as white as snow; though they are red as crimson, they shall be like wool'"** (Isaiah 1:18).

You don't have to set yourself free from guilt. Jesus already did it for you. You are now free to stop hating yourself and free to speak patiently and kindly to the people around you.

_____

_____

_____

_____

_____

February 16
it's in the Word

People do know a few things about God all on their own. They know he exists—every culture on earth involves stories about a power greater than man. All of nature sings of intelligent design, of order, of brilliant engineering. People sense that God (whoever he/she/it may be) is good, and their consciences make them nervously aware of a certain accountability.

But God's rescue plan through Jesus Christ is revealed knowledge, not inherent knowledge. And God absolutely insists that people acquire this knowledge through other people. Those who know share what they know. **"How, then, can they call on the one they have not believed in? And how can they believe in the one of whom they have not heard?"** (Romans 10:14).

The amazing stories of Israel's Old Testament history demonstrate that God will spare no effort to do what he alone can do. But he absolutely refuses to do for us what he has enabled us and empowered us and commissioned us to do, and that is to share Jesus with one another.

Share what you know. Share whom you know.

_____

_____

_____

_____

_____

from failure to winner

Circuses, carnivals, and all manner of traveling shows for millennia have featured psychics and mind readers. They make their money off gullible customers and generally tell them things they would like to hear. They're frauds, of course. But aren't you glad that nobody can really read your mind?

Think of all the garbage that's in there. Think of the old hatreds, stewing like toxic sludge at the bottom of your soul. Think of the pride that refuses to let you say, "I'm sorry." Think of the wet fog of depression that makes you feel unworthy of anything good or noble. Think of the dull recollections of the times you cheated or hurt other people. Think of the dreams of your youth that have crashed.

There is someone who can read your mind. **"O LORD, you have searched me and you know me. You know when I sit and when I rise; you perceive my thoughts from afar"** (Psalm 139:1,2). That knowledge is safe with him, though. He knows how great your failings are, and it was for just such a person as you and for needs just like yours that he sent his Son to live for you, die for you, and rise again for you.

His perfection makes up for all your failures. Through faith in him, you may claim the gift of a holy reputation in God's royal court. Seen through the lens of Christ, you look like a winner to God.

_____

_____

_____

_____

_____

February 18

America is blessed

The Old Testament historical and prophetic books have a lot to say about the relationship between the Israelites and their country. As we read those words, it's a little tricky for American Christians to navigate specifically which of those things might apply to us today.

Here is what America is not: we are not the new Israel. Believers in Christ are the fulfillment of the prophecies of Israel's restoration. We are not God's chosen people. God certainly loves America, but he loves and has richly blessed many other countries too. We are not a theocracy, i.e., a form of government where our laws come straight from the Bible and direct guidance for governmental decisions comes straight from God.

Here is what America is: a place richly blessed by God; a place that enjoys many spiritual freedoms, including the right to believe and practice our faith and to share it freely; a place richly blessed with the financial resources to spread the Word beyond its borders through missionaries and mass media; and your place to find joy in serving others.

"Shout for joy to the Lord, all the earth. Worship the Lord with gladness. . . . It is he who made us, and we are his" (Psalm 100:1-3).

_____

_____

_____

_____

_____

February 19

when children stray

Every parent feels rejected by his or her children at some point, and rejection always leaves wounds. It is one thing, however, to see your children squander money, drop out of school, or hook up with a high-risk boyfriend or girlfriend. It is far more devastating to see your children appearing to reject Jesus Christ.

You trained the child right. You taught her to pray. You took him to Sunday school and worship. But now you have a prodigal. What do you do?

When your prodigal son or daughter has stopped listening to you, you have to give him or her to the Lord and let him use whatever tough-love therapy he thinks necessary. Not all pain is destructive—some is therapeutic. The Lord sometimes allows his dear ones to be hurt to bring them to their senses.

The father in Jesus' heart-rending parable patiently waited for his prodigal son: **"While he was still a long way off, his father saw him and was filled with compassion for him; he ran to his son, threw his arms around him and kissed him"** (Luke 15:20). As long as they're alive, there's hope.

_____

_____

_____

_____

_____

just talk

Maybe I'd pray more if it didn't look so weak. When I'm praying, I must look like I'm talking to myself, mumbling impossible things to nobody. Everybody craves a sign, power, and control, isn't it so? Wouldn't it have been cooler if upon becoming a Christian, you got a light saber to use? or blue lightning bolts? or a million dollars in gold ingots? Instead, God simply invites you to talk to him.

Talk is cheap, right? Maybe so, but not when you address your heavenly Father in the name of Jesus. Whether you speak your message out loud, sing it, whisper it, or just think it in your head, God hears you and guarantees to process your request.

What may look like a small person simply making weak sounds then becomes mighty. The apostle James has a simple, forceful, direct way of helping us understand God's ways. He says, **"The prayer of a righteous man is powerful and effective"** (James 5:16).

Did you grasp that? Every time you pray, you set something into motion. Every time you pray, something in the universe changes. You have never wasted a prayer in your life. Not a one falls to the ground unheard and unanswered. Your prayer talk makes you *powerful* and *effective* for God's work and your needs.

_____

_____

_____

_____

_____

is it okay to want wealth?

Loving money more than God is indeed a sickness. St. Paul warned in 1 Timothy 6:9-11 that some who had been eager to get rich had fallen into traps, temptations, and many foolish and harmful desires that plunged them into ruin and destruction. Some had wandered from the faith and pierced themselves with many griefs.

However—the fact that money is abused does not mean that it is evil in and of itself. Money is not intrinsically evil. Money is like electricity—it is portable, convertible energy that can get things done.

Money is one of God's gifts, and as such we receive it with gratitude and joy. I have never met anyone who had absolutely nothing. Even the poorest people I've ever known had a little and needed to manage it wisely. Properly understood, there is nothing at all to be ashamed of in seeking to build your family's financial strength.

In fact, God helps you do that with his blessings. **"Misfortune pursues the sinner, but prosperity is the reward of the righteous"** (Proverbs 13:21). **"The blessing of the LORD brings wealth"** (Proverbs 10:22).

_____

_____

_____

_____

_____

February 22

trust like Abraham

If there's anything that people can't stand, it's being told what to do. It's not just teenagers who rebel against authority. The sinful beast that lives in each of us wants to be god and lord of our lives. We are all born saying no to our Creator. Even after we have been brought to faith, we have to work daily to subdue our drive to disobey.

The Lord picked out one of his believers in the Chaldean city of Ur, not far from what is now the Iraqi city of Basra, and directed him to pack up and move to Canaan, many hundreds of miles on the other end of the Fertile Crescent. **"The Lord had said to Abram, 'Leave your country, your people and your father's household and go to the land I will show you.' . . . So Abram left, as the Lord had told him"** (Genesis 12:1,4).

Abram (his original name before God changed it) could not possibly have known all the reasons God had for the move, *but he went anyway.* He had to leave his house to live in a tent, leave his familiar surroundings to live with strangers, and leave behind most of his family and friends. *But he went anyway,* because God directed him to. God blessed him by making him the patriarch of the Israelite nation and father of all believers. But in about 2091 B.C. he didn't know that; all he had to work with was the command.

Abraham is my hero for obeying God even though he didn't know where he was going. Abraham is my hero for trusting that God's ways are always good ways.

God gives you friends

"It is not good for the man to be alone," said God, as he created the first woman. It still isn't good for people to be isolated. He made us to be social creatures. He also created the concept of the church because it is not good for people to be in spiritual isolation.

Satan has an easier time picking off the strays. Left to ourselves we can get lost, eat things not good for us, and fall prey to any one of the thousand or so temptations that the devil has found successful in destroying people's bodies and souls.

"They devoted themselves to the apostles' teaching and to the fellowship, to the breaking of bread and to prayer" (Acts 2:42). Every one of those divine activities builds up people's faith and spiritual strength. Every one is a gift from God intended to be enjoyed by a spiritual family.

I need my Christian friends. I need someone to tell me if I'm getting weird in my beliefs. I need someone to tell me if I am rationalizing a sinful lifestyle. I need encouragement when I am down and a posterior kick when I am being stubborn. So do you. Do you have a congregation? Love it! Do you need a congregation? Find one!

February 24

I hurt

"Stuff happens." I saw that on a bumper sticker once. Stuff happens to our bodies. People I know well have been in car accidents, sports accidents, and home accidents. People I am close to have arthritis as a daily companion. Their pens no longer move, and their musical instruments must now lie silent. I know some of their world. When my back goes out on me, I just collapse onto the floor as waves of agony sweep over me.

Modern medicine has greatly reduced the amount of physical pain in our lives. But there is plenty left. We live a lot longer than we used to. But guess what—that just means that we are frail longer.

Here's what God says about your pain: **"He has not despised or disdained the suffering of the afflicted one"** (Psalm 22:24). In other words, pain does not mean that you are being punished. To the contrary, God will make your pain work for his loving agenda in some way. None of your suffering is meaningless. Everything will be brought together to serve a greater purpose.

Your pain will have limits—it won't last a minute longer than the Lord decrees. **"Find rest, O my soul, in God alone; my hope comes from him"** (Psalm 62:5).

_____

_____

_____

_____

_____

my faith is so weak

"I wish my faith was stronger." "I wish I could believe like my grandmother." "I don't have much of a faith." "My faith is so weak." Sound familiar? Do you worry about your lapses in faith?

One of the great things about the Bible is the unflinching honesty in its stories. We are given heroes to look up to, but most of them also had terrible weaknesses, which are described without blinking. Noah got drunk; Abraham was ready to let his wife, Sarah, join the pharaoh's harem; Samuel and David were both terrible parents; Hezekiah was a reckless show-off.

Faith's source is God's Word. Faith's object is not you; it's Christ. Faith's power is not in the believer, but in the One who spoke the promises. When Peter looked too much at himself, he began to sink. When he was listening to Jesus, he could walk on water just like the Master. **"Why are you downcast, O my soul? Why so disturbed within me? Put your hope in God, for I will yet praise him, my Savior and my God"** (Psalm 43:5).

_____

_____

_____

_____

_____

February 26
I'm afraid of dying

"Do not go gentle into that good night.
Rage, rage against the dying of the light."

Welsh poet Dylan Thomas' famous words were written for his dying father, grown weak and frail, urging him to fight against death. You know those feelings, don't you?

Have you also not felt the dread of being forced to let go of someone you love? Have you also not felt the dread of the dying process? What makes dying even more stressful is the realization that we brought death into the world, that it is God's righteous punishment on human evil, that a grim judgment awaits. We know deep down inside that dying is not a sweet, natural part of the great circle of life, as Mufasa and Rafiki tell us in *The Lion King*.

The king and poet David felt it too. **"Be merciful to me, O Lord, for I am in distress; my eyes grow weak with sorrow, my soul and my body with grief. My life is consumed by anguish and my years by groaning; my strength fails because of my affliction, and my bones grow weak"** (Psalm 31:9,10).

David found peace in believing in the coming Savior who would grant him immortality. Through Christ the dying process for you is only the road home. Through Christ death is not the dying of the light, but entrance into the light.

_____

_____

_____

_____

_____

February 27
cultivate humility

Radio humorist Garrison Keillor once asked his mother, "Mom, am I good-looking? Her modest, Midwestern reply: "You're good-looking enough, dear."

Humility is learned behavior. By nature, we are miniature Satans: full of ourselves, prideful, interested in only one agenda in life: ours. We imagine that we are the center of the solar system—no—the galaxy. Other people are just bit players and props in the drama of Me.

It is natural to crave attention and to boast. It is Christian to praise others first and wait patiently for others to discover our own brilliance. Our Lord Jesus is both our example and teacher, the divine Redeemer who came to earth not to be served but to serve.

Can you accept this? **"Let another praise you, and not your own mouth; someone else, and not your own lips"** (Proverbs 27:2). Do you have the patience to wait for others to discover your good features?

_____

_____

_____

_____

_____

relax!

Do you ever have panic attacks—when you feel as though your life is being swept up in a tornado of bad things and you are helpless? Do you get exhausted from worry because your whole life seems to be teetering on the edge? Do you assume that things will always turn out for the worst? Does your mind race while you are trying to fall asleep? Do you jump when the phone rings, dreading the call that loved ones are dead in a ditch?

Relax. You were created by a loving, omnipotent genius who designed you for a life of joy, not fear. You were rescued by God's Son, Christ Jesus, who lived for you, died your death for you, rose again as a prototype of your own rising, and guarantees your forgiveness as your personal intercessor. Your needs matter to your heavenly Father, and you have but to ask.

"Do not be anxious about anything, but in everything, by prayer and petition, with thanksgiving, present your requests to God. And the peace of God, which transcends all understanding, will guard your hearts and your minds in Christ Jesus" (Philippians 4:6,7).

The Father's kind wishes for you are carried out by legions of holy, mighty angels who leap to do his bidding. You are loved. You are safe. You are immortal.

_____

_____

_____

_____

_____

March

"This is the confidence we have in
approaching God: that if we ask anything
according to his will, he hears us."
(1 John 5:14)

March 1

God is involved

Did you ever have an ant farm when you were a kid? Ant farms are made out of two slides of glass with just a very thin layer of dirt. You watch the ants lay their eggs and bustle around doing ant things. But you don't go down there with them. You're not involved in their life; you just look at them.

That's not how God works. He's involved. He knows how many hairs are on your head. He engraved your name on the palms of his hands. To top it off, in the person of Jesus Christ he became human like you. He doesn't just watch you—he came to live in your world. How can you not just praise him for that level of commitment? King David said, **"I will praise you, O Lord, with all my heart; I will tell of all your wonders"** (Psalm 9:1).

God's Word guarantees that God is engaged in your life. He's not looking at you like an ant in his ant farm, watching detached and aloof and critical, but he interacts with you as someone he's connected to by blood. Remember that Jesus ascended into heaven with his body. He is still human, still looking out for you, still crazy in love with you.

_____

_____

_____

_____

_____

offer support at home

"The wife must respect her husband" (Ephesians 5:33).

It's hard to be a good wife these days. Godly wives get very little incentive in the media to respect their husbands. Men are regularly portrayed as blundering, lazy dolts who do nothing but drink beer and watch sports. Men make messes, are childish and violent, and have only one thing on their minds. How can Christ's sisters not feel resentment toward their husbands and scorn in their hearts?

How do TV commercials make you feel when they portray other husbands and lovers buying cars, jewelry, and luxury vacations for their mates on Valentine's Day and you got maybe a card and some lousy chocolates?

Respect him anyway. If not for him, then for Christ. Your husband can never grow into the leader you long for if you refuse to follow. Every home leader starts out as a rookie and has to grow into his role. A woman will have more in the end if she looks for and then praises Christ-like leadership in him than if she scolds and nags him over his perceived failures.

Men really can learn and generally are eager to please. They can develop into awesome partners who bring great gifts to their wives' lives. Ask any widow.

_____

_____

_____

_____

_____

God is omnipotent

How strong are you? How much of your world can you control? Can you bench-press 5,000 pounds? Can you lift a mountain? Can you change the weather? Can you create a living thing by speaking a word? Well, of course you can't.

But your God can. God is omnipotent. That means that there is no limit to his power. When God came to earth in the person of Jesus Christ, his disciples watched in awe as he showed total mastery over all creation. The gospel of Mark tells how Jesus' disciples were amazed when he silenced a violent storm that had threatened to swamp their boat. They said, **"Who is this? Even the wind and the waves obey him!"** (Mark 4:41).

You and I daily are humbled by our own small size, weaknesses, and limitations. Isn't it good to know that wherever you sail your little boat today, the master of wind and wave is riding along?

_____

_____

_____

_____

_____

a servant's attitude

The beautiful truth that Jesus Christ found joy in serving you doesn't stop there. He redeemed you not only to get you to heaven someday but to initiate your personal transformation *right now* and to make you more like him *right now* and to make you useful in bringing benefit to the lives of other people *right now*.

The joy in serving others is not learned on the streets. Strutting and talking and bravado generally rule there. It doesn't play well in the movies either. The traits of beauty and strength that we idolize in people usually turn out to be pretty *self*-serving, don't they?

You know where the attitude of a servant is best taught and modeled? Right in your home. **"Train a child in the way he should go, and when he is old he will not turn from it"** (Proverbs 22:6).

You probably can't respect a boss until you've first learned to respect your father. You probably won't serve others well until you've first learned to serve your mother. The younger parents start with "joy in serving" therapy for their children, the better.

_____

_____

_____

_____

_____

God cares

I. Love. You.

We are all starving to hear those three words. They are consumable. We burn them up to keep going in a hostile and cruel world, to keep going when our own self-doubts and self-hatred gnaw at our self-confidence. We can never hear those words enough.

How could you want to pray to a God who didn't love you? You might bargain with such a god or try to pay him off or earn some points with rituals, but you couldn't bare your soul.

The One who invites your prayers made himself low for you. He emptied himself, taking the very nature of a servant. He was born in a barn, lived simply, taught the Word, bore scorn, was arrested and unjustly convicted, and endured the scourge and the cross in order to break the power of sin's curse over you. On the third day, he triumphantly rose from death and promises a similar resurrection to all who trust and believe in him.

Why did he do all of those things? Because he loves you. And so you can **"cast all your anxiety on him because he cares for you"** (1 Peter 5:7).

_____

_____

_____

_____

_____

honor God with your firstfruits

It takes no brains to be an impulse spender. Advertisers and marketing people study your behavior, your preferences, and your life patterns to determine best when to jump you with their seductive spending come-ons. Food shopping, for instance, is no longer just food shopping. You are bombarded with marketing messages from the moment you drive into the parking lot, from the huge window signs to the hanging TV sets chattering at nobody to the point-of-purchase displays surrounding you as your cart crawls forward to the checkout clerk.

Let your gifts to your heavenly Father come not only from a passionate heart but also from a brain that plans. **"Honor the LORD with your wealth, with the firstfruits of all your crops; then your barns will be filled to overflowing, and your vats will brim over with new wine"** (Proverbs 3:9,10).

Do you get the point? When you set aside God's portion first, two things happen: first, you show that God really is #1 in your life, worthy not of occasional leftovers but worthy of top billing; second, you can expect that a delighted God will bless you back with his spiritual and material gifts so that you can give again.

_____

_____

_____

_____

_____

loyalty to Christ

Nicodemus must have worked long and hard for his position in Jewish society's elite. He was a member of the sect of the Pharisees—an exclusive club of religious achievers who had also made it financially. They thought personal wealth was a necessary "proof" of God's favor. Membership was not hereditary—you had to earn your way in. Even better—Nicodemus was a member of the supreme ruling council, the Sanhedrin.

Jesus' words and teachings had the ring of truth that Nicodemus had been missing all his life. His first conversation with Jesus had to be clandestine so he would not lose his position in the social register. Likely he watched in silence on the night of Jesus' "trial" as his proud Council became nothing more than a kangaroo court, which spent hours bribing witnesses to support a predetermined verdict.

But then he said, "Enough." He decided to out himself as a follower of Jesus. **"With Pilate's permission,** [Joseph of Arimathea] **came and took the body away. He was accompanied by Nicodemus, the man who earlier had visited Jesus at night. Nicodemus brought a mixture of myrrh and aloes, about seventy-five pounds"** (John 19:38,39).

Myrrh was usually bought and sold in small vials. Seventy-five pounds was worth a king's ransom. Though Jesus had been executed like a criminal, Nicodemus wanted him to be buried like a king. Nicodemus is a hero of mine. He reminds me of whose approval I need most.

What holds you back from more public loyalty to Jesus?

_____

_____

take care of the seniors

It is a natural impulse in us all to look down on those we think dumber than we are and to take advantage of those weaker than we are. We fawn over the beautiful, rich, and powerful and despise losers.

Can you respect someone in a wheelchair? Is it a worthwhile use of your time to help elderly relatives stay in their home a while longer? Are you too busy and important to be bothered with helping people with shaky hands and bad hearing?

"If anyone does not provide for his relatives, and especially for his immediate family, he has denied the faith and is worse than an unbeliever" (1 Timothy 5:8). Jesus' love is all about flowing downhill. Everything he did was for people dirtier than he, poorer, sicker, more ignorant, broken, unworthy, and lost. But he found joy in serving, and he smiles and promises us that we will find fulfillment in his steps.

Look around in your family. Who needs you today?

_____

_____

_____

_____

_____

March 9

deliverance from troubles

It's bad enough to feel like you're sinking down with troubles that can't be fixed. What's even worse is when you feel all alone, that nobody knows what you're going through and nobody cares.

If you are wearing the holy robes of Jesus through Baptism (see Galatians 3:27), then neither of the above will ever be true of you. If you are a believer in Christ, then God not only sees you and everything about you, but he claims you and accepts responsibility for how you are doing. No pit is so deep that he can't pull you out; no floodwater is so high that he can't reach where you're at to lift you up.

Here is a psalm for all God's children who feel as though they are drowning in trouble right now: **"This poor man called, and the Lord heard him; he saved him out of all his troubles. The angel of the Lord encamps around those who fear him, and he delivers them"** (Psalm 34:6,7).

Your Father sees you. Your Savior is with you. His Spirit lives within you. His angels are all around you. At just the right moment, you will experience divine rescue.

_____

_____

_____

_____

_____

I'm with him!

One of my favorite memories is the sight of a little girl wearing a princess costume holding her daddy's hand . . . in a hardware store. She walks with him in this big strange place, happy and confident because she's with her protector. Can you still remember what it's like to be only 3 feet tall? Everything looks much bigger and scarier when you feel small.

Just like that little girl, we are given the gift of walking around with God in public. The "churchy" word for that is *extol*. In Latin it means "to pick up and carry around." The blessing God gives his church is that we get to extol him. We get to praise our God in public and carry him around with us during the day. Each day you can say, **"In God I trust; I will not be afraid. What can man do to me?"** (Psalm 56:11).

This week as you walk around at home, in the store, at work, and at church, you can be confident that you are walking around with your protector. Doesn't that make you feel safe? and proud? Say with a happy heart, "I'm with the big guy. I'm with God. I'm with him!"

_____

_____

_____

_____

_____

I'm disabled

Does anyone in your family have a disability? Do you? My close family has been touched by polio, hydrocephalia, spina bifida, and Williams syndrome (missing genes inhibit full physical growth).

Jesus met many disabled people and loved them all. **"Another time he went into the synagogue, and a man with a shriveled hand was there"** (Mark 3:1). What do you suppose it was like to have a shriveled hand? Kind of hard to play most sports, wouldn't you think? A little tough to impress girls, maybe? Employers might think twice before hiring such a man.

Jesus healed the man in the synagogue instantly, miraculously, with a word. His heart hurt with compassion for his hurting brother. And yet his mission on earth was not primarily to patch up every disabled person. There were still plenty of disabled people on earth when he left, and there are even more today.

Jesus' first mission was to demonstrate in word and deed that God's Son, the world's Savior, had come to earth to teach, suffer, die, and rise again. His greatest gift to us *right now*, disabled and "abled," is not restoration of broken bodies but restoration of our broken souls through the forgiveness of our sins.

Complete restoration of our bodies will come later.

_____

_____

_____

_____

_____

thank you for the rescue, Lord

You know, Lord, that I try to be responsible and take care of my own business. I don't want to be a burden on anybody. I try to handle everything, and I mean everything. Maybe I am a little too confident in my ability to tackle every problem.

Maybe that's why it takes me so long to ask for help. I don't want to seem like I'm begging. I admit it—I'm proud. But when I needed big help for a big problem, you were there for me. I know there was divine intervention—there is no other possible explanation for the solution. I am giving you all the credit. I don't know if you just spoke a word or sent an angel or just reached down. **"You give me your shield of victory, and your right hand sustains me; you stoop down to make me great"** (Psalm 18:35).

I will continue to strive to be self-reliant. But I'm going to work harder on being humble enough to ask for help when I need it. I'm going to enjoy knowing that you always have my back and are *actually working to make me great (!)*, and I'm going to praise you in advance for all the things you must be doing for me that I don't even notice. Thank you. Thank you! You are the best!

_____

_____

_____

_____

_____

the cure for pride

Every year tearful people stand in front of the casket of someone who died sooner than anybody ever expected. When someone has passed, it is no longer possible to say, "I'm sorry." "It was my fault." "Let's not fight anymore." "I miss your friendship."

Pride is a terrible master. It keeps us so aware of our own wounds and hurt feelings that we don't notice the pain in others, even hurts that we have caused. Pride makes everything always all about *Me*. Pride turns misunderstandings into arguments and arguments into fights. Pride makes people sullen, brooding over the changeless past.

Pride seduces you into thinking that you are innocent and have it all together. St. Paul learned the hard way: **"If you think you are standing firm, be careful that you don't fall!"** (1 Corinthians 10:12).

Jesus has the cure. Jesus *is* the cure. First he demonstrated true personal humility. He came to our world and emptied himself of all heavenly splendor, taking the form and nature of a slave. He submitted to the laws of God and Caesar and kept them all for us. He surrendered to a miserable death on the cross of atonement. Risen and glorified, he now calls us to believe in him and to be like him, "proud" to be a humble servant. This is the cure for pride—to find joy in making other people's lives better.

_____

_____

_____

_____

you will be resurrected

Your odds of winning a multimillion-dollar jackpot in the lottery are terribly small. It's about 195,000,000 to 1 that you have wasted your money.

But every believer in Christ will be a winner on the great day of judgment. Luck, odds, and gaming skill have nothing to do with it. Your winning ticket was purchased for you as all your debts were paid, paid in full, when the Son of God suffered, died, was buried, and rose again. **"And I—in righteousness I will see your face; when I awake, I will be satisfied with seeing your likeness"** (Psalm 17:15).

You can handle any adversity knowing that you win in the end. You can endure financial, physical, and emotional hardships cheerfully knowing that the game will be reset and you will start over in heaven. Your body will be restored to the perfection God originally intended. The entire universe will be re-created without any evil, sickness, or death.

Waiting for you is resurrected human #1, the first installment of the great resurrection, your Savior Jesus. You will be satisfied to see his likeness, satisfied indeed, for you shall see him face–to-face, never again to die.

_____

_____

_____

_____

_____

believe the blessing promise

People have always craved shortcuts to get what they want. That's why Ponce de Leon searched for the fountain of youth; that's why Harry Potter and his friends studied magic; that's why Willie Sutton robbed banks; and that's why people gamble.

Does it surprise you that there are some simple paths you can choose that will significantly improve your home life? No, not chanting *Leviosa!* or *Alohomora!* The secret? Fearing the Lord. **"Blessed are all who fear the Lord, who walk in his ways. You will eat the fruit of your labor; blessings and prosperity will be yours. Your wife will be like a fruitful vine within your house; your sons will be like olive shoots around your table. Thus is the man blessed who fears the Lord"** (Psalm 128:1-4).

Realize two things. First, *fear* in this sense does not mean to be terrified. It means to respect God, prize your relationship with him above all things, pay attention to his Word, be proud to be identified with him, and make your life decisions based on his will.

Second, God blesses those who fear (i.e., respect and obey) him. *Bless* means that the almighty God intervenes in your life and changes its course to make it better for you. He makes good things happen for you that wouldn't have occurred otherwise.

Your whole family will love living in a blessed home.

I'm afraid of being abandoned

A relative of mine adopted a child from overseas. He told me that when the little girl was handed over from the foster mom, the mom chose to walk away abruptly without any good-byes. The little girl clung like a terrified animal to her new adoptive mom and for months afterward exhibited major fear behaviors. How could you not? Do you think she still has abandonment nightmares? Do you ever have abandonment nightmares?

Were you ever the kid left behind at a gas station or restaurant? Do you find it hard to trust people because you assume that they will dump you sooner or later? **"My acquaintances are completely estranged from me. My kinsmen have gone away; my friends have forgotten me"** (Job 19:13,14).

Your baptism is the place to start in regaining your self-confidence. When you were baptized, the omnipotent God of the universe accepted an obligation to act as your Father throughout your life. He washed away your sins through that wonderful water and committed himself to you unconditionally.

He will never lose track of you. He will never stop caring about you. In fact, he's crazy about you.

_____

_____

_____

_____

_____

St. Patrick: missionary to the Celts

In American popular culture, the middle of the month of March becomes a silly season. Stores, schools, and bars are festooned with green in honor of St. Patrick's Day. Leprechauns, pots o' gold, and shamrocks abound. The day means little more than an excuse to drink beer and build up some real or pretend Irish pride.

The real Patrick was known for something else entirely. He was British, not Irish, living in the A.D. 400s. Kidnapped as a teenager by Irish marauders, he was taken to Ireland. There he was forced to work as a slave-shepherd among the wild Celts. He managed to escape and eventually made his way back to Britain.

But Patrick chose to go back to Ireland and devote the rest of his life to bringing the Christian gospel to the Irish people. Imagine that—the freed slave went back to his enslavers. It's the same thing St. Paul did with a runaway slave named Onesimus. He wrote to the onetime master Philemon, **"I am sending him—who is my very heart—back to you . . . no longer as a slave, but . . . as a dear brother"** (Philemon 12,16).

This is how powerful the gospel is—to turn enemies into friends and slaves into missionaries.

_____

_____

_____

_____

_____

I love to see my kids worshiping you

Lord, you know I love my kids. I love 'em even when they're naughty, even when I'm grouchy and irritable, even when they disappoint me, especially when they disappoint me. When I see their acts and words of rebellion against you, I feel fear gnawing at my heart. What if they grow up to be unbelievers? What if they recklessly throw away their faith?

That's why it is such ecstasy to hear their words of worship and see their faith-deeds. What pleasure it is to sit with them in church and see them engaged. I love to hear their voices singing. I love to discuss with them what we learned as we travel home. I share your Palm Sunday (and Palm Monday) thrill at the sight and sound of children worshiping their God: **"From the lips of children and infants you have ordained praise"** (Psalm 8:2 and Matthew 21:16). Their hosannas matter.

I hope to leave my children a legacy, a noble inheritance. I hope to leave them financial assets when I pass on to help stabilize their finances. I hope to have passed on a moral legacy, a decent and honorable way to live. I hope to have taught them to love their country and their community. Most of all, I hope that my faith in you will live on in their hearts.

_____

_____

_____

_____

_____

in Jesus' name

Just before he was arrested, tortured, and murdered, and knowing that all this was about to happen, Jesus spent some intense hours with his disciples. He gave them important information about carrying on with their lives and ministry when they would no longer have his physical presence in their midst.

He especially wanted them to know that their close relationship with the Father would continue, because their Savior would still be their personal link to his throne. **"My Father will give you whatever you ask *in my name*. Until now you have not asked for anything *in my name*. Ask and you will receive, and your joy will be complete"** (John 16:23,24).

When you listen to Christians pray, you will often hear them end their prayers with "in Jesus' name," or the more formal, "through Jesus Christ, your Son, our Lord, who lives and reigns with you and the Holy Spirit, one God, for ever and ever." Mentioning the proper name of Christ is a sweet custom. But that's not all Jesus meant—just to attach his proper name like a mattress tag to your heavenly communications.

Praying in Jesus' name means believing that he is your Savior, that your designation in heaven has been changed from "damned" to "saved," that you are now considered God's child, and all this only because of Jesus.

It also means that you pray according to his name in the sense of his self-revelation, that is, that you are following his charge to put God's agenda first.

_____

_____

control your appetites

We are all barraged by advertising seeking to remove some of our money from us. We have to develop sales resistance or we'd all be bankrupt in 24 hours. But it's hard. Not only do advertisers work overtime at tempting us to indulge our passions and fantasies, but easy credit seduces us into borrowing ourselves into huge debt.

Learning how to say no to yourself is an exceptionally valuable skill. When my mother and her sister were young during the Great Depression, they used to beg their papa for treats and store items they'd see while riding in their car. "Take a good look," he would say as he kept driving. They didn't like it at the time, but later they came to realize the value of learning to control their appetites.

"In the house of the wise are stores of choice food and oil, but a foolish man devours all he has" (Proverbs 21:20). Cultivating the grace of self-denial means that you will likely be spared the stress of living on the edge of financial ruin all the time.

Do you control your appetites . . . or do they control you?

_____

_____

_____

_____

_____

the last shall be first

One of the most curious ironies in the New Testament is that Jesus' disciples often needed help understanding his parables. They got caught up in the details and couldn't see where they fit in. It seems as though Jesus' enemies, the Pharisees, had no trouble grasping it when their ways were being condemned in his stories.

"The Pharisees, who loved money, heard all this and were sneering at Jesus. He said to them, 'You are the ones who justify yourselves in the eyes of men, but God knows your hearts. What is highly valued among men is detestable in God's sight'" (Luke 16:14,15).

Since the Pharisees drew their members from the upper middle class, they all had money. They encouraged one another to conclude that their money proved that they enjoyed God's favor (self-justification). Jesus added one of his trademark "backward" statements—in God's eyes, wealth is no guarantee of integrity, nor is poverty a guarantee of God's punishment.

Though the world listens to braggarts, God prefers the humble. Though the world adores the rich and famous, the Lord lifts up the lowly. Though the world admires people with many servants, God prefers those with servant attitudes.

So tell me—whose approval are you hungry for?

_____

_____

_____

_____

_____

don't judge

Somehow even people who have never read the New Testament have managed to learn certain words from Jesus' Sermon on the Mount: **"Do not judge, or you too will be judged."** (How have those words gotten so famous?) Jesus continues, **"For in the same way you judge others, you will be judged, and with the measure you use, it will be measured to you"** (Matthew 7:1,2).

"Don't judge," people say, and by that they mean, "You are not allowed to criticize anything I say or do." That's not what Jesus meant, however. Other portions of his Word permit and encourage and even command us to rebuke and correct what is evil.

So what is this "judging others" that Jesus forbids?

1. Condemning the person instead of the sinful action.
2. Imagining that you are superior to someone else.
3. Imagining that you are someone's judge.
4. Enjoying finding fault with people more than building them up.

Bring others to Jesus. Don't bring them down.

_____

_____

_____

_____

_____

God's angels are everywhere

On the surface of things, it certainly seems as though Satan is lord of the earth, doesn't it? There are a half dozen major wars going on at any given time. Suicide bombers throw away their own lives to take as many others to the grave as they can. Drug merchants coldheartedly sell chemicals that enslave people and destroy their health and families. Little children are neglected and beaten; the unborn are killed by the hundreds of thousands each year.

That's what it looks like on the outside. Behind the scenes there is another reality. God is still in charge of every aspect of this sinful and broken world, and he is making everything work together for the good of those who love him. Behind the scenes his holy angels work to carry out his long-range plans, plans that always have a happy ending for all believers.

"He will command his angels concerning you to guard you in all your ways; they will lift you up in their hands, so that you will not strike your foot against a stone" (Psalm 91:11,12). Think of that! Nothing in your life happens by accident. You are under the constant loving surveillance of a God who guarantees your eternal happiness and has many divisions of angels ready to carry out his detailed instructions. Don't be afraid!

_____

_____

_____

_____

_____

I'm so frustrated

All right, admit it. You're angry with God.

Your home's breadwinner has been unemployed for a terribly long stretch. You have a lingering illness that keeps you from developing your career. You work so hard to save a little money and the markets collapse and your investments shrink or evaporate. You are hit with the tragic death of someone you loved very dearly.

"God, why did you let that happen?" **"Why have you rejected us forever, O God? Why does your anger smolder against the sheep of your pasture?"** (Psalm 74:1). Realize that God's people for millennia have been confused by their hardships and suffering and wondered if God has stopped loving them. Why does he let bad things happen to us? Worse—what if he's sending them? Or worst of all, what if they are punishments?

Realize these things: (1) God no longer punishes his children. All the punishing has been done on the cross of Christ. There is no condemnation for those who believe in Christ. (2) Earth is broken. Everybody suffers. You won't experience heaven on earth. You will get heaven in heaven. (3) God sets limits on your pain. (4) God solemnly promises to make everything in your life, even hardships, *especially* the hardships, work for you in the long run.

Cut him some slack. Wait. You'll see.

---

accept help from your friends

I'm always amazed at how applicable the core principles of A.A. are for a variety of life problems beyond just alcoholism. A.A. counselors often have to work very hard to get people to take the first step and to admit that they have severe problems. Sometimes major interventions are needed.

Another core principle is this: an alcoholic cannot turn his or her own life around but needs help. That's a hard one for me to learn. When I'm struggling, I'm often too proud to accept help. Maybe you've thought, "Nah, I'll just keep going a little while longer; I'll be fine. I can take this; this ain't nothing. I've been through worse."

The Bible says, **"Listen to advice and accept instruction, and in the end you will be wise"** (Proverbs 19:20). I'll tell you this: in my own life I have already been straightened out a number of times. Fortunately, God made me listen to what brothers and sisters had to say, and they got my brain back on a better track. But I'm not done yet. I need you—not only to pray for me but to keep me on the right path.

I also need you to have a humble spirit and to be willing to let the people around you tell you a thing or two as well.

Your family and your church are a God-designed buddy system to keep you on his path.

_____

_____

_____

_____

_____

I hurt

Pain in and of itself is not bad. In fact, it's actually good. Pain messages tell the truth. They tell you that something is wrong, perhaps very wrong, and they tell you exactly where the problem lies. Without pain messages you could easily bleed to death or suffer serious and life-threatening infections.

That said, pain makes life miserable. Chronic pain—fibromyalgia, migraines, neuralgia—makes it miserable all the time. Pain drains energy and leaves you exhausted. Pain keeps you from being productive, makes you crabby, and turns your life inward.

Usually when people say "this day and age," they are groaning from the decline in morality and rise of crime and cruelty. "This day and age," however, has also provided us with a wide array of legal narcotics that ease even severe pain and provide peace and rest to people recovering from major surgeries or to people dying of painful illness.

Pain can also be redemptive. St. Paul said, **"I want to know Christ and the power of his resurrection and the fellowship of sharing in his sufferings, becoming like him in his death, and so, somehow, to attain to the resurrection from the dead"** (Philippians 3:10,11). Pain makes us see our need for God. Pain helps us share the experience of Christ himself. Pain cures us of our fantasy that earth is a paradise and makes us long for heaven.

_____

_____

_____

_____

_____

one is enough

The seventh book of the Bible is cursed with a confusing name. Judges sounds like dry reading, like ancient legal briefs or summaries of dusty court cases.

It's nothing of the sort. A better title would be "Leaders" or "Champions." These chapters illustrate God's favorite way of bringing about major change in the lives of his people—he sends one person. The book of Judges is all about the power of one.

The first of these judges, or let's call them transformational leaders, is Othniel. His story illustrates the power of just one person to make a huge impact on a whole society. Israel had lost its spiritual moorings and gone after the Canaanite god Baal. God allowed invading bands from nearby Aram to torment them for eight years. They cried out to him for help. What did he do? He sent one man:

"The Spirit of the Lord came upon him [Othniel], so that he became Israel's judge and went to war. The Lord gave Cushan-Rishathaim king of Aram into the hands of Othniel, who overpowered him. So the land had peace for forty years, until Othniel son of Kenaz died" (Judges 3:10,11).

Never say, "I am only one." Never say, "What can just one person do?" Sometimes one is enough to initiate the change God wants.

_____

_____

_____

_____

_____

there's always hope

One of the pleasures of life, available to rich and poor alike, is to experience your steady changing of the seasons. What a beautiful divine rhythm you have built, Lord. Each season has its own matchless beauty—the glistening white blanket of new-fallen snow; the first crocus and daffodils and tulips of spring; the long golden days of summer; the fiery colors of autumn forests.

Anyone who has spent even one winter in the north half of the U.S. has to be impressed at your miracle of rebirth. How can any living thing survive a stretch of subzero temperatures? Everything looks dead. But every year, just like clockwork, you send more sun and warmth and your frozen world bursts back into life. **"He hurls down his hail like pebbles. Who can withstand his icy blast? He sends his word and melts them; he stirs up his breezes, and the waters flow"** (Psalm 147:17,18).

We love spring for many reasons, Lord. We're delighted to emerge from our igloos and enjoy the outdoors again. We love the Easter story of our resurrected Savior. And we see enacted for all your amazing power to bring life out of what seems to be dead. There's always hope—spring always follows winter—you always have the last word, and that word is *life*.

Thank you, Lord.

_____

_____

_____

_____

_____

the Mr. Hyde inside

In 1885 Scottish author Robert Louis Stevenson conceived of a marvelous "bogey tale," as he called it, to illustrate the duality of human nature. He called it *The Strange Case of Dr. Jekyll and Mr. Hyde.* It was a great hit with the reading public. People resonated immediately with the good doctor's daily dilemma of an internal struggle to keep the beast in him at bay.

Someday we will be without sin. In heaven we will be whole. In heaven we will never again have to wrestle with the Mr. Hyde inside.

In the meantime, we labor at self-control. A loving God shares his power with us, power that streams into our minds and hearts through his wonderful Word. He promises that we can rebuke the devil, and he will flee from us.

We can also rebuke the junior version of the devil within us. **"A man of knowledge uses words with restraint, and a man of understanding is even-tempered"** (Proverbs 17:27).

_____

_____

_____

_____

_____

March 30
hope for the hopeless

Children are by nature optimistic and resilient. When they're small, they haven't yet seen the full range of human cruelty. They believe in fairies, ghosts, and handsome princes on white horses. They know that every story will end with everyone living happily ever after.

But years of disappointment and frustration can beat the hope out of a person's heart. After a while, you not only expect loss and failure, but some people even sabotage their own efforts as a self-fulfilling prophecy—"See, I knew I would fail." We all need hope. It is the oxygen of the human spirit. But like oxygen it is consumable, and we must learn how to find it and breathe it.

The Bible and the sacraments bring the life-giving O_2 of the Holy Spirit (whose very name in both Hebrew and Greek means "wind" or "breath"). **"May the God of hope fill you with all joy and peace as you trust in him, so that you may overflow with hope by the power of the Holy Spirit"** (Romans 15:13).

Reconnected to the message of God's deeds for us and God's love for us, even a hopeless heart can start beating again. Those stories are all true! Yes he did. Yes I can.

_____

_____

_____

_____

_____

there is no condemnation

The Lord Jesus, God from all eternity, took on human flesh and came to live on earth in person for a number of reasons. But the chief of them is to free those who all their lives were held in slavery by their fear of death, as the writer to the Hebrews puts it in the second chapter.

Jesus lived a replacement life for us, submitting to all laws of God and man and keeping them all perfectly. He offered his body to abuse and suffering, knowing that in this way the punishment that we deserved was being diverted totally upon him. Finally, he surrendered to death itself, and through the great exchange that happened on Calvary, our death became his death and his innocence became ours.

The upshot? **"There is now no condemnation for those who are in Christ Jesus, because through Christ Jesus the law of the Spirit of life set me free from the law of sin and death"** (Romans 8:1,2). Here is why you need never fear God again. Your sins were pardoned, all of them, objectively, freely, long ago, without reference to your performance. It is inheritance, not wages. It is yours—all who believe it have it.

God really means it—no condemnation means no condemnation. You can exhale now.

_____

_____

_____

_____

_____

April

"'I know the plans I have for you,' declares the LORD, 'plans to prosper you and not to harm you, plans to give you hope and a future.'"
(Jeremiah 29:11)

April 1

morning is best

Okay, okay, God doesn't keep business hours. He is available for worship, praise, and prayer 24/7. There is no bad time.

But, forgive me for saying so, morning is best. King David thought so too. **"In the morning, O Lord, you hear my voice; in the morning I lay my requests before you and wait in expectation"** (Psalm 5:3).

Here's why: through prayers of repentance and the comfort of the gospel, you can start your day not only with a hot shower but with a rinsed spirit. When you start your day certain of the forgiveness of your sins, every morning is fresh and new. When you commit your day's agenda to the Lord, you can then trust that he will guide and shape it according to what fits into his master plan and what is good for you.

When you start your day with the Lord, you can get his help right away instead of waiting until you are burdened, frustrated, and exhausted by trying to do everything yourself. And when you start your day with the Lord, you will see the people around you as blessings, God's instruments, in serving him and accomplishing the mission for which he made you in the first place.

a wife is a good thing

"Take my wife. Please." For decades comedian Henny Youngman made a living off that line. It wasn't just a gag. As with all comedy, there was enough truth in that contemptuous statement that husbands resonated with it and laughed. Thus it became part of his brand. I doubt if too many women thought it funny.

I don't think God does either. At the beginning of time, God noted that it was not good for the man to be alone, and so he made a helper suitable for him. Now many thousands of years later, together is still better than alone. A believing wife is a man's faith encourager #1, his truth teller, comforter, image manager, and nurturer of children.

A good wife helps her guy better understand how the female half of the world thinks and operates. She is a great advisor on fashion, appropriate social behaviors, tending relationships, and how a home ought to look. Any husband can make a list of his wife's failings (as she could his). A much better exercise is for every husband to take inventory of how richly God has blessed his life through his wife.

Men, say this with me: **"He who finds a wife finds what is good and receives favor from the Lord"** (Proverbs 18:22). Ask any widower.

_____

_____

_____

_____

_____

I'm too far gone

Are you a *Star Wars* fan? Remember how Darth Vader fought off all of Luke Skywalker's attempts to bring him back to the good side? Vader thought that he was too far gone. He had resigned himself to service to the evil emperor.

Perhaps you have felt that your sins are too great for God ever to love and accept you. Perhaps your years of guilt and shame keep you from God's house and from enjoying the fellowship of God's other children. Perhaps you are so aware of your unworthiness that you just can't bring yourself to pray.

The Bible says in Romans 5:20, **"Where sin increased, grace increased all the more."** In other words, God's forgiveness is greater than your greatest sin. Christ is greater than Satan. God's mercy is greater than your guilt.

Perhaps you know someone who feels that he or she is too far gone and is resigned to fear and damnation. You can be God's agent of hope. Feel the love. Share the love.

_____

_____

_____

_____

_____

April 4
children are a miracle

Lord, how can I thank you enough for my children? I know, I know — I complain enough about them and scold them too much, but I am really and truly grateful that you honored us by giving them to our home.

When I was single, I guess I knew in theory that **"sons are a heritage from the LORD, children a reward from him"** (Psalm 127:3). But the reality is far more amazing. The nine months of wonder as a new life grew . . . the incredible process of childbirth . . . the first cries and first cuddles — Lord, how can anyone who has seen the drama in a birthing room stay an atheist?

My children *are* a heritage. They *are* a reward from you — help me always see them in that way. Thank you for their laughter, their foolishness, their innocence, their questions, their energy, and the amazing things that come out of their mouths.

Today I rededicate them to you. You designed and fashioned them, Father. Lord Jesus, you redeemed them. Spirit, you live in them. Keep them yours now and always. Keep their guardian angels on duty, as you have promised. Help them grow into adults who will find joy in serving you and building your kingdom. Lord, thank you for my miracle children.

_____

_____

_____

_____

_____

celebrate your God

Need a lift today? Let the Bible tell you just how wonderful your God is. Here are just four of his marvelous characteristics: **"The LORD is gracious and compassionate, slow to anger and rich in love"** (Psalm 145:8).

The Lord is *gracious:* Sometimes you don't generate very wonderful, cozy, cuddly feelings in other people's hearts, least of all in God's. Still, God treats you better than you deserve. He has decided to love you, regardless of your past. That's what grace is.

The Lord is *compassionate:* God suffers with you. When politicians say they feel your pain, they don't even know who you are. But God feels your pain, knows who you are, *and* does things to help you because your pain is now personal to him through Christ.

The Lord is *slow to anger:* Aren't you glad Scripture doesn't say, "God, you have a hair-trigger temper"? Or, "You never forget when I mess up"? Or, "You keep accurate, detailed records of all my debts"? Don't you love it when God is patient with you and cuts you some slack?

The Lord is *rich in love:* He isn't stingy with you. He gave everything he had—his one and only Son—to buy you the forgiveness you could never earn or deserve. If he didn't withhold his dearest treasure, he will surely give you the littler things as well.

_____

_____

_____

_____

_____

keep it moving

One of the wondrous features of the teachings of Christ is that God's world works seemingly backward from our everyday experience. According to Jesus' teaching, God measures greatness through humility. Getting what you need by serving others. Winning by yielding.

Here's another "backward" gospel principle: *you get more by giving more.* **"One man gives freely, yet gains even more; another withholds unduly, but comes to poverty. A generous man will prosper; he who refreshes others will himself be refreshed"** (Proverbs 11:24,25). Doesn't that sound counterintuitive? If you do things for other people, then you will have *less* time, money, and energy for yourself, right?

Here's the mystery component: it's God who enters our lives quietly to make things happen for people who adopt his agenda for their lives. We don't live in a zero sum universe. Our God is a God of abundance. The One who once multiplied loaves and fishes to feed a multitude can see to it that faithful and generous men and women will have everything they need and more.

Now—if he could only persuade you to believe that. Go ahead. Call his bluff.

_____

_____

_____

_____

_____

who, me? judgmental?

Scots poet Robert Burns offered some immortal lines on the difficulty of self-awareness: "O wad some Pow'r the giftie gie us. To see oursels as ithers see us!" Why can we see so clearly the flaws in others and be so unaware of our own? If only we could see ourselves as ithers see us.

You and I, for instance, are probably just as judgmental as the people we resent for being judgmental. When Jesus told his disciples in the Sermon on the Mount not to judge so they wouldn't be judged, he wanted to warn them of the terrible sin of hypocrisy—thinking you are morally superior to other people, innocent of sin, more valuable to God, worthy of greater honor.

In fact, we are in as much need of Christ's mercy as any other person. Sin eats away at everything we think, say, or do, everything stained and twisted by the selfishness we drag around. Without Christ we too would wear a toe tag for hell.

So? So **let us stop passing judgment on one another** (Romans 14:13). As fellow lepers, we can simply pass on the healing gospel of Christ. Our judgmental words can be replaced with words of kindness and encouragement.

_____

_____

_____

_____

_____

love is better than money

Loving money and loving people are actually diametrically opposite forces. If you love money, basically you are just loving yourself, because you crave the power and pleasures and comforts that money brings. When you love other people, you are actually choosing to spend yourself, your energy and time, to make someone else's life better. You are giving rather than taking.

At one time or another we have all believed that acquiring money would bring happiness. It never does. The opposite is true: **"Better a meal of vegetables where there is love than a fattened calf with hatred"** (Proverbs 15:17). You will find the greatest satisfactions in your life in the ways in which you have served other people's needs. It's as though *they* have the keys to *your* happiness.

When we spend our first energy tending our relationships, including our relationship with God, all of our needs will be met. If you spend your life chasing money, you will end up with nothing. There are no checkbooks in coffins. But you can take people with you to heaven.

In Christ, love can survive the grave.

_____

_____

_____

_____

_____

April 9

I feel like I'm drowning

Navy survivors of the bombing of Pearl Harbor in 1941 had terrifying tales to tell of being below decks in sinking or capsized ships. Trapped behind bulkheads, air supply dwindling, they watched the water level rise. Some escaped; many hundreds didn't.

Is your personal load of bad news coming all at once? **"Save me, O God, for the waters have come up to my neck"** (Psalm 69:1). God must be letting it happen for a reason. Let go of your own agenda for a minute and try to imagine God's.

Many of the rescued sailors at Pearl Harbor were freed not by their own efforts—they couldn't put the smallest dent in ship steel. They were freed by divers with underwater cutting torches. They "prayed" for help by banging wrenches on the hull to show where they were.

Sometimes the waters rise in our own lives because we are too proud or stubborn to ask for help, or blow it off when God first sends other people as our "rescue team."

Here is a promise from One who loves you and finds no joy in your misery: **"Therefore let everyone who is godly pray to you while you may be found; surely when the mighty waters rise, they will not reach him"** (Psalm 32:6).

_____

_____

_____

_____

_____

I have a place in God's church

All kinds of wonderful things happen when you become a believer, whether you become part of the body of Christ as a little child or as a retiree. Your status with God changes from enemy to child. Your future changes from condemned to saved. Your spiritual appearance changes from filthy to glorious in God's eyes.

Another marvelous benefit is that you acquire an enormous number of new friends and family members. As you are connected to Christ, you are automatically connected to his brothers and sisters. Isn't that amazing? No Christian can possibly say, "I am alone." **"Remember that at that time you were separate from Christ, excluded from citizenship in Israel and foreigners to the covenants of the promise, without hope and without God in the world. Consequently, you are no longer foreigners and aliens, but fellow citizens with God's people and members of God's household"** (Ephesians 2:12,19).

Are you part of a congregation? You have a network of people to worship with, pray with, serve with, laugh with, grow with, and learn with. Through your church you can be an important encourager of other strugglers. And there you can let people minister to you. Then you will know how you matter in God's scheme of things.

_____

_____

_____

_____

_____

tomorrow is not guaranteed

"Life is short—eat dessert first," read the sign. Perhaps you've seen it or one like it, such as its variation, "Life's too short to . . ." (there follows some frugal or sacrificial behavior that you are encouraged to abandon, the idea being that we should eat, drink, and be merry for tomorrow we die).

Actually, life is short. Psalm 39 offers a grave rebuke to all who drift along in their lives, putting off worrying about their relationship with God for another day: **"You have made my days a mere handbreadth; the span of my years is as nothing before you. Each man's life is but a breath. Man is a mere phantom as he goes to and fro"** (Psalm 39:5,6).

That means first things first. *Now* is the day of salvation; now is the moment for repentance of sin and faith in Christ Jesus. **"The night is nearly over; and the day is almost here,"** Paul wrote in Romans 13:12. Does that sound morbid? Not at all! In fact, it is liberating to realize that we are but stewards of God's treasures and servants of God's people. Set free from the fear of death by the death of Christ, we can enjoy every day knowing that an unlimited supply awaits us on the other side of the grave.

_____

_____

_____

_____

_____

what a fool believes

Q: What do the book of Proverbs and Mr. T have in common? A: They both have nothing but scorn for fools.

The dominant topic in Proverbs is godly *wisdom* — acquiring it, living it, enjoying its fruits, and shunning the thoughts and actions of fools. Wisdom in Proverbs is described as more valuable than money, jewels, or gold, and it needs to be pursued and prized more than anything else on earth.

Godly wisdom is nothing less than hearing, believing, and living the words of God. An example: **"A fool shows his annoyance at once, but a prudent man overlooks an insult"** (Proverbs 12:16). How true! If we feel that we have to retaliate for every slight, every dig, every bump we encounter from people along our way, we will be in a constant state of conflict, fighting our way through life.

How much better to adopt the mind of Christ, who in humility bore abuse from others. Our stress level will go down and our life enjoyment level will go up when we choose not to hear and dwell on put-downs from the peanut gallery. If God likes me, I'm golden.

_____

_____

_____

_____

_____

April 13

it's time

If you ever come to my house, one of the first things you'll see is that I have this thing about clocks. There's something about the ticking and chiming that soothes my soul. I must have an inner dread about being late.

Jesus always knew what time it was—time to heal, time to teach, time to rebuke, time to go on a retreat, time to attend celebration dinners. His Father let him know when it was time to die. Jesus told his disciples that their traveling teaching ministry was almost over. **"From that time on Jesus began to explain to his disciples that he must go to Jerusalem and suffer many things at the hands of the elders, chief priests and teachers of the law, and that he must be killed and on the third day be raised to life"** (Matthew 16:21). He knew that his royal entrance into Jerusalem on Palm Sunday would be his last.

A miracle happened amidst the palms. Crowds of people recognized that the quiet man on the donkey colt was their Messiah. Their hosannas showed that they knew what time it was—their King was riding into their lives and claiming their allegiance.

Do you know what time it is on Palm Sunday? It's time for you to quit dithering and claim, or re-claim all over again, Jesus Christ as your Lord and King. Through his Word, through the splash of baptismal water, through his body and blood given in the Supper, Jesus comes to you as personally today as he did back then. The palms call you: worship him *now*.

_____

_____

_____

connected to Christ

We all resonate with President Teddy Roosevelt's dictum, "Speak softly, but carry a big stick." Power trumps talk, doesn't it? In late 1907 Roosevelt sent *16* U.S. battleships on a 43,000-mile journey around the globe to show off America's growing fleet. Painted pure white with gilded scrollwork, the "Great White Fleet" forcibly made the point that America was now a first-rate military power.

Displays of power, however, do not convert people to faith in Christ. You might think that resurrection from the dead, the ultimate in miracles, would have brought everybody in Israel and the ancient Near East to faith. It didn't happen when the "other" Lazarus was raised (John 11) nor with the resurrection of Christ himself, nor with the resurrections performed by Paul and Peter.

Jesus said to a rich man in hell, **"If they do not listen to Moses and the Prophets, they will not be convinced even if someone rises from the dead"** (Luke 16:31).

Ah, but all who *do* listen to Moses and the Prophets and who believe their message have already begun to live again. Connected to Christ, we are connected once again to the life force of the universe. His unshakable Word promises that we ourselves will rise from the dead and that we will see the resurrected Redeemer with our own eyes. His Word is enough.

_____

_____

_____

_____

_____

pay your taxes cheerfully

I will admit to being a tax grumbler. There. I've said it and am ashamed. Perhaps you too have grumbled while filling out your Form 1040. Many first-century Israelites resented Roman taxation as well. Jesus' enemies once tried to play on those popular resentments to trick him into advocating tax evasion.

"Jesus, knowing their evil intent, said, 'You hypocrites, why are you trying to trap me? Show me the coin used for paying the tax.' They brought him a denarius, and he asked them, 'Whose portrait is this? And whose inscription?' 'Caesar's,' they replied. Then he said to them, 'Give to Caesar what is Caesar's'" (Matthew 22:18-21).

I love seeing national forests and wilderness areas, driving on interstate highways, enjoying the security of strong armed forces, and trusting a strong judicial system. Why am I not more willing to shoulder my portion of the burden of paying for all those wonderful things? Just selfishness, I guess.

I'll be better this April 15. I promise.

_____

_____

_____

_____

_____

the beauty trap

Do you know any anorexic men? I didn't think so. Men are anxious to some extent about their appearance, but the pressure on women to be thin and beautiful is on a whole different level. Cosmetic surgery has become an enormous industry. Makeup, hair, clothes—think of the time and money that women feel they must invest in these things.

It's one thing to try to clean up and look nice. It's another entirely to live in daily self-hatred. The other day I saw a video about a young woman lamenting how she looked. What depressed her was not the usual "deficiencies"—hair, nose, shape, etc. She was despairing because she had "man shoulders." Good grief. The celeb shows had even made this girl hate her shoulders. It's a battle you can never win— there's always somebody around who is taller, thinner, cuter, with better hair, skin, clothes, and jewelry.

You cannot escape the culture. What you can escape is the self-torment of wishing you were somebody else (even a magazine model). One of the blessings of the gospel of Christ is to allow us to accept ourselves and identify and enjoy our own unique gifts and blessings. Here's Jesus' voice: **"The Lord has anointed me to preach good news to the poor . . . to bind up the brokenhearted, to . . . provide for those who grieve in Zion—to bestow on them a crown of *beauty* instead of ashes"** (Isaiah 61:1,3).

Whose admiration do you most crave? Crave God's. Through the lens of Christ's work, your "pictures" look nice to him. In fact, you're beautiful.

take heart!

The span from Palm Sunday to Easter Day is usually called Holy Week. It was the greatest burst of God's saving works that the planet had ever seen, surpassing even creation itself. It encompassed the Savior's mighty victory over mankind's most terrible enemies: sin, Satan, death, and hell.

For most of that week, however, Jesus' disciples were under a severe strain. Many of the things Jesus told them made no sense to them at the time, and what they did understand they didn't like hearing. On Thursday they celebrated one last Passover meal with Jesus, then tasted the first ever Communion meal. Jesus washed their dusty feet, one by one, as a powerful demonstration of servant-leadership.

Most of those evening hours were taken up by a lengthy teaching session. It was a sobering preview of the warfare and hardships that awaited them and anyone who openly serves the Lord. But it was also a calm and serene proclamation of final victory to all who were bound together with Jesus in faith. **"I have told you these things, so that *in me* you may have peace. In this world you will have trouble. But take heart! I have overcome the world"** (John 16:33).

Here is hope for all believers today who groan and are afraid. The Bible tells us that our lives are hidden in Christ. Outwardly it may seem that we are wasting away. The reality is that our lives are in Christ's wonderful hands. When your life is full of trouble, take heart! Christ has overcome. He won; you win.

_____

_____

_____

there will be justice

The sinking feeling in the pit of your stomach. The long scratch on the paint of your new car, keyed by some callous vandal. The broken window. Your missing purse. A silent and invisible pickpocket nabs your wallet in a crowd.

An arsonist burns down a building that provided jobs to dozens of people, now unemployed. A mugger leaves a shaken victim who will never feel safe again. Teenagers knock a grade school kid off his bike and steal it.

We can't escape. The world we live in is broken. The cruel, the greedy, the violent take advantage of their fellows. Sometimes they are caught. Often, terribly often, they are not, and they live on to damage more lives another day. Where is justice?

Here it is: **"Be sure of this: the wicked will not go unpunished, but those who are righteous will go free"** (Proverbs 11:21). God sees and knows; he remembers and waits. The Day is coming when there will be no secrets and no escapees. Those who trust in Christ are forgiven and welcomed. Those whose crimes are unforgiven will receive what the Judge thinks they deserve.

_____

_____

_____

_____

_____

give in proportion

The way the IRS works, you can earn quite a bit of money before your income becomes taxable. All those below a certain level are excused from having to fund governmental services—they can ride for free.

God doesn't manage his world that way. One of the most shocking stories in the New Testament is the story of the widow's mite. A woman gave a contribution of several cents to her God at the temple. Jesus saw her do it and praised her for it to his disciples.

His point: all of God's children are blessed and entrusted with the King's treasures; all of God's children are invited to return an honorable proportion to him. All of God's children can enjoy the thrill of sharing their treasures so that the ministry of the Word can keep going out to people.

The concept is elegantly simple: **"On the first day of every week, each one of you should set aside a sum of money in keeping with his income"** (1 Corinthians 16:2).

_____

_____

_____

_____

_____

April 20

kindhearted women

One of the profoundest influences on my life from ages 1 to 14 was my grandmother. She went straight to work after seventh grade, never attended high school, never drove a car. She never made the newspapers or a "Who's Who" listing in her city. But she was a shining light in my life. She had time to play with me and listen to my childish chatter. She made me feel important.

Gossip magazines and TV shows fawn over the wealthy, their cars and romances and homes and escapades. The celebrity industry, however, while adoring you on your way up will mock you when you fall. Money gets people's attention but not their affection.

"A kindhearted woman gains respect, but ruthless men gain only wealth" (Proverbs 11:16). Do you have any kindhearted women in your life? Women who spent time with you when you were small, praised and encouraged you on the way up, and made you feel important?

Here's a task for you today. Right now! Put this book down and list five kindhearted women who have encouraged and built you up. Are any still alive? How soon can you thank them?

_____

_____

_____

_____

_____

joy in humble service

Lord, I know some people who are absolutely miserable. They know they have made some terrible and selfish choices. They feel depressed and guilty all the time. They have found out the sad truth that Satan is lying when he promises happiness and satisfaction.

But I have found the reverse to be true also. When I listen to you, when I adjust my values to you, when I dare to do your will, my life is good! I love that feeling! I don't like the urge to run away from you, avoiding you, fearing you. I love the sense of your smile and approval.

I have found your words to be true: **"The LORD takes delight in his people; he crowns the humble with salvation"** (Psalm 149:4). I know my sinful past is washed away; I know your powerful Spirit is at work in me, changing me and leading me. I love my life whenever I think that you are delighted in me. I love wearing my crown of salvation—it makes me feel that I can endure any hardship and overcome any obstacle.

My Savior is my hero and example. He came not to be served but to serve. Help me believe, *really* believe, *always* believe that you call great those who serve other people humbly.

_____

_____

_____

_____

_____

without fear

Man-made religions find human guilt and fear very useful in getting people's attention and in getting them to do what the organization wants. Voodoo, for instance, thrives on threats and curses. For another, the (false) teaching of purgatory made even believers dread the day of their death, for then would come countless years of torment to "pay" for their sins.

Fear and guilt come from the law, amplified by our consciences. But the gospel of Christ drives out fear. Have you noticed how God's angel messengers at the dawn of the New Testament age kept saying the same thing to startled and terrified saints—"Don't be afraid"?

When Zechariah finally was allowed to speak, he showed that he got it. Inspired by the Spirit, he uttered marvelous words at the birth of his miracle son: **"Praise be to the Lord, the God of Israel, because he has come and has redeemed his people . . . to rescue us from the hand of our enemies, and to enable us to serve him** *without fear"* (Luke 1:68,74).

The joyful service that you render to your God is not to amass points so that you can qualify for heaven. Or frantically to undo some of your old sins. Or to get him to like you. Remember: No fear. We like to serve him because he likes us.

_____

_____

_____

_____

_____

remember whom you serve

Wouldn't it be silly if a receptionist answered the phone and didn't know the name of the company she was representing? Wouldn't it be silly if a sales rep never mentioned the name of his company? Wouldn't it be silly if an employee forgot that she was an employee and imagined that she was the owner?

Silly but believable. People do the same thing to God all the time. We all go through foggy stretches where we get confused about our mission in life. We forget that we're all managers in God's company, that our great purpose in life is to give God glory, receive and reflect his love, and act as his agents in bringing benefit to the lives of other people. That's why you were created. That's why you were redeemed.

What is your life's main purpose? Here's one way to put it: **"In all your ways acknowledge him"** (Proverbs 3:6). Isn't it amazing how much easier our daily decision making gets when we begin the day by saying, "God, I am working for you today. Thanks for letting me into your company."

_____

_____

_____

_____

_____

April 24

I'm disfigured

There was a reason why the phantom of the opera wore a half mask. The right side of his face was disfigured, and he was ashamed of it.

Life is hard. Life is even harder if your face or skin is disfigured. Our society worships and adores physical beauty and assigns much less value to people who aren't good-looking. A cleft palate, rosacea, and severe acne all make people feel like second- or third-class members of society. They are self-conscious in front of people and know that their looks will close doors throughout their lives.

"While Jesus was in one of the towns, a man came along who was covered with leprosy. When he saw Jesus, he fell with his face to the ground and begged him, 'Lord, if you are willing, you can make me clean'" (Luke 5:12).

Leprosy brought a triple curse. Not only did it blotch your skin, but certain types caused nerve death in one's extremities, causing that tissue to die. Worst of all—it was thought to be contagious, and lepers were utterly quarantined and isolated from human contact.

Jesus' heart hurt when he encountered people who suffered from leprosy. He himself knew what it was like to be ugly. He himself was **"disfigured beyond that of any man and his form marred beyond human likeness"** (Isaiah 52:14). Then and now he responds with compassion, miraculous medical care, special blessings like reconstructive surgery, and hope for a better future.

---

leading God's way

You might call Samuel the last of the judges and the first of the prophets. He was the bridge between tribal societal organization and the monarchy of Israel. As God's personal representative to the Israelite nation, he wielded considerable power. Like the traveling justices in the Old West, he had a prophetic and judging circuit that he would ride. And yet, unlike American politics, he did not see his authority as a convenient way to enrich himself and make his life more comfortable.

"As for me, I am old and gray. . . . I have been your leader from my youth until this day. Here I stand. Testify against me in the presence of the LORD and his anointed. Whose ox have I taken? Whose donkey have I taken? Whom have I cheated? Whom have I oppressed? From whose hand have I accepted a bribe to make me shut my eyes?" (1 Samuel 12:2,3).

Politics has always been awash in money, as people seek to buy influence or power or escape from the consequences of their sins. Who of us is free of the belief that having money is good and having a lot of money is great?

Samuel is my hero because he showed that at the end of your life, what brings the greatest satisfaction is not how much money you made (and spent) on your own pleasures. It is in how useful you have been to God and his saving purposes.

last word

When there are two or more strong-willed people in a family, there is often a struggle over who gets the last word. It's a control game—even when you yield, you're only pretending to yield if you can get in one last shot, one last attempt to control the discussion.

I don't like it when I get one-upped by my family and friends. But I will tell you that I am delighted and relieved and totally fine with my God's having the last word in my life. I try to make myself useful to him, make good plans, take risks, buy, sell, build, save, invest, and organize. But I know myself well enough by now to know that there are streaks of selfishness, blindness, and foolishness in all I do.

This word from the Word gives me comfort: **"In his heart a man plans his course, but the LORD determines his steps"** (Proverbs 16:9). God is my safety net. He is the director of my play. He is my backstop, umpire, and best friend. I can't wait to thank him face-to-face.

In the meantime, I can go forward, knowing that he gets the last word in all I do. You can too.

_____

_____

_____

_____

_____

marry only fellow Israelites

Do you know anyone who is party to an arranged marriage, i.e., where the parents chose their child's spouse? That custom is rare in America but more common in countries like India.

In Old Covenant times in Israel, the heavenly Father set boundaries around a select group of marriage prospects; he wanted marriage to stay within Israel. Here was his law: Moses told the Israelites, **"When the Lord your God brings you into the land you are entering to possess and drives out before you many nations . . . do not intermarry with them. Do not give your daughters to their sons or take their daughters for your sons, for they will turn your sons away from following me to serve other gods"** (Deuteronomy 7:1,3,4).

This was not just Jewish chauvinism. It was a matter of survival. Israelite people frequently broke this commandment, and the unions with unbelievers usually turned out to be spiritual disasters. Even great King Solomon, the wisest man on the face of the earth, had his heart turned from God by his foreign, idol-worshiping wives.

The point was not to preserve Israelite culture. The point was to keep the often wayward Israelites from throwing away their faith in the God of Abraham.

_____

_____

_____

_____

_____

choose wisely whom you marry

Okay, that was then and this is now. What does God have to say about our marriage pool in New Covenant times? Contrary to what many Americans have believed for centuries, there are no racial restrictions on marriage partners in the New Testament. Various states did indeed adopt miscegenation laws, but those laws didn't come out of the New Testament.

First Corinthians chapter 7 shows that an unbelieving spouse who becomes a Christian does not have the right automatically to divorce his or her still-unbelieving spouse. The hope is that the new believer's loving words and example may draw the unbeliever into listening to the Word.

But for a Christian to choose to marry someone he or she knows is an unbeliever poses huge risks. That person could become a spiritual boat anchor, dragging you down, draining your spiritual energy, making fun of your commitment, adding resistance to a life that has enough problems already. St. Paul's advice: **"Do not be yoked together with unbelievers. For what do righteousness and wickedness have in common? Or what fellowship can light have with darkness? . . . What does a believer have in common with an unbeliever? What agreement is there between the temple of God and idols? For we are the temple of the living God"** (2 Corinthians 6:14-16).

Listen to your Christian friends and family. Think before you leap.

_____

_____

_____

where are you, God?

I'm here to tell you that I hate being confused. I try so hard to understand my world, but sometimes I just don't *see* God's hands at work, I don't *see* Christ's victory, and I don't *see* all of God's people looking like winners. Why do humble, suffering, righteous people have to bear additional heavy blows? Why do abusers and neighborhood destroyers get away with their evil work? Why is my life so hard so often?

David was confused sometimes too: **"How long, O Lord? Will you forget me forever? How long will you hide your face from me? How long must I wrestle with my thoughts and every day have sorrow in my heart? How long will my enemy triumph over me?"** (Psalm 13:1,2). God chooses not to explain everything. He chooses to let us struggle sometimes. He chooses to not provide us with extensive advance information, advance supplies, or constant hand-holding.

What he does do is invite us to look at his track record of promise keeping. What he does do is point us to Calvary, where the war was won. What he does do is invite us to trust that he will make the littler things fall into place, each at just the right time. His time. **"I trust in your unfailing love; my heart rejoices in your salvation. I will sing to the Lord, for he has been good to me"** (Psalm 13:5,6).

_____

_____

_____

_____

_____

somebody stop me

A letter from a troubled *Time of Grace* viewer: "Am I truly saved though I continue to sin?"

That cry from the heart is a common experience with all Christians, including St. Paul: **"I know that nothing good lives in me, that is, in my sinful nature. For I have the desire to do what is good, but I cannot carry it out. . . . Who will rescue me from this body of death?"** (Romans 7:18,24). It is a hard truth that sin will live within us until we are raised up on judgment day and personally transformed in body and soul. In heaven we will never sin again, nor even desire to do so.

In the meantime, we find ourselves in the middle of a war. But it's a war that Christ has already won. When your sins trouble you, as they should, look not to yourself, your worth, your record, your achievements, nor even your good intentions; but look to the cross of Christ. Who will rescue us from this body of death? Jesus did.

His death once and for all paid your obligations in God's court. You are declared not guilty. With that triumphant verdict and with new confidence, you can return to the battle, seeking to honor God with your life for his matchless gift of a Savior.

_____

_____

_____

_____

_____

May

"Create in me a pure heart, O God,
and renew a steadfast spirit within me."
(Psalm 51:10)

you are your children's refuge

There's a reason why children retell stories about bogeymen and monsters under their beds. It's because they know their world is scary and dangerous and they need to know that there is a place for them where they can be safe. Daddy's strength is a huge wall holding off the monsters to give them time to grow up.

Where does Daddy get his strength from? In the earlier part of his life, Solomon was still following the miraculous wisdom that God gave him. He shares an important insight about family security: **"He who fears the LORD has a secure fortress, and for his children it will be a refuge"** (Proverbs 14:26). God's Word and wisdom help men to control their own sinful and violent impulses, and his divine forgiveness helps a man to be a patient, disciplined, and kind husband and father.

A little girl needs a daddy who thinks she is a princess, beautiful and precious. If her heart is secure in that manly admiration, she doesn't have to throw herself at bad boys for attention when she's a teenager. Little boys need a daddy who shows them that real strength is shown in self-control, self-discipline, and self-sacrifice. The feeling of manhood is not automatic—it needs to be conferred by another man.

A man who is strong in the Lord will know how to be strong for his family.

_____

_____

_____

_____

_____

pray for your country

"Ask not what your country can do for you; ask what you can do for your country." With those stirring words, President John F. Kennedy inspired new patriotism in his American listeners as he delivered his inaugural address in 1961. Two months later he signed the Peace Corps into law, a form of national service that would ultimately draw more than 200,000 mostly young people.

There are two particularly poisonous attitudes toward government that Satan will seek to inject into your soul and spirit. One is to resent taxation, grumbling and cheating wherever you think you can get away with it. The other is to assume a bushel basket of government benefits as entitlements, as though you were *owed* a comfortable life from Washington, D.C.

God uses both good and bad governments as his servants knowingly and unknowingly to carry out his will. Through the messages of his Old Testament prophets, God lets you peek behind the scenes of what he is up to on the world stage. It is no surprise to see how he blessed Israel through its good kings. It is a great surprise to see how even the terrible invaders, Assyria and Babylonia, were carrying out his loving and saving plans. He told the people of Judah, who were about to go into exile, **"Seek the peace and prosperity of the city to which I have carried you into exile. Pray to the Lord for it, because if it prospers, you too will prosper"** (Jeremiah 29:7).

If Israelites could pray for their conquerors, how much more will Christians want to pray for our wonderful country, our America?

_____

_____

your cash is trash

Money is a wonderful tool, isn't it? It is a lever of power—it makes things happen. We can trade it for food, mechanical transportation, clothing, and a home.

Money is a wonderful tool, but it makes a terrible master. People who become addicted to it find it a fickle and abusive lover. It promises happiness if you only get more, but more only leaves you wanting still more.

It will be taken from you when you die. All of it. It will not be available to you when you stand before your Maker to give account for the way in which you spent your life. **"Wealth is worthless in the day of wrath"** (Proverbs 11:4). **"Whoever trusts in his riches will fall"** (Proverbs 11:28).

What now? See your money as God's gift. He's the owner, you the manager. Invest it in his kingdom, in service to others, in taking care of your family, and in leaving a legacy. Look at your heavenly Father as your real security and trust his clear promises to take care of you. And make Jesus Christ your greatest treasure. He alone is what you need on the day of wrath.

_____

_____

_____

_____

_____

women can be strong too

In most hero stories it seems that the script usually reads that the man is the brave and courageous and visionary one and the woman is the compassionate and emotional and intuitive one. Deborah is a hero of mine because she stepped up when none of the male leaders, including Israelite commander Barak, had the courage to act.

Sisera, the Canaanite king of Hazor, a fortress city in the north of Israel, had been terrifying the Israelites for two decades with his raiding and attacks. He had nine hundred iron chariots under his command! When God finally had Israel's attention and repentance, he sent word that a divine rescue was on the way. **"Then Deborah said to Barak, 'Go! This is the day the Lord has given Sisera into your hands. Has not the Lord gone ahead of you?'"** (Judges 4:14).

The Lord brought about such a complete victory that Sisera's entire army was destroyed. And because Barak had been so hesitant, even with a direct divine prophetic promise, God gave to another woman, Jael, the significant honor of slaying Sisera.

Deborah was also a phenomenal poet. May I suggest that today would be a good day for you to enjoy her stirring poem of praise to God in Judges chapter 5?

_____

_____

_____

_____

_____

brotherly hatred

We might wish to think that our families are bulwarks of strength against the hostility of a cruel and heartless world. Ah, if only 'twere so. The sad reality of our existence is that families can harbor as much or even more conflict. Some of the worst damage to people's bodies and souls is done by their own relatives.

"Joseph went after his brothers and found them near Dothan. But they saw him in the distance, and before he reached them, they plotted to kill him" (Genesis 37:17,18). Jacob's family was rancid with favoritism, simmering resentments, and hatred. It is only God's intervention that kept Joseph, the spoiled 11th son, from being killed by his brothers. Yes—that family. The preservers of the faith and ancestors of the Messiah.

Family members have a unique opportunity to hurt one another, but they can choose to see their homes as a place to begin in acting out Christ-like love and a Christ-like servant-spirit. How can we ever love our neighbors if we have not first mastered how to love our sisters and brothers?

Do any long-standing resentments, grudges, cruelties, failures, or misunderstandings spoil your family relationships? God spent a lot of time on Joseph and helped him grow up. Joseph in turn helped his brothers mature and repent of their horrible hatred. How can you be God's instrument of healing in your family?

_____

_____

_____

_____

who, me? a thief?

Theft is one of the most discouraging of all crimes. How your heart sinks to discover your car stolen or your home broken into. How the victims fantasize about sweet revenge on the thieves. We despise them.

Do you know any thieves? Is it possible you are one? Perhaps you've never stolen a car. But is God talking to you along with the Israelites that the prophet Malachi addressed? **"Will a man rob God? Yet you rob me. But you ask, 'How do we rob you?' 'In tithes and offerings.' Bring the whole tithe into the storehouse"** (Malachi 3:8,10).

God thinks that the entire earth belongs to him and that all our material possessions, including our income stream, come from him. God thinks that he has spectacularly blessed each one of us. When people refuse to return to God an honorable portion of that God-given income, he views it as robbery.

This would be a great moment to pause and review your charitable giving plan. Would God call your offerings to him honorable? pathetic? mediocre? robbery? admirable?

_____

_____

_____

_____

_____

talk or pain

One of the reasons why the school of hard knocks is so effective is that it doesn't allow for any dropouts. The laws of economics are like the law of gravity—they are in force whether you like them or not, whether you believe in them or not. Nothing of value is free. You get what you pay for. You get what you work for.

I believe that there also are some simple laws of education. People have basically two ways to learn and adapt their behaviors: talk or pain. They can learn by listening to their teachers and elders, by reading books and studying the behaviors and experiences of others. Or they can learn the hard way, suffering the consequences for being lazy, dishonest, undisciplined, or mouthy.

God loves education, especially the teaching and learning of his Word. Your choice—you can do this hard or you can do this easy. **"He who scorns instruction will pay for it, but he who respects a command is rewarded"** (Proverbs 13:13).

So what kind of life are you choosing for yourself? Do you find the Bible boring, obsolete, and a waste of your time, or are you thirsty for its wisdom?

_____

_____

_____

_____

_____

I'm sick

We all expect to get sick now and then, and that doesn't bother us particularly. But when serious illness strikes, it can turn our lives upside down. Sickness shatters our illusion of control. Major sickness can destroy your savings, your career, your future. Prolonged sickness can also rock your faith in God's protection, love, and care.

God is there for us when we need him. When we put our trust in him, we give him the chance to make the illness work for us. Once when Jesus' friend Lazarus was seriously ill, everybody around him was panicking. But in John 11:4, Jesus simply said, **"This sickness will not end in death. No, it is for God's glory so that God's Son may be glorified through it."** He then demonstrated his power by raising Lazarus from the dead and by raising up a strong faith in those who were there.

Even if you can't see it right away, God will make your life better in some significant way. Even more important, he uses major illness to advance *his* agenda. Your life becomes a canvas for him to paint on. Your sickness will be for God's glory.

_____

_____

_____

_____

_____

God will never leave me

I spent a lot of nights in high school waiting for a bus on a dark corner after late practices or events. One of the bitterest experiences for all bus-dependent people is to arrive at the corner seconds too late and to watch the bus you need pulling away. Perhaps that sounds like small potatoes, but it's miserable at the time. That "left behind" panic lingers in the mind; it is an ongoing fear that many have.

"They left without me" means that you're not very valuable. "They left without me" means that maybe they thought of you as a drag on their fun. "They left without me" means that you don't belong.

Your God will never leave you. Here is his promise to every believer: **"I am the Lord, your God, who takes hold of your right hand and says to you, Do not fear; I will help you. Do not be afraid"** (Isaiah 41:13,14).

When bleak feelings of abandonment sweep over your soul, visualize a kindly Father taking you by the hand and holding on tightly. Imagine how safe you are when the Lord of all walks at your side. Believe him when he assures you that he is guiding your steps to the place where you can live with him forever. After the dark valley of the shadow of death comes the house of the Lord forever.

_____

_____

_____

_____

_____

two ears, one mouth

Okay, let's get right at it. Why is it so hard to get people to listen to you? For the same reason *you* don't like to do it. Listening is an act of surrender—you surrender the agenda to the speaker. You lose control of the conversation. The speaker will probably start telling you what to do (God forbid). You probably know everything the person is going to say (blah, blah, blah; yada, yada, yada). Listening seems weak.

Except that it's good. And godly. And smart. **"He who answers before listening—that is his folly and his shame"** (Proverbs 18:13). You can't learn when you're talking. Listening shows respect to someone else. Listening first helps you avoid revealing that you don't know what you're talking about. Listening first gives you time to organize and focus your thoughts, so that when it is your turn, your words will have greater impact.

Practicing listening to other people is also excellent training to help you listen better to God.

_____

_____

_____

_____

_____

nothing matters

Some people come to a point in their lives that is worse than fear, worry, or panic. That place is called apathy. Numbness of spirit. Don't care. Nothing matters.

Apathy is a coping mechanism for people who feel overwhelmed. They give up so they won't have to feel bad anymore. Since their feelings send only pain messages, the only thing to do is cauterize them. Then the pain will stop.

The problem is that sensations of being loved then also stop. The more people wall off their hearts, the more impossible relationships become. Then every human interaction becomes just business; a hard, cold game where the strong survive and the weak become roadkill.

Can you feel apathy creeping into your spirit? Let the heat of God's love, his desire to interact personally with you in your life, melt some of that ice. Want to fly again, sing again, care again? "[The Lord] **satisfies your desires with good things so that your youth is renewed like the eagle's"** (Psalm 103:5).

_____

_____

_____

_____

_____

wounded healers are the best

The people whose spiritual talk I most care to listen to aren't people with perfect hair and physiques, perfect lives, and plenty of money. The best witness is not given by the super successful. If Donald Trump says, "Trust in God and everything will be fine," I'd say, "Yeah, right," because the Donald can buy his way out of whatever trouble he may be in. But if someone who has buried a child says, "The Lord Jesus was there for me to comfort my heart," *that* I find believable. That's a powerful witness. She's earned the right to be taken seriously.

I call those people "wounded healers." When somebody has been broken and the Lord has patched him or her back together, that's a compelling testimony in our world. People won't suspect you of being a hypocrite when you then talk about Christ.

If you've been wounded, not only will God put you back together, but he also will re-invite you to be part of his work team. The brokenness of your past does not disqualify you from being useful because it's God's agenda, not yours. He reminds you, **"My grace is sufficient for you, for my power is made perfect in weakness"** (2 Corinthians 12:9).

Perhaps your pain, failures, or disabilities will become a perfect canvas on which God can paint beautiful things.

_____

_____

_____

_____

_____

it hurts when I laugh

Have you ever noticed how joy and sorrow are never too far apart from each other? It's as though they are twined around each other, bound up into our lives, and both are present in each experience. **"Even in laughter the heart may ache, and joy may end in grief"** (Proverbs 14:13).

"The wedding was beautiful, but if only the groom's father were still alive." "I got the promotion, but we have to move." "That cute guy asked me out, but now his ex-girlfriend hates me." It's part of life in this broken world. All of nature is in bondage to decay, and we can't escape it until Jesus returns.

Forewarned is forearmed. Since you can anticipate the streaks of sadness, you will not slip into fantasies that your world will soon be Utopia. Expect sorrow, but don't let it spoil your joy. Look for joy; expect it; celebrate it. See your joys as proof that God still cares for you and is sending good things to ease your journey.

Lift up your eyes to your coming heavenly home where sorrow will be banished. Every sad tear will be wiped from your eyes.

_____

_____

_____

_____

_____

loveless marriage

Some people grieve because the years are slipping past and they have not found a spouse. Their biological clocks are ticking and their bells are tolling. It was never their heart's dream to be single.

But being trapped in a loveless marriage is even worse, because your situation is now more or less permanent. What do you do when none of your needs is met and you feel used? What do you do when you feel like someone else's emotional punching bag? Where do you go with your resentment? How do you not feel envy at all the other happy couples?

Lord, have mercy! Lord, help us! A nice but plain woman named Leah used a trick to snare a husband in Jacob. When he realized the ruse, he didn't make her go back to her father's house, but he didn't like it much and always blamed her. **"The Lord saw that Leah was not loved"** (Genesis 29:31). Leah tried to please Jacob and win his love by bearing him children. The names she gave her boys are heart-wrenching signs of her desperation for her husband's approval.

Do you know anyone who feels trapped in a loveless marriage? Can you provide a sympathetic heart, words of encouragement, and prayer for godly wisdom?

_____

_____

_____

_____

_____

share your hope

Ever feel like you're going through life with such a heavy weight on your back that you can't stand up straight? Have you also experienced the relief that comes when God sends help? I hope you remember to thank God when he sends that blessed relief. But there's something else you need to do.

When you are standing up straighter, you have a chance to pass on the hope you have to the sufferers and stragglers and strugglers around you. But you can't do that if your spirituality is bottled up into a silent, personal thing. We were built for interaction with one another. We're made to be puzzle pieces—beautiful, colorful, with only part of the overall divine design.

The grand picture only comes together when you are put together with other people. **"Praise be to the . . . God of all comfort, who comforts us in all our troubles, so that we can comfort those in any trouble with the comfort we ourselves have received from God"** (2 Corinthians 1:3,4).

So open up a little, okay? Tell your personal story of God's rescue to the people around you who are scraping by. Share your hope, share your comfort, share your joy. When you do that, you'll notice they'll be standing a little straighter too.

_____

_____

_____

_____

_____

feed my lambs

Ora na azu nwa—Nigerian Igbo proverb.

Some of you who are single or married without children may be thinking, "Well, this whole parenting thing is for somebody else." Not true. The African proverb is right—it really does take a village to raise a child.

You may not have a child but are connected by blood, marriage, and faith to many young ones. God considers you a key part of the discipling process. Parents are often exhausted and overwhelmed by the day-to-day care of their children. They need and welcome as many Jesus-loving, hug-giving adults in their lives as possible.

After his triumphant resurrection, Jesus commissioned believers to feel a sense of communal responsibility for children. He told his main man Peter, **"'Simon son of John, do you truly love me more than these?' 'Yes, Lord,' he said, 'you know that I love you.' Jesus said, 'Feed my lambs'"** (John 21:15).

Whether you're an auntie or uncle, a Sunday school teacher or a neighbor, a community or church volunteer, a coach or a teacher, Jesus is thrilled that you are willing to be part of his village, thrilled that you place such high value on his little people, thrilled that you are helping to feed his lambs.

_____

_____

_____

_____

_____

God is listening

What makes you think God is listening when you pray?

There is only one satisfactory answer to that urgent question: we know he's listening because his Word tells us. We don't have the divine ability to see what's going on in the spirit world. We can't see how the sound energy in our voices, or the mental energy in our thoughts, reaches all the way up to heaven. It is enough for us to know that he hears. We will let him worry about the physics.

His Word never lies, and his Word says this about how important he sees your communication efforts: **"The Lord is far from the wicked but he hears the prayer of the righteous"** (Proverbs 15:29). That prayer connection is not given to all. Only through faith in Jesus Christ are we declared righteous enough to be called God's children. Only through faith in Christ are our messages received, answered, and then processed. Only through faith in Christ are the angels of heaven directed to carry out God's kindly intentions toward us.

Here is honor indeed—the Lord of the universe chooses to listen to you. Little you.

_____

_____

_____

_____

_____

is alcohol my friend or foe?

Wine is one of God's gifts to the human race. It eases stress and brings a smile—Psalm 104:15 says that it **"gladdens the heart of man"** (women seem to like it too). Jesus created 120 gallons of it to bless a wedding reception and even chose it as part of his holy meal of love and forgiveness.

But our sinful minds and damaged willpower are vulnerable to Satan's temptations. Careless alcohol use can make us act crazy or become its slaves. Even saints sometimes get stupid: **"Noah, a man of the soil, proceeded to plant a vineyard. When he drank some of its wine, he became drunk and lay uncovered inside his tent"** (Genesis 9:20,21).

Do you think people set out in life to become alcoholics? Do you think people crave the experience of alcohol withdrawal, liver damage, DWI arrests, uncontrollable vomiting, and slavery to liter after liter of vodka? Of course not.

When slaves of alcohol cry out to God for deliverance, he sends it. Pay attention—listen to his Word for strength, forgiveness, and direction. Listen to your family members and accept their help in cutting through the lies and pretending. Listen to your AA counselor and support group. **"Apart from me you can do nothing,"** Jesus said (John 15:5). With him you can do all things.

_____

_____

_____

_____

_____

the Holy Spirit

I know this may sound a little crazy, but one of my prayer heroes is the Holy Spirit. Yes—there is actually a lot of praying that has gone on within the Holy Trinity itself. Seriously!

You recall, of course, how often Jesus prayed to his heavenly Father during his time on earth. Now at the Father's right hand, Jesus pleads for the believers on the basis of his saving work. Did you know that the Spirit is a terrific pray-er also? **"The Spirit helps us in our weakness. We do not know what we ought to pray for, but the Spirit himself intercedes for us with groans that words cannot express"** (Romans 8:26).

Aspiring writers who desire their work to be published should realize that they need an editor. Editors clean up and tighten up early drafts so that the final copy says just what the author needs it to say. Isn't it a spectacular comfort to know that our sometimes incoherent, sometimes stammered, sometimes selfish, sometimes misdirected prayers go to the Father, not only through the name of Jesus but also through the editorial desk of God the Holy Spirit? Amazing!

This means that you can feel free to pray even when you fear your thoughts aren't completely collected, or when you're having trouble putting your feelings into words. The Holy Spirit will bring perfect prayers to the Father. Every time.

_____

_____

_____

_____

_____

get rich slow

There will always be people who want to get rich quick, and they will always be followed closely by people ready, willing, and able to take advantage of that craving. Gambling casinos, lotteries, carnival games of chance, "can't miss" investment deals, and "insider" stock tips will separate the get-rich-quick crowd from what money they do have. As you may know, there's only one winner in the gambling business—the house.

The godly alternative is not joyful poverty but to seek to build your family's financial strength in a godly way. You might call it a "get rich slow" strategy. **"Dishonest money dwindles away, but he who gathers money little by little makes it grow"** (Proverbs 13:11). Getting up and going to work each day, saving your paychecks, living small, learning to make do, patiently investing in a sound financial plan, and deferring expensive pleasures will grow your assets.

Materialism is indeed a disease. But the way to avoid it is to let God teach you how to make, save, spend, and give money. It gives him pleasure to be generous with us. It also gives him pleasure to see us build financial security so that we can be generous with others.

_____

_____

_____

_____

_____

I oughtta get more, right?

One of the hardest tasks in running any business is determining salaries and benefits. Human resource committees and officials do a lot of research to figure out what the market is paying. Larger firms hire expensive consultants to help them get their compensation and benefit packages just right.

Generally, seniority with the company gets rewarded, right? Not in God's heavenly HR scheme. Read Jesus' parable of the workers in the vineyard. **"'These men who were hired last worked only one hour,' they said, 'and you have made them equal to us who have borne the burden of the work and the heat of the day'"** (Matthew 20:12).

Have you been a Christian for a long time? Do you feel any twinges of resentment that people in your past who were party animals and hell-raisers might come to the Christian faith late in life and be accepted to the same heaven where you are planning your everlasting retirement?

Might it help to remember that you have no right to set even your sinful big toe into God's holy presence? Your forgiveness, gifts, accomplishments, and immortality are all gifts of his grace, not rewards for your achievement. We must never take for granted the mercy shown us to the point where we resent that mercy being shown to someone else. Rejoice with the angels over even one bad boy who repents.

_____

_____

_____

_____

_____

restore one another

When Adam and Eve committed that first sin against God, they hid when they heard him coming. If you could have seen them crouching in the bushes, would you have laughed at them? Probably not. You know exactly what they were feeling, because you've been there—shame, fear, rationalization, and mutual blaming.

When you know someone in your family or church has been rebelling, does that make you despise them? I hope not. You've rebelled enough yourself. Don't judge other sinners. Restore. The Bible says, **"If someone is caught in a sin, you who are spiritual should restore him gently"** (Galatians 6:1).

Your church is a support network for you. But it is also a search-and-rescue team, and you're part of it. You have not only God's permission to speak for him; you have his command and plea to do so. When continual, habitual sin takes over people's lives and destroys their relationship with God, don't turn away. Don't condemn. Don't laugh. Don't feel superior.

Don't let people hide from their Savior. Only in Jesus will people ever find relief from the guilt in their souls.

_____

_____

_____

_____

_____

pride makes you deaf

It's not too hard to spot pride in other people. Pride makes people full of themselves, contemptuous of other people, totally into their own agendas, no empathy for the struggles of others, quick to brag, quick to take credit, and quick to blame. Pride makes you deaf to opinions and suggestions other than your own.

God hates it too. **"Pride goes before destruction, a haughty spirit before a fall"** (Proverbs 16:18). **"When pride comes, then comes disgrace, but with humility comes wisdom"** (Proverbs 11:2). Here's the question: how do you know if pride is a problem for you? And another: what can you do about it?

First, listen carefully to advice from those close to you, especially your spouse, your boss, and your coworkers. If the people God put closest to you tell you that you sound arrogant, you probably are.

Second, listen to God. Imitate your Savior Jesus, who humbled himself all the way to the cross. Prize service more than power, praising more than being praised, and listening to others more than talking about yourself. At one point in his life, King David got too big for his own good, but he learned humility from God. You can too.

_____

_____

_____

_____

_____

where you need to be

The great heroes of the Bible, whose lives are held up for us to imitate, whose writings we study and read, were superheroes of faith. But they could also be super-criminals, super-fools, super-idiots. They sometimes embarrassed themselves and brought shame to the Lord. Samson, Gideon, and Jacob, for instance, were deeply flawed individuals.

But get this—God used them anyway! One of the coolest things about the way God works is that he gets his best work done by some of the most unpromising, broken material you can ever imagine. If you think, "I'll never be good enough, so I'll leave it to others," you'll flounder around wondering what you're doing here.

I've got good news for you from 1 Corinthians: **"Now you are the body of Christ, and *each one of you* is a part of it"** (12:27). Hang on, it gets better: **"In fact God has arranged the parts in the body, every one of them, just as he wanted them to be"** (12:18).

God not only gave you unique gifts for service. He also placed you on his team to carry out his agenda. That is why you're here on this earth and not in heaven already. And he's got you right where he wants you, in an environment where you can help move his agenda and with relationships God can use.

_____

_____

_____

_____

_____

good drugs

Drugs are everywhere in our country. EMTs arriving on accident scenes use drugs to stabilize people in injury traumas or health crises. Good. Sad and desperate people buy crack and crystal meth to ease the pain of their lives and to get numb. Bad. Hospitals have thousands of drugs on hand, ready for any health emergency. Good.

The best drug of all, however, is not a chemical at all. It does not need a doctor's prescription, and there is no downside risk of addiction or overdose. **"A cheerful heart is good medicine,"** says Proverbs 17:22. This is not to say that painkillers or mood-leveling medications are useless or wrong. The point: as a Christian you are not completely at the mercy of your moods. You *can* choose your attitude because of the things God has told you in his Word.

Your body is a thing of beauty, designed by God to be his temple. You are loved with an everlasting love. Your sins are forgiven. The angels of heaven hover with divine protection. Your life is a divine mission that only you can perform, and at its end you will be welcomed into glory forever. You are immortal.

When you ponder these joyful things, how can your heart not be cheerful? How can you not feel better at once?

_____

_____

_____

_____

_____

the doxology

Did you ever notice that the conclusion to the Lord's Prayer as we speak it in church is not found in the Bible? Protestants almost universally end it by saying, "The kingdom and the power and the glory are yours, now and forever" (or "For thine is the kingdom . . ." if you still use the King James Version).

Even though that *doxology* (a short statement of praise to the Trinity) is not in the Bible's prayer, it still makes a great finishing statement to Jesus' teaching. It explains why we have such confidence that all the things we ask for will be granted. It reaffirms our promise to make the Lord's name hallowed, work to extend his gracious rule in people's hearts, and make obedience to his will a life priority.

St. John heard a magnificent song from ten thousand times ten thousand angels who surround the throne of God: **"Worthy is the Lamb, who was slain, to receive power and wealth and wisdom and strength and honor and glory and praise!"** (Revelation 5:12).

A doxology like that one is a great way to end any prayer:
- We affirm that God is our supreme Ruler, our King.
- We affirm that God is able to do all we ask and more.
- We pledge to give him the honor and glory when he takes care of us as we ask.

And when you say "Amen" at the end, you put your personal exclamation point on what you just said. "That's the truth!"

_____

_____

_____

_____

blessed are the peacemakers

It is good to remember the brave men and women who have served, or fallen in service to, our country. They fought to preserve the freedoms with which God has blessed our nation—the very freedoms that give us the liberty to worship our God.

But freedom does not mean absence of conflict. Do you ever feel as though you are in the middle of your own war? What's the level of conflict in your life right now? Do you get along with your boss and coworkers? Been laid off? That will crank up your internal stress level. How about your home life? What's the mood in your home right now?

God in his wonderful Word tells us that we can be players in this game of shaping and influencing the level of conflict in our world. **"Do not let any unwholesome talk come out of your mouths, but only what is helpful for building others up according to their needs, that it may benefit those who listen. Be kind and compassionate to one another, forgiving each other, just as in Christ God forgave you"** (Ephesians 4:29,32).

Anyone can ramp up anger. Jesus Christ calls us to make peace between people. We who have been loved and forgiven unconditionally can do no less than share that same attitude with the people around us, whether we think they deserve it or not. Do you love to argue and win fights? Do you think you can let Jesus teach you to find even more joy in making peace?

_____

_____

_____

can I get rid of doubt? I doubt it

A friend of mine who doesn't go to church told me once, "I wish I could believe. I'd like to believe." Next to idolatry, i.e., the desire to worship something or someone other than the Lord, doubt is among the oldest of sins. Satan massaged Eve's appetite for independence and planted doubts in her mind that sprouted into flagrant disobedience and rebellion.

Do you have trouble understanding and accepting God's lordship over you? If so, you have company. **"Immediately the boy's father exclaimed, 'I do believe; help me overcome my unbelief'"** (Mark 9:24). All Christians have a mixture of doubts and faith in their hearts; the struggle to master fear and doubt is part of our mission.

Our own reason, emotions, and experiences are vulnerable to satanic manipulation. Only God's Word drives out fear and doubt. Only the Word has satisfactory explanations to the origin and purpose of the human race; only the Word tells the truth about good and evil; only the Word reveals what is coming next at the end of our lives. Pray for faith. Read the Word. Hear the Word. Believe the Word. Receive the Supper. Give God your doubts.

_____

_____

_____

_____

_____

why am I so impatient?

Who do I think I am?

I must think I am the supreme commander of the universe. I want everything, and I want it now. It's good to have a plan and move forward in life. It's good to dream big and not settle for the status quo. But I hate it when other people expect me to get in line with their agendas. So why do I do that to other people?

You must think I'm pretty ungrateful, Lord. I want more than I have, and that makes me crabby, feeling sorry for myself. Is there hope for me? Can you teach me how to wait? I know that's how your heroes of old learned your ways: **"I waited patiently for the LORD; he turned to me and heard my cry"** (Psalm 40:1).

It's impossible to mistake your love for me. Love is the only answer for what could have led you to punish your Son for my sins. It's impossible to mistake your wisdom—the world around me is so beautiful and well ordered. You are a genius beyond all understanding. I know your strength and power have no limits.

Please help me relax and enjoy you and the people around me more. Help me get my life more in tune with your agenda. What *you* want is more important than what *I* want.

_____

_____

_____

_____

_____

who, me? a liar?

Why do people lie?

You know why. Because it's *easy.* Because we're *lazy* and want to avoid work and responsibility. Because we feel *guilty* and don't want to admit our wrong. Because we're *afraid,* afraid of the consequences of our actions. We lie because we are all born liars. No one has to take Beginning Lying or Advanced Lying in school because we get good at it all by ourselves.

Truth telling is learned behavior. When you became a Christian, the personal transformation began. Your past is forgiven and you have the Spirit's power in the present. When you learned that the Lord hates a lying tongue, you began to resist, to believe that the truth is always better.

That personal transformation is a work in progress, and you and I must struggle with it our whole lives. It is not optional for a Christian: **"If anyone considers himself religious and yet does not keep a tight rein on his tongue, he deceives himself and his religion is worthless"** (James 1:26).

Let's practice. Say with me: "I did it." "It's my fault." "It's a weakness of mine." "I was wrong about that." "Will you forgive me?"

_____

_____

_____

_____

_____

what if she is cheating?

Scripture gives us strong direction to commit to marriage till death us do part. Scripture condemns quick and easy divorce. Scripture connects us with the power of the Spirit to heal sin's wounds and change our behaviors. Scripture tells us that love always hopes, always perseveres.

But sometimes the marriage bond is broken by the ultimate betrayal. Jesus himself, in warning against casual divorce, grants an exception in the case of adultery by a partner: **"I tell you that anyone who divorces his wife, except for marital unfaithfulness, and marries another woman commits adultery"** (Matthew 19:9).

What to do when that happens? Time for careful planning. Time to get sober advice from trusted family members and friends. Time to see your pastor. If the innocent spouse decides that the marriage is irretrievably broken by the partner's adultery, he or she may seek a divorce without sinning.

Even better is the possibility of reconciliation. Permission from God to seek a divorce is not a mandate. It is one of my joys to know happily married couples who overcame a serious breach of trust years back. Perhaps you know some too. Perhaps you are one of them.

_____

_____

_____

_____

_____

June

"Do not conform any longer to the pattern of this world, but be transformed by the renewing of your mind. Then you will be able to test and approve what God's will is—his good, pleasing and perfect will."

(Romans 12:2)

in the direct presence of God

If you listen for it, you will hear the word *heaven* pop up in people's talk now and then. "Heavenly" desserts, chocolate treats, Caribbean cruises, and therapeutic massages are all nice. Unfortunately, the things we call heavenly on earth are pale shadows of the grand reality.

In heaven your pain will be gone. You will get back all the Christian friends and loved ones that you laid to rest. You will live in absolute security, bothered no longer by Satan and his temptations. You will never sin again.

But the best is that you will be very, very close to, actually in the personal presence of, our God. You will be very close to the ultimate source of life, goodness, and love, and you will feel it throughout your being.

In Revelation, John writes, **"I heard a loud voice from the throne saying, 'Now the dwelling of God is with** [people]**, and he will live with them. They will be his people, and God himself will be with them and be their God'"** (21:3).

_____

_____

_____

_____

_____

the covenant was temporary then

Back in the days of the Wild West, vast federal lands were loosely organized into "territories." Townspeople, farmers, and ranchers dreamed of the day when they could attain the privileges of statehood. They all assumed that the territorial government was only a stepping-stone to full participation in American government and life.

God's massive layers of rules in the Old Covenant were not just divine hazing. Embedded in all the regulations were important truths about how sinful people could be reconciled with their holy Creator. **"These** [i.e., provisions of the ceremonial religious laws] **are a *shadow* of the things that were to come"** (Colossians 2:17).

Shadows show the rough outline of the illuminated object. Shadows give advance notice of something coming. Shadows aren't the reality, but their dark forms show that something substantial is behind them.

These covenant shadows were *designed* to be temporary. **"'The time is coming,' declares the Lord, 'when I will make a new covenant with the house of Israel and with the house of Judah'"** (Jeremiah 31:31). That time came. It is your privilege to live in the time of this New Covenant.

_____

_____

_____

_____

_____

now your covenant is eternal

Hollywood never just releases a movie. Studios invest millions in advance publicity. One of their tried-and-true techniques is to issue a "trailer." In real life, trailers are pulled *behind* something. In Hollywood, trailers go *ahead,* showing snippets and fragments of the movie to lay out the basic plot premise and tease and gain interest from moviegoers.

Throughout the Old Testament, God issued little trailers, glimpses of the glory of the Savior Jesus. Every one of the ceremonial laws of Israel's "childhood" pointed to the thrilling battle of good and evil that the Son of God would win. **"These** [i.e., provisions of the ceremonial laws] **are a** *shadow* **of the things that were to come;** *the reality,* **however,** *is found in Christ"* (Colossians 2:17). **"Now if the ministry that brought death, which was engraved in letters on stone, came with glory . . . will not the ministry of the Spirit be even more glorious?"** (2 Corinthians 3:7,8).

The Ten Commandments are a symbol of the Old Covenant. God's laws, holy and perfect as they are, demand a holiness in us that we could never achieve. In and of themselves they produce only death and damnation for us. Only through faith in Christ can we find forgiveness and life. The New Covenant is based on freedom in our forgiveness. It will last beyond the grave; it is everlasting.

_____

_____

_____

_____

_____

June 4

you promised!

Every father figures out a cheap solution to kid problems—promise them anything. Works every time—at least at first. Every father also overpromises, going to that well just a little too often, and then the kids call your bluff. "Hey—you said we were going to McDonalds." "Hey—you promised to take us to the state fair!" "Hey—you said this was the year we were going to see the ocean."

When you're busted by your kids, you realize that some damage has been done. Your credibility is shot, at least for now. Your ability to buy family peace with a promise is gone—they don't believe you anymore. **"Hope deferred makes the heart sick, but a longing fulfilled is a tree of life"** (Proverbs 13:12).

How's your heart doing right now? Have you been severely disappointed? lied to? let down? One of the most beautiful aspects of our relationship with God is that he never overpromises. He means everything he says. He delivers on time, every time.

Think back to the blessings that only God could have sent—the financial relief, the love of friends, the joy of family—and pause to remember and enjoy the fulfillments of your longings. God is good!

_____

_____

_____

_____

_____

he's everywhere

Do you remember the old *Chickenman* superhero spoof? "He's everywhere! He's everywhere," the crowd would chant. Well, no he isn't. Nobody is everywhere, though it's a pleasant fantasy to think that a superhero like Batman could keep vigil over the entire Gotham City.

If only people really believed that God is everywhere. It would terrify unbelievers, leading them to repent, and it would provide great comfort to believers. But guess what— God *really is* the ultimate security cam: **"The eyes of the Lord are everywhere, keeping watch on the wicked and the good"** (Proverbs 15:3).

Think of the ramifications: he tracks and remembers all human activity. He is intensely interested in what every human being is doing (his capacity is so infinite that he can even track each bird in nature). You can totally rest easy about evil and justice because he will take care of it in his time.

And you never have to fear that you've been abandoned. God sees everything in your life. He cares about you and is committed to you accomplishing your mission in life. He is never out of radio contact and will be there when you need a rescue.

_____

_____

_____

_____

_____

I feel like a hypocrite

It's hard to tell your teenage kids not to smoke when you do. It's hard to get them to take their studies seriously when they keep hearing stories about how you wasted your years in college. It may seem hard to bring someone to take God more seriously when you have some things about your own life that are common knowledge that you're ashamed of.

If you needed a completely clean record in order to speak up for God, nobody would ever be allowed to utter a word. Noah, David, Solomon, and Peter did great things for the kingdom and were great witnesses, but they were also miserable sinners.

Here is St. Paul's honest confession: **"Christ Jesus came into the world to save sinners—*of whom I am the worst. But for that very reason I was shown mercy so that in me, the worst of sinners, Christ Jesus might display his unlimited patience as an example for those who would believe on him and receive eternal life"*** (1 Timothy 1:15,16).

Sometimes a humble, forgiven bad boy is more believable than a smug know-it-all.

_____

_____

_____

_____

_____

personal integrity

Adam and Eve were created in the image of God. They were born loving and wanting the right things, hating and rejecting what was wrong. Their reckless experiment in disobedience destroyed that image in themselves and their descendants. Bottom line—you and I were born in Satan's image. And thus what comes easy to us are characteristics from Satan's mind-set: selfishness, disrespect, pride, revenge, cruelty, lies, lust.

Through the splendid intervention of Jesus Christ, the poisonous deeds of our past, present, and future were forgiven by God. Through the planting of faith in our hearts by the Spirit, we tap into that forgiveness and receive it. Through the prompting of our Spirit-Counselor, we develop an interest in living our new identity and becoming more Christ-like.

But that's work. Every feature of Christ-behavior is learned behavior. We need God's Word and God's power to make those changes. **"Whoever gives heed to instruction prospers, and blessed is he who trusts in the Lord"** (Proverbs 16:20). Do you want to prosper? Do you want blessings in your life? Go ahead—call God's bluff.

_____

_____

_____

_____

_____

time to change your spiritual clothes

"That's just how I am" is a phrase we use when we don't want to change. That's how husbands excuse their tempers or wives their ancient grudges. That's how students excuse their mediocre grades or employees their rudeness to customers. It's also how Christians excuse their self-chosen immaturity.

Here's a paradox: God accepts you just as you are, warts and all. But he absolutely will not settle for your staying just as you are. As the gospel message of his unconditional love sinks in, he calls you to change yourself to be more like him, using his Word and Spirit and power.

The Bible's words: **"You were taught, with regard to your former way of life, to put off your old self, which is being corrupted by its deceitful desires; to be made new in the attitude of your minds; and to put on the new self, created to be like God in true righteousness and holiness"** (Ephesians 4:22-24).

Here's what to take off: a spirit of whining, envy, self-pity, and lying. Here's what to put on: a spirit of praise, gratitude, humility, and service.

If you're not sure where to start on your own life, just ask the people you live with. They will know right away where your changes need to begin.

_____

_____

_____

_____

_____

do disabilities disable faith?

A *Time of Grace* viewer asks, "What about those who are unable to comprehend God's salvation due to intelligence deficiency?" I understand the question. The Christian faith is deep and complex and demands great wisdom and mental sharpness to grasp it. But at the end we will not be judged on the basis of how much we know or understand, but on this alone—are we connected to Christ?

Religious snobs have always looked down on little children and the disabled as though they couldn't believe, as though faith were impossible for them. In fact, St. Paul reminded Timothy that he had known the Scripture's message *from infancy.*

Jesus told his disciples on several occasions that not only *could* little ones believe but that adults needed to model *their* faith on that of children. He said once, **"See that you do not look down on one of these little ones. For I tell you that their angels in heaven always see the face of my Father in heaven"** (Matthew 18:10,11).

Any time faith is created in a person through the Spirit's work, it is a miracle. It may be that the Spirit has an easier time with a disabled person than a college professor.

_____

_____

_____

_____

_____

it's good to be hungry

It's good that you don't always get what you want. It's good that you have to wait, that unfulfilled longings make your heart and soul restless. It's good to be hungry.

Is that crazy talk? Does that sound like the talk of a Christian who's lost his marbles? Well, ponder this: **"The laborer's appetite works for him; his hunger drives him on"** (Proverbs 16:26). Think about it from God's point of view. If we were totally full and satisfied in every way, we would slow down and stop. Why work? Why exert yourself? Who needs other people?

Our needs and longings and unfulfilled desires provide the drivers to move us to grow and develop, to seek and explore, to work and toil, to need people and helpers and friends and build relationships for survival.

Some degree of struggle and hardship and hunger is also good for us to remind us of our dependence on God. If we had everything, our prayers would droop and finally cease. Don't curse your struggles. Let them drive you on. Let your hunger work for you.

_____

_____

_____

_____

_____

still angry after all these years

One of my kids, roughly age 6, was glowering in his bunk bed. "Do you like being angry?" I asked. "Yes," he said.

Do you like being angry? Or do you hate it but can't get the anger out of your heart? Time does not heal wounds. The infection only grows as the weeks slide by. What to do? Well, the first step is realizing the danger. Unresolved anger keeps you in an emotional prison. It eats out your soul like sulfuric acid. You will damage yourself and others.

God once saw the sickness in a man's heart and tried to intervene: **"The LORD said to Cain, 'Why are you angry? Why is your face downcast? If you do what is right, will you not be accepted? But if you do not do what is right, sin is crouching at your door; it desires to have you, but you must master it'"** (Genesis 4:6,7).

Bathing your soul in the gospel message will help relieve your own guilt, and it will inspire you to be merciful to the person you believe caused your pain. Pray for peace, peace in your heart. Give your anger to God and let him take care of the other guy.

_____

_____

_____

_____

_____

one way

When people die, their grieving relatives want badly to believe that their loved one is now enjoying life in heaven. Even flagrantly unspiritual rogues and thugs have relatives who construct lovely scenarios of paradise with which to comfort themselves. In their view everybody gets a piece of pie in the sky by and by. They are wrong.

Others want very much to be open-minded and nonchauvinistic about spiritual things. In their view all steeples (and minarets) point to heaven. All ways are as equally good. In their view all religions and philosophies can be "true" for the individual believer. They are wrong.

Still others believe that leading an okay moral life, i.e., being more or less as good as anybody else in the neighborhood, should qualify you for a heavenly reward. They too are wrong.

Here is the truth: **"Salvation is found in no one else, for there is no other name under heaven given to men by which we must be saved"** (Acts 4:12). That name is Jesus Christ. There is only one way, and he is it. Believe it. The people in your life need to know this. Tell them.

_____

_____

_____

_____

_____

she's so pretty and talented; I hate her

The seeds of self-hatred, self-doubt, and depression lurk in the heart of every person. So do resentment and envy of other people. Why is he so successful? Why does she have so many male admirers? Why does his family have all that money and mine has nothing? Why is she so pretty and I'm so not? It's hard to affirm other people when you feel so needy. How can you fill someone else's cup when you feel empty?

Here is one of the marvelous secrets of happy living that only the Bible can reveal because the concept is so counterintuitive. Ready? Here it is: when you really want something from someone else, like love, acceptance, and praise, you go first and give. **"Encourage one another and build each other up"** (1 Thessalonians 5:11), says St. Paul.

That is also one of the magic secrets of a happy marriage. Don't wait to turn on the charm, kindness, and support until your partner is worthy of it. Go first. You know what? It works. Kind words (i.e., treating people better than they deserve) release love and kindness in others, and those will come back to you in even greater abundance. I guess we shouldn't be surprised. Isn't that how Christ treats us?

_____

_____

_____

_____

_____

'tis God's gift

During the 2008 presidential campaign, candidate Barack Obama's connections with his longtime pastor, Rev. Jeremiah Wright, caused him some severe personal and political discomfort. Wright's church in Chicago is intensely Afrocentric, and Wright himself has such contempt for America's racist past (and, he would say, present) that he used language from his pulpit calling on God to damn, not bless, America.

Rev. Wright is not alone. Some find it tempting to mock and deride our country because of its faults and failings. Sociologists say that the current generation of young adults has no confidence in any institution of any kind, including the national government.

St. Paul lived and worked in an empire with far fewer civil rights than ours. The Roman Empire officially sanctioned the murder of his Savior Jesus. And still he wrote, **"There is no authority except that which God has established. The authorities that exist have been established by God"** (Romans 13:1). That would seem to include China, Zimbabwe, and Cuba.

With all their flaws and shortcomings, national governments prevent things that God thinks are far worse: chaos and anarchy. God bless America.

_____

_____

_____

_____

_____

why am I still alone?

Every person on earth has unfulfilled longings, and that includes Christians. Some of the saddest groans come from single people who would really love to be married. If God says it's not good for the man (or woman) to be alone, they think, why then am I still alone?

There seem to be no good answers. Is there something wrong with me? Am I such a loser? Am I that ugly? Am I being punished? Doesn't God care enough for my dreams and hopes to do anything for me?

The truth for each person is unknowable, at least till we reach heaven. But God invites people to find fulfillment in whatever their situation—it's all good. He seems to want it both ways: **"It is good for a man not to marry"** and **"Since there is so much immorality, each man should have his own wife"** (1 Corinthians 7:1,2).

Lonely singles should realize that being trapped in a marriage to the wrong person is far worse. Perhaps the lonely Christian needs to wait until the right person is ready. Perhaps some things have to change in his or her own heart. Perhaps the person is overlooking a great potential partner close by. Watch for God's surprises. Never give up.

_____

_____

_____

_____

_____

receiving gifts

We learn about gifts pretty early in life. One sure way to get a child's attention is simply to say the word *Christmas*. Kids immediately associate the concept with presents, that is, cool free stuff that various people give you.

Giving and receiving gifts expresses and strengthens relationships. Gifts send messages: "I love you." "You are important to me." "I appreciate what you do for me." "Thank you for everything."

Giving and receiving gifts also can symbolize strong mutual obligations. **"When Abraham's servant heard what they said, he bowed down to the ground before the Lord. Then the servant brought out gold and silver jewelry and articles of clothing and gave them to Rebekah"** (Genesis 24:52,53). Rebekah joyfully accepted these treasures because they communicated powerfully the commitment of Isaac's proposal of marriage.

Tell me the truth—what are your most precious possessions? It wouldn't surprise me if many of them are gifts from people who mean a great deal to you.

_____

_____

_____

_____

_____

be persistent

Parents don't like it when their children beg and their spouses nag. If you are asked for something and the answer's no, you don't like to hear about it again and again. Wouldn't it be logical to assume, then, that God would be irritated if we ask for something more than once?

Logical? Yes. But in fact, the very opposite is true. He does not see repeated prayers as nagging or begging. **"Jesus told his disciples a parable to show them that they should always pray and not give up. . . . 'Will not God bring about justice for his chosen ones, who cry out to him day and night? Will he keep putting them off?'"** (Luke 18:1,7).

In Jesus' little story, a widow pestered a judge for justice until he relented. Instead of criticizing the woman for being such a pest, Jesus held her up as a hero and invited all believers to be just like her.

When our first prayer doesn't seem to be granted, we don't know for sure when God is saying no permanently, or when his answer is "maybe," or when the answer is "later." What we do know is that the Father not merely tolerates but welcomes and even praises persistent pray-ers. Pray and don't give up!

_____

_____

_____

_____

_____

build your reputation

A friend of mine had a T-shirt that read, "If I had known I was going to live this long, I would have taken better care of myself years ago." Ain't that the truth! And it's true not only of health issues, but sex, money, and crime as well. Mistakes and sins of the past never go away, and many come 'round to bite us later.

Every year idealistic and excited people try to get a loan to buy their first home only to find out that they had ruined their credit rating long ago. Because of their reputation, no bank will lend them a dime. If you suffer a jewelry theft, or if you total your car, those things can be replaced. If you ruin your reputation, you will find that it is ten times harder to restore.

"A good name is more desirable than great riches; to be esteemed is better than silver or gold" (Proverbs 22:1). Tell the truth. Pay your bills. Live within your means. Keep your word. Do what you say you're going to do. Wait till you can afford it. Do I sound like your father? I do? Thank you!

_____

_____

_____

_____

_____

they will come streaming in

It's hard for the old guard when they realize that the ethnic group that founded their community/congregation/ school/whatever is drifting away and being replaced by "people not like us." It's easy to criticize the insularity of the first generation of Jewish Christians, who were dismayed about letting Gentiles into their congregations. Realize, however, that for centuries the Jews had thought they were the only believers (and would always be the only ones). They were the chosen.

Two dysfunctions arise from such insularity. One is that as your tribe fades, you become afraid and pessimistic. The other is that as new peoples pour into your community, you fear that the heritage and traditions will be lost and soon the message itself will be lost. Isaiah assures fearful Jewish believers and nervous old guardians today: **"Lift up your eyes and look about you: All assemble and come to you. . . . Then you will look and be radiant, your heart will throb and swell with joy"** (Isaiah 60:4,5).

Outreach works. If you really care about reaching out to people not like you, it will happen, and new believers sooner or later will outnumber the original ethnic group. *Pssst*—wanna know a secret? It's okay. In fact, it's God's ongoing plan.

_____

_____

_____

_____

_____

June 20
I wasn't thinking

You know the old saying about sticks and stones, how words don't hurt. What baloney! Words hurt worse than fists, and the heart-pain they give can last a lifetime.

When children are told that they will never amount to anything, they may believe it their whole lives. When a man tells a woman she's stupid, her self-confidence may permanently be broken. When a woman treats her man like a child, he may live down to her expectations indefinitely. When a person blabs a secret about a friend in public, the friendship may be over at that moment.

"Reckless words pierce like a sword, but the tongue of the wise brings healing" (Proverbs 12:18). The word *reckless* means that you weren't thinking when your tongue was flapping. We all need to grow in the skill of tongue management.

In the meantime, we can use our mouths for their God-intended purpose—to bring soothing and healing to the injured victims of Satan's attacks. It is amazing to me what great things can be done in a person's soul by a few words: "You look pretty today." "I liked what you said yesterday." "You did a great job." "I appreciate you."

_____

_____

_____

_____

_____

God and my limitations

A source of never-ending surprise to me and my wife is how different our four children are from one another. How could each have such distinct personalities and skill sets coming from the same two biological parents?

It gives us great pleasure to see them develop their gifts. It also gives us pain to see them struggle with things they are not good at, whether that's advanced algebra, saving money, or managing a relationship. I hope they know that their parents will always love and accept them just as they are.

Did you know that God is even more interested and passionate about helping you develop your life? He and the angels clap and cheer when you succeed. But get this—he does not despise you or hate you or give up on you when you struggle. He knows all of your limitations: **"As a father has compassion on his children, so the LORD has compassion on those who fear him; for he knows how we are formed, he remembers that we are dust"** (Psalm 103:13,14).

Isn't it sweet to entrust your life to the One who knows all your weaknesses, bad secrets, and brokenness and likes you anyway?

_____

_____

_____

_____

_____

who, me? a Pharisee?

There used to be a yeast company in my town. Its pungent, musky smell wafted over the near west side on production days. Yeast's ability to reproduce rapidly makes it an indispensable ingredient to beer and bread. God chose to use this wonderful substance as a metaphor for sin—something that metastasized quietly and dangerously. At Passover time the Jewish housewives were to get rid of every trace of yeast in their kitchens and eat only unleavened bread.

Jesus warned his disciples, and he warns you and me, with a similar word picture: **"Be on your guard against the yeast of the Pharisees"** (Matthew 16:6). Huh? Who, me? A Pharisee? You're kidding, Jesus. Pharisees are other people. Them, not me.

Jesus rebuked the Pharisees for imagining that they were good enough for God as is, that they didn't need a Savior, that their wealth proved God's favor, that they were superior to the "sinners." He condemns those attitudes in us as well. The legalistic and loveless spirit of the Pharisees is alive and well in the world today, and it must not be allowed to live in our hearts and minds.

It must not live in our congregations either.

_____

_____

_____

_____

_____

soon I can praise you face-to-face

Lord Jesus, you took on my humanity and were born just like me. You honored the human race by living among us and as one of us. You offered your body on the cross, were buried like us, and rose again not only in spirit but in body too.

When you ascended into heaven, you brought your body with you! You took our humanity to the very throne room of heaven. You are now bonded to us into eternity. We praise you and worship you! We are honored by your total commitment to the rescue of the human race.

As for me, I can live joyfully and confidently because you have guaranteed my ultimate victory over death, grave, and hell. I can bear anything, undergo any hardship, absorb any sorrow, face any satanic attack, or endure any loss when I know that I will soon be with you.

I'm not worried about what I will leave behind here on this earth. You will replace it all and give me much more. But my greatest treasure in heaven, Lord Jesus, is *you.* I can't wait to see you face-to-face. I am eager to give you my love and worship in person. **"And I—in righteousness I will see your face; when I awake, I will be satisfied with seeing your likeness"** (Psalm 17:15).

Come soon, Lord Jesus.

_____

_____

_____

_____

_____

be proud of God

Of all the things teenagers do that cause hurt to their parents, being ashamed of them in public is one of the worst. I did it to my parents, and my own kids have repeatedly done it to me. Even though I expect it and even understand it to some degree, it still hurts that they think my wife and me too old, too slow, and too out of it to be associated with.

I don't suppose God is too thrilled when the children he adopted by faith into his royal family, his royal priests, think themselves too cool to be identified with him in public. How that disdain must hurt his fatherly heart!

St. Paul had much to be ashamed of himself. In his earlier life he thought himself a great champion for God and his law. Later he discovered that he was a poseur and a fraud. He was actually at war with his Savior. His conversion experience changed forever how he viewed himself and the privilege of representing God wherever he went.

His changed philosophy: **"I am not ashamed of the gospel, because it is the power of God for the salvation of everyone who believes"** (Romans 1:16).

Can people tell that you're a Christian at your school? where you work? on your block?

_____

_____

_____

_____

_____

June 25
whatcha lookin' 4?

Isn't it funny how your mind-set can become a self-fulfilling prophecy? What I mean by that is that you usually find what you are looking for and what you expect.

If you expect other people to let you down, if you are bracing yourself at all times, refusing to trust anybody, bitter about past betrayals and certain the next one is coming any minute, you will probably find evidence today or tomorrow that someone must have it in for you.

On the other hand, if you assume that there is good in people, if you decide to choose the most optimistic explanation for their words and actions, if you assume that God is going to do some amazing things for you today, you will probably find that too. **"He who seeks good finds goodwill, but evil comes to him who searches for it"** (Proverbs 11:27).

There are mountains of evil in our world, but there is also amazing good—and great beauty and heartwarming .miracles and wonderful people. Satan indeed is strong, but God is stronger. Mercy has triumphed over judgment; life has triumphed over death; love has triumphed over hatred. Look for mercy, life, and love, and you will find them.

_____

_____

_____

_____

_____

June 26

Immanuel: God with us

Does it ever bother you that you are invited to worship a God that you can't see? If there really is a divine Maker of this world, why doesn't he hang around to let us get to know him? God's seeming absence from this planet has led some to fear that we are all alone here and that there is nobody and nothing greater than man.

Ah, but that's not so. The Bible says that **"in Christ all the fullness of the Deity lives in bodily form"** (Colossians 2:9). Think of it—God himself actually took on human flesh and entered our lives. The prophet Isaiah says that the child born through a wondrous virgin birth should be called "Immanuel," which in Hebrew means "God is with us."

Next time you feel isolated and alone, fearful that nobody is listening when you pray, just whisper, "Immanuel!" That will help you remember, "God, you are right here with us!"

_____

_____

_____

_____

_____

it's her fault

Home sweet home? Alas, not always. You'd like to think that your home would be a steady refuge from conflict in the business world, but sometimes it's the reverse—the bitterest quarrels and deepest pain arise between people who on other occasions say that they love each other.

How can that be? Well, remember that sinful parents give birth to sinful children, who are little ego monsters by nature. They don't need to go to school or summer camp to learn how to argue and talk back. Remember that a marriage joins two sinners together and inevitably our inborn and ingrown selfishness sprouts.

What to do? Train yourself to listen for the signs of temper, emotion, fatigue, and miscommunication. Respect what out-of-control mouths can do to destroy a relationship. **"Starting a quarrel is like breaching a dam; so drop the matter before a dispute breaks out"** (Proverbs 17:14).

It's not necessary for you to show that you're right all the time. You can yield gracefully if you choose. You can manage your brain and mouth to show that healing is more important in your home than being right.

_____

_____

_____

_____

_____

aging

Help! My body is betraying me. American culture is all about worshiping youth and beauty and strength. How can you not be depressed about the way in which your body is steadily breaking down?

Decline in our looks is bad enough—who in his right mind welcomes wrinkles, skin blotches, gray hair, flab, and male-pattern baldness? Even worse is the slow erosion of our health—onset of diabetes, prostate trouble, cartilage loss in knees and hips, hypertension, and cataracts. Moses nailed it 3,500 years ago: **"The length of our days is seventy years— or eighty, if we have the strength; yet their span is but trouble and sorrow, for they quickly pass, and we fly away"** (Psalm 90:10).

But there are some splendid features about aging that I have come to appreciate. (1) Every day I live I am one step closer to being in heaven with the Savior and people I miss. (2) With age have come serenity, wisdom, and greater inner peace. God's marvelous agenda is becoming clearer to me. I'm starting to get it. (3) There are things I can do for God in my 60s that I couldn't have done in my 20s (and I trust that if I make it into the 80s, God will have opportunities for me unique to that age).

Aging doesn't mean that our efforts become less important to God. On the contrary, sometimes God entrusts his biggest jobs to geezers—Moses was 80 when he led Israel out of Egypt, and Abraham was 99 before God thought him ready for fatherhood.

_____

_____

_____

obey your parents

You've seen what happens when a child has not learned to obey, haven't you? "Sally, come here. Sally! I mean it, right now. Please, Sally, if you come here, I'll take you to McDonalds. All right, Toys 'R' Us too."

It's disgusting, isn't it? When parents don't teach their child that they will say something one time and expect it to be done, that child has learned, "I have power. You don't mean what you say."

A child who has never learned to obey his or her parents probably will never be a very good employee, and what's worse, may never learn to obey God. How can children obey somebody they cannot see if they have not learned the basic concept of allowing themselves to be guided by their own parents? If they can't learn to obey you, putting a plaque of the Ten Commandments in their bedrooms isn't going to help them obey God.

That's why teaching joyful obedience deserves our fullest, strongest attention. After commissioning his apostles to make disciples of all nations, Jesus added, **". . . teaching them to obey everything I have commanded you."** For their encouragement and strengthening he added, **"Surely I am with you always, to the very end of the age"** (Matthew 28:20).

_____

_____

_____

_____

_____

for others

We all have a selfish streak by nature. When we become aware that we are able to access God's throne through prayer, our first instincts are to care only about ourselves. But just as spiritual growth helps us see the joy and fulfillment that come from serving other people, growth in prayer maturity leads us to think of other people's needs before our own.

St. Paul invited his Asian brothers and sisters to pray for him while a prisoner in Rome, awaiting his trial in imperial court. **"Pray also for me, that whenever I open my mouth, words may be given me so that I may fearlessly make known the mystery of the gospel, for which I am an ambassador in chains. Pray that I may declare it fearlessly, as I should"** (Ephesians 6:19,20).

The formal word for this kind of praying is *intercession*. I personally have been sustained by the prayers of other wonderful people in stretches of my life when I have been too distracted or lazy to pray for myself. You will not know until you get to heaven how your life has been blessed by the faithful prayers of people who love you.

Could I dare to ask you to pray for me today so that I may proclaim the gospel fearlessly?

_____

_____

_____

_____

_____

July

"The LORD delights in those who fear him,
who put their hope in his unfailing love."
(Psalm 147:11)

grace? what's that?

Every trade and every craft has its own jargon. That special "inside talk" sometimes uses ordinary English words but gives them totally different meanings. For instance, you may have a sister, i.e., a female sibling. In carpenter talk, though, a "sister" is a short piece of wood that is used to reinforce a joint between two ceiling or floor joists.

In day-to-day conversation, the word *grace* means that someone moves fluidly and beautifully. We admire a dancer's graceful steps or a figure skater's graceful twirls. It can be a woman's name. It can mean a prayer of thanks before you eat: to "say grace."

But when you read it in the New Testament, and you will see it a lot, it means something else entirely. It means nothing less than that God chooses to love the unlovable, just because. **"God demonstrates his own love for us in this: while we were still sinners, Christ died for us"** (Romans 5:8). *Grace* means that God went first to rescue us. *Grace* means that the purchase of our freedom was 100 percent God's doing. *Grace* means that the pressure is off you to perform, that you can always find a resting place in your Savior.

Grace means that God's love for you is unlimited and unconditional. You can exhale now.

_____

_____

_____

_____

_____

you can't have it both ways

In God's view you can't be partly married or partly single any more than you can be partly pregnant. You're either one or the other. What a plague on society when single people live together as though they were married or when married people act like they're single.

In God's view the issues are pretty simple: **"Marriage should be honored by all, and the marriage bed kept pure, for God will judge the adulterer and all the sexually immoral"** (Hebrews 13:4). Contrary to what many today think, the Sixth Commandment, which forbids adultery, has not been repealed.

God's ways are beautiful, fulfilling, and they work. Every alternative that sinful human beings have invented has turned out to be unfulfilling, hurtful, self-oriented, and destructive. Seriously—don't you have enough problems in life without asking for God's judgment too?

You honor God's creation of marriage not only when you are married but also in the way you conduct your dating life.

_____

_____

_____

_____

_____

God's awesome creation

Whenever I get frustrated with people or paperwork or staring into a computer screen, I have found respite in getting outside. How marvelous, how complex, how subtle, how perfect, how beautiful is the world you made, Lord. If I crouch down close to the ground, I can see not only the flowers but the drops of dew, the bugs crawling on the ground, and the bees doing their pollinating. I can smell earth, feel the sun's warmth, and touch the waxy chlorophyll factories, a.k.a. leaves, that you use to grow your plants.

At night I can look up and like Abraham derive immense comfort from the stars you put there. **"He determines the number of the stars and calls them each by name. Great is our Lord and mighty in power; his understanding has no limit"** (Psalm 147:4,5). Great flaming gas balls in the sky—Lord, they seem to serve no purpose other than their stunning beauty in the night sky and as aids to navigation. Did you put them there just for us?

If you not only made them with a word but take inventory of them and even care enough to have a personal name for each, all 50 billion of them just in our galaxy among the billions of galaxies, well, that tells me that you are capable of keeping track of me and my life too. You are awesome.

_____

_____

_____

_____

_____

July 4
love your country

It's not too hard to be nice to nice people. It takes Jesus' love operative in us to choose to be nice to unpleasant people.

In the same way, it isn't hard to love your country when you like your leaders and approve of their policies. It takes the Spirit's power to speak and act supportively as a good citizen when you don't like your government, or worse, when your government is persecuting you.

You might think that the early Christians, hammered as they were between hostile local Jewish authorities and a persecuting imperial government in Rome, would nourish a separatistic and resentful mind-set. The Spirit led the apostles (most or all of whom would suffer persecution) to exactly the opposite counsel: **"Submit yourselves for the Lord's sake to every authority instituted among men: whether to the king, as the supreme authority, or to governors, who are sent by him to punish those who do wrong and to commend those who do right. For it is God's will that by doing good you should silence the ignorant talk of foolish men"** (1 Peter 2:13-15).

Non-Christians might assume that Christians will make terrible citizens, since we acknowledge a power higher than an earthly king and claim a heavenly citizenship. The reverse is true. Biblical Christians make the best citizens and can silence critics by working for their communities and showing respect for their government. Today would be a great day to honor yours.

_____

_____

_____

baptize them

God desires so strongly to create saving faith in the hearts of your children that he not only gives you his powerful Word to share with them, but he gives you also another means by which the Spirit can come to live within them: Holy Baptism.

In Old Testament times, newborns were welcomed into a relationship with God and the believing community through the offering of animal sacrifices and ritual circumcision. In New Testament times, Christ has opened up membership in the heavenly family through the **"washing with water through the word"** (Ephesians 5:26). If you thought that getting your kids' immunization shots gave you peace of mind from measles, mumps, and rubella, imagine the peace you can enjoy knowing that your little ones wear robes of the holiness of Jesus Christ.

On Pentecost Day itself, the birthday of the New Testament church, Peter gave this promise to thousands of amazed listeners: **"Repent and be baptized, every one of you, in the name of Jesus Christ for the forgiveness of your sins. . . . The promise is for you and your children"** (Acts 2:38,39).

I think that the reason why some people hesitate is that they think their kids are too young to understand these great things. Hey—you don't need to understand a legacy or bequest to receive it legally. Baptism is God's gift for all, and that includes your children.

---

ask God for help

One day a small boy tried to budge a heavy stone but couldn't move it. His father, watching, finally said, "Are you using all your strength?" "Yes!" the boy cried. "No, you're not," his father answered. "You haven't asked me to help."

The Bible teaches a critically important life truth, one that many people don't grasp. Here it is: God has resources to give his children, but he intentionally withholds them.

Q: Why?

A: *Because he is waiting for his children to ask for his help!*

God is interested in your physical and material success. But he is far more concerned with the development of a faith relationship with you. He considers the Need/Prayer/Answer/Thanksgiving rhythm crucial to the faith-building process and uses it again and again.

Here is the pattern: **"I sought the Lord and he answered me; he delivered me from all my fears. Those who look to him are radiant; their faces are never covered with shame"** (Psalm 34:4,5). Do you get the premise of the promise? My Father cares about me. My Father listens to me. My Father chooses the time to respond. My Father helps me. It's all good. I am glad I trusted him.

_____

_____

_____

_____

_____

God and my legacy

One of the most famous Bible misquotes is, "Money is the root of all evil." The Bible actually says that "the *love of money* is a root of all kinds of evil." Scriptural warnings against the addictive power of materialism do abound, as well as warnings against cravings for fame. You may wish that your investments turn out to be lucrative, but what adjective is usually used with the word *lucre?* Yep, *filthy.*

And yet wealth and fame are not evil in themselves. In fact, God loves to bless believers with those very things as they seek to leave a legacy for their children. **"Blessed is the man who fears the LORD, who finds great delight in his commands. His children will be mighty in the land; the generation of the upright will be blessed. Wealth and riches are in his house, and his righteousness endures forever"** (Psalm 112:1-3).

While you may have to endure poverty, that doesn't make it a career goal. Seeking to build your family's assets so that your children and grandchildren can become financially secure and become generous givers is a great goal. The God we worship is not a god of scarcity but the God of abundance. **"[He] is able to make all grace abound to you, so that in all things at all times, having all that you need, you will abound in every good work"** (2 Corinthians 9:8).

Do you have a will?

_____

_____

_____

_____

_____

significance

One of Sir Arthur Conan Doyle's best Sherlock Holmes stories is entitled, "The Red-Headed League." A man with flaming red hair was hired to go to an office and copy out the *Encyclopedia Britannica* longhand day after day for a handsome salary. It turned out that this "work" was meaningless—a criminal had hired him simply to get him out of his house so he could dig a tunnel from its basement into a bank vault.

"Then he went on his journey. The man who had received the five talents went at once and put his money to work and gained five more. So also, the one with the two talents gained two more. But the man who had received the one talent went off, dug a hole in the ground and hid his master's money" (Matthew 25:15-18).

Do you ever fear that your life has little significance? God expects no more, but also no less, than that you go to work for him with whatever talents you've been given. He is all-powerful, of course, and it's not that he *needs* our work. But it gives him special delight when we get in tune with his agenda and *choose* to work for him.

Remember what you've been praying? *Whose* kingdom come? *Whose* will be done on earth as in heaven? Every offering and tithe you give, every hour you donate, every word you speak in his service, every prayer you send to heaven *really matters.*

_____

_____

_____

_____

you can make a difference

Have you ever tried to get someone else to change a destructive behavior? It seems impossible, doesn't it? People are resistant to change, and they tend to push back when they feel pushed by someone else. It seems impossible to get someone else to quit smoking, quit living together in adultery, or quit wasting money on lottery tickets and the slots. In the same way, it may seem impossible to reignite someone's cold, dead faith.

But it can happen. Your God wants you to know that it is possible to bring someone back from spiritual suicide. You can influence positive change in another person. Your words and actions can make a difference.

"My brothers, if one of you should wander from the truth and someone should bring him back, remember this: Whoever turns a sinner from the error of his way will save him from death and cover over a multitude of sins" (James 5:19,20).

The most thrilling words you will hear in heaven are Christ's, when he says, "Welcome home." The second most thrilling phrase will be heard by those who turned a sinner from the error of his way, when he or she says, "Thank you for saving my life."

_____

_____

_____

_____

_____

July 10

omg

People today use the terms *cussing* and *swearing* to refer to just about any vulgarity or "adult talk." But the word *swearing* has a very distinct meaning—to call on God as your witness, as the gold standard for truthfulness, to punish you if you are lying. The real sense lingers on in court and with the inauguration of public officials as they place a hand on a Bible, which theoretically means that they realize that they are accountable to a higher power.

"Oh, God!" "Oh, my God!" "Swear to God." Those words have lost their meaning in today's conversations. Their only purpose is to serve as an intensifier, as the speaker tries to amplify the emotion of what was just said.

The words, however, mean that you are calling on God as your witness that you are not lying. Here is how Jesus felt about having his name used in that way: **"Do not swear at all: either by heaven, for it is God's throne; or by the earth, for it is his footstool. . . . Simply let your 'Yes' be 'Yes,' and your 'No,' 'No'; anything beyond this comes from the evil one"** (Matthew 5:34,35,37).

What you will find is that if you develop a reputation for speaking only the truth, you won't need to trot God's name out as if he were your chief character witness.

_____

_____

_____

_____

_____

church people can be cruel too

Military personnel are trained in recognition of the enemy, and military intelligence strains every resource to identify the enemy's location and movements. But every combat veteran knows the sad reality that great harm can also be done by people on our side, people wearing our uniforms. Sometimes it is called "friendly fire." In the first Battle of Bull Run during the Civil War, for instance, uniforms of both Confederates and Union men were not of a consistent color, and gunners sometimes belatedly realized that they were blasting away at their own troops.

Sad to say, Christians can expect to face hostility not only from secular unbelievers, but from people within the organized church. Church people are human; while thinking that they are serving God they can be as wrong, misguided, and cruel as any unbeliever. Jesus warned his disciples to expect friendly fire: **"Be on your guard against men; they will hand you over to the local councils and flog you in their synagogues"** (Matthew 10:17).

Jesus knew that sad reality from his own bitter experience. The most intense hatred he faced during his brief ministry was from the church leadership of his time: the Pharisees, priests, and legal scholars. It was they who arranged to arrest him and convict him of a capital crime in an illegal late-night kangaroo court.

Consider yourself warned. Now you know.

_____

_____

_____

God's strength shown in my weakness

When you are stressed, two agendas compete in your heart. One is Satan's. He will try to spin your hardships, especially economic hardships, as proof that God is incompetent. Or weak. Or senile. Or absent. Or dead. Or that he has given up on you, loves you no more and probably never did, and you are left alone to languish in your struggles.

The other agenda is God's. It is a great surprise as you grow in your Christian faith to discover that God gets his loving and saving plans accomplished not only by giving us things but also by taking things away. He blesses us both with pleasures and with hardships.

St. Paul knew both bounty and privation, and he had learned to see God at work in both scenarios. He had learned to be thankful for his easy days. But he had learned also the value of drawing strength from God when he was empty. **"That is why, for Christ's sake, I delight in weaknesses, in insults, in hardships, in persecutions, in difficulties. For when I am weak, then I am strong"** (2 Corinthians 12:10).

When you are empty, you can watch God make a way out of no way. You can watch the miracle of manna, miracle bread, reenacted before you. You can accept his hardships as antimaterialism therapy. You can celebrate his just-in-time providing of everything you need. Ahem. *Need.*

_____

_____

_____

_____

_____

your attitude matters

If I've messed up and somebody's going to try to straighten me out, it sure helps if that person comes in humility. Because, immature as I still am, if I feel that somebody is talking down to me, I'll push back and do the opposite, just to demonstrate that you can't push me around.

When you see someone whose life is spiraling downward and summon up your nerve to get involved, attitude is everything. Perhaps you're so aware of your own failings that you would feel like a hypocrite getting into someone else's business, or fear that you will be rejected. Love them enough to risk their rejection. Speak with a repentant heart and a soft voice.

James reminds us, **"Who is wise and understanding among you? Let him show it by his good life, by deeds done in the humility that comes from wisdom"** (James 3:13). That humble wisdom doesn't come easily. If you have it, it's because you've learned some of your life lessons the hard way.

Your words may be just that much more believable if you've fallen and been helped back to your feet, if you have benefited from someone else's spiritual help.

_____

_____

_____

_____

_____

Christ is our model

People need heroes to look up to, to know that at least somebody has figured out life and figured out how to be successful. Who are your heroes? Achievers in sports, finance, fashion, or music?

People crave heroes also to know how to live. We pay attention not only to the achievements of athletes, musicians, and movie stars, but we crave details of their personal lives as well. A huge magazine, TV, and online industry has arisen to satisfy that craving. We want to know about the stars' relationships, cars, mansions, and lifestyles.

Living a godly life is plenty hard. Satan attacks and tempts from the outside, and we struggle with the old sinner still within us. We need both information on how to please God and also the will and inspiration to keep at it. Jesus Christ provides both. He gives us his Word to teach our minds. He gives us his Spirit to live within to give us strength.

And he leads by example. He is our greatest hero. **"Your attitude should be the same as that of Christ Jesus: Who, being in very nature God, did not consider equality with God something to be grasped, but made himself nothing, taking the very nature of a servant"** (Philippians 2:5-7).

I want to be like him.

_____

_____

_____

_____

_____

he's alive again

Remember the story of the prodigal son? When he returned, the father threw him a big party, but the older "good" brother didn't approve. The good son got not a tongue-lashing, but a patient explanation of what goes on in a parent's heart. When a young adult runs away from his or her parents' guidance, their hearts are sick with fear. When a child comes back, it is as though he or she rose from the dead, and the sense of relief is overwhelming. Of course there will be a celebration.

"'My son,' the father said, 'you are always with me, and everything I have is yours. But we had to celebrate and be glad, because this brother of yours was dead and is alive again; he was lost and is found'" (Luke 15:31,32).

In our work of spiritual reclamation, let us always remember that broken sinners are restored not by the law (commandments, shame, pressure, works, incentives) but by the pure gospel (the Father's unconditional love, Christ's unconditional forgiveness, the Spirit's patient working of faith).

And when you have been a bad boy or bad girl, always remember that God's greatest desire is to embrace you once again and give you a plate of veal, not to give you the punishment that you so richly deserve. Mercy triumphs over judgment.

study her

One of the teasers and puzzles that sustains interest in a marriage over many decades is the fact that you never fully comprehend your partner. Men and women are tantalizingly wired differently from each other. Their perceptions about money, romance, communication, time, and appropriate social behaviors can be significantly different.

God built us with these differences to enrich our lives. Satan would like to use them as wedges to drive us apart. Spouses who assume that their partner thinks just like them will grow frustrated and irritated.

The apostle Peter had a mother-in-law, so he must have had a wife too. She undoubtedly taught Peter a lot about how the female half of the human race perceived things. **"Husbands, in the same way be considerate as you live with your wives"** (1 Peter 3:7). In this passage, the Greek words translated "be considerate" literally mean to live with your wife "according to knowledge." In other words, study her. Pay attention to her words, face, needs, nonverbal communication. Attune yourself to her—don't assume that she looks at the world as you do.

Wives, you can help your husbands in their study of you. Begin sentences occasionally with the words, "I want . . ." They speak a different dialect of English from you—do not assume that they can read your mind. Marriage is a dance— pay attention to your partner.

_____

_____

_____

_____

remember who you are

Imagine that someone was trying to steal your inheritance by keeping you from claiming your rights as a son or daughter of royalty. Imagine that the strategy was to get you to doubt that you really had royal blood at all.

Satan is trying to steal your joy and persuade you to doubt your legal identity. Don't let him. Through your adoption papers (i.e., baptismal certificate) God is named as your Father. St. Peter called you no less than God's chosen people, God's royal priests.

Your royal identity ironically explains why your life is so hard sometimes. **"The Lord disciplines those he loves, as a father the son he delights in"** (Proverbs 3:12). What a comfort it is to know that our loving Father has an eye on our hardships to make sure that we are not overwhelmed. What a comfort it is to know that none of our suffering is in vain—he will make every bit of it work for our good in one way or another. What a relief it is to know that he guarantees a happy ending and that only the middle chapters are hard.

My Father in heaven delights in me! Seriously!

_____

_____

_____

_____

_____

July 18
Hannah's sacrifice

Has anyone in your family struggled with infertility? Have you? One of the seeming injustices of human life is that people who have no business having children seem to conceive easily, while couples with secure homes and lives and empty arms try and try and wait for a baby that never comes.

Hannah was one of those infertile women with a broken heart. What made matters worse was that she had to live in a polygamous marriage. Her co-wife had children, and she provoked and taunted Hannah about it. Hannah prayed intensely and vowed that if God gave her a son, she would give him back to God. Her prayer was answered, and she kept her vow.

She told Eli the high priest, **"'As surely as you live, my lord, I am the woman who stood here beside you praying to the LORD. I prayed for this child, and the LORD has granted me what I asked of him. So now I give him to the LORD. For his whole life he will be given over to the LORD.' . . . Then Hannah prayed and said: 'My heart rejoices in the LORD'"** (1 Samuel 1:26–2:1).

Only a mother could fully appreciate the cost of her sacrifice. She called her little boy *Sh'mu-El* ("heard by God"), and he became a great leader of the nation. Hannah is my hero.

_____

_____

_____

_____

_____

July 19
don't be shy

Do you remember the awkwardness you felt when you attended somebody else's family gathering for the first time? How uncomfortable it was to meet your date's parents and feel them look you up and down? How nervous you were that you would say the wrong thing or fail to perform the way you were supposed to? How glad you were to get out of there?

I suspect that one of the fears that keeps Christians from praying more often, and keeps them from enjoying the prayers they do offer, is that they are uncomfortable. They know they haven't lived the way they should; they feel sheepish and guilty about asking for things they know they don't deserve; they are not so sure they know the etiquette of the heavenly court.

Here is good news for everyone who believes in Jesus as his or her Savior. You aren't *partially* forgiven—you are *completely* forgiven. You aren't merely *tolerated*—you are *loved!* **"Let us approach the throne of grace *with confidence, so that we may receive mercy and find grace to help us in our time of need*"** (Hebrews 4:16).

You are given the right of citizenship in eternal life in heaven. Claim it! You are given the right to be called a son or daughter of God. Claim it! You are given the right to approach God himself any time, with any petition. Don't be shy!

_____

_____

_____

_____

_____

balance sheet

Do you find yourself doing personal inventory every now and then? You know, mentally reviewing your assets, your personal balance sheet as it were?

Perhaps you reflect with satisfaction on your steadily growing mutual funds, IRAs, 401(k)s, and annuities. Maybe you are counting the months until you make that last mortgage payment and the house is finally yours, not the bank's. Or you smile at the steady promotions and raises you've received or your wonderful new car or much bigger house.

Not to overdo the buzzkill, but every one of those things not only *can* be taken from you but *will* be taken from you. Your best friend, Jesus, urges you to put the forgiveness of your sins and his guarantee of resurrection and immortality at the top of your personal balance sheet: **"Store up for yourselves treasures in heaven, where moth and rust do not destroy, and where thieves do not break in and steal. For where your treasure is, there your heart will be also"** (Matthew 6:20,21).

The only way out of the grave is Jesus. The only things you can take with you to the next life are people. How do those two truths influence your agenda for today? Is it evident to Jesus and the people in your life that they are more important to you than money?

_____

_____

_____

_____

_____

guests in God's world

All of us struggle every day to try to get control of our environments. We try to build financial wealth so that we won't suffer need. We try to take care of our health so we don't feel pain or suffer illness. We try to manage our relationships to reduce stress. It is humbling, though, to realize that we aren't in control of very much.

Actually, this world doesn't really even belong to us. We are guests in someone else's world; we are actors in someone else's play. **"The earth is the Lord's, and everything in it, the world, and all who live in it; for he founded it upon the seas and established it upon the waters"** (Psalm 24:1,2). **"Every animal of the forest is mine, and the cattle on a thousand hills"** (Psalm 50:10). It is humbling to realize that we were created for God's benefit, that everything really belongs to him, and that we really own nothing.

But it's exhilarating too. The *Creator* of the universe is also our heavenly *Father*. The great Power uses his power to bless and protect and prosper us. The great Owner of all wealth loves to give gifts to his children. The great Engineer is planning even now how he will guide your steps in this world to get you home to his.

Here's a thought: The same Being who created the Grand Canyon loves you dearly.

_____

_____

_____

_____

don't sweat the small stuff

Psychologist Richard Carlson is given credit for this wonderful two-part advice on dealing with stress: (1) Don't sweat the small stuff. (2) It's mostly all small stuff.

Most of us find ourselves getting wound up over issues that, in the larger scheme of things, are not all that important. We want so badly to be right that we fry relationships to prove our point. We argue and argue, but to what end? We hold ancient grudges, but what is the point? We assume that we are cursed, that we are doomed to have everything go wrong for us in the end. When we are looking for bad news, we can usually find it.

God has a better way. Just as he chooses to forgive us, giving fresh supplies of grace and mercy each morning, he invites us to show that same bigheartedness to the fools and sinners who surround us.

"A man's wisdom gives him patience; it is to his glory to overlook an offense" (Proverbs 19:11). We don't have to be right all the time. We don't have to point out every sin and flaw in the people around us. We can let go of the judging and trust that God will get it right in the end.

What matters is enjoying God's love for us and loving the people around us.

_____

_____

_____

_____

_____

perfectionism

Do you have friends who always seem to criticize and never praise? Worse—did your own mother simply make demands on you and never let you know that you had done anything well? Do you still live in fear of her criticism? Do you dread your father's constant disapproval of your decisions? Worst of all—do you beat yourself up because nothing you have ever done seems good enough?

What makes people so perfectionistic? Perhaps they grew up on a steady diet of criticism. Perhaps they are even more insecure than you. You can't control what other people say to you, but you can decide whether to accept their judgment or not, and you can control how you talk to other people.

Here is St. Paul's therapy for healing strained relationships: **"Be kind and compassionate to one another, forgiving each other, just as in Christ God forgave you"** (Ephesians 4:32).

There has been only one perfect human being, and his name is Jesus. Get this—through your faith in him, God considers you as perfect as Jesus is. If he likes you and accepts you, you can like and accept yourself.

_____

_____

_____

_____

_____

everything just seems hopeless

"Keep Hope Alive" was Jesse Jackson's campaign slogan when he ran for president in 1988. And yet those words are more than just throwaway political placards and yard signs. Social change is impossible in communities that have given up. America's inner cities need to keep believing in America's central promise of freedom and equality under the law.

Do you know the taste and odor of despair? Of seeing nothing positive? Does your marriage seem permanently broken? As a single parent, do you fear that you will never find anyone to marry? Do you have addictive behaviors of many years that seem impossible to change?

You may have run out of ideas, run out of strength, maybe even run out of the desire to keep struggling. But just because you have run out of strength doesn't mean that God is powerless too. Just because you're out of ideas doesn't mean that God's brain is dry. Just because you can't see the way out doesn't mean that God has lost his eagle's height view.

Here is a promise to all of God's children who need a breath of heavenly oxygen: **"A righteous man may have many troubles, but the LORD delivers him from them all"** (Psalm 34:19).

_____

_____

_____

_____

_____

servant angels

Everybody works in heaven. Jesus said once, "The Father works, and I also work." That is, the three persons of the triune God not only exerted themselves tremendously when they designed and built the universe, but they work each day to maintain and sustain it.

The angels work too. They don't just hover around in great winged clouds, waiting to see what's going to happen, watching God and watching us. They are God's spirit-agents, carrying out his gracious will on our behalf. **"Are not all angels ministering spirits sent to serve those who will inherit salvation?"** (Hebrews 1:14).

When you say your prayers this evening and take inventory of your day and plead for help with your finances, your health, your family, your job, and your home, take a moment and thank the Lord for the invisible army of servants that he sent which is working on your behalf even while you speak.

Someday you may be told of the guidance, whispers, and nudges by which they got you where God wanted you. Someday you may be told about the bulletproof protection they provided against disaster and against the evil one.

_____

_____

_____

_____

_____

what are they doing here?

Poor people make rich people uncomfortable.

It's not just the huge income gap. There can be a big difference in people's value systems and behaviors too. There's a reason why some people want to live in gated communities with an ex-marine security officer at the guardhouse. There's a reason why many social gathering places are members-only.

Christians can't control private clubs and exclusive suburbs. But they can control how people are treated in their congregations. The Bible teaches that all people, regardless of income level, are broken sinners who need the gospel of forgiveness and who need the Spirit's help to rebuild. All believers, rich and poor alike, are important members of the body of Christ; all have needs, and all have gifts to share.

In addition, poor people have a special place in the eyes and heart of the Lord, and he watches how they are treated. **"Has not God chosen those who are poor in the eyes of the world to be rich in faith and to inherit the kingdom he promised those who love him?"** (James 2:5). Every visitor to your congregation deserves attention and respect. Every member, regardless of what his or her personal balance sheet looks like, deserves dignity. Let's learn to get comfortable with one another.

_____

_____

_____

_____

July 27
you lack nothing

One of the most cherished phrases in the Declaration of Independence is the assurance that in America you are guaranteed the right to life, liberty, and the pursuit of happiness. It is important to note that the government of the United States does not guarantee your happiness, only your right to pursue it.

God is better than our government. He doesn't merely set up a game in which you are able to pursue your own righteousness and holiness with him. His holy and pure commandments are beyond the ability of sinners to keep perfectly. By giving you forgiveness of your sins through the blood of Jesus, he thereby gives you his favor. By giving you his favor, he obligates himself to act toward you like a Father and throws open the gates of heaven.

How is that not a cause for great joy? **"Rejoice in the Lord and be glad, you righteous; sing, all you who are upright in heart!"** (Psalm 32:11). That doesn't necessarily mean that you are grinning or giggling all the time. What it does mean is that even in your days of hardship and pain and tears, you have the quiet confidence that you are a winner. When you have Jesus, you have everything. When you have Jesus, you lack nothing. When you have Jesus, you are immortal like him. When you have Jesus, your eternity is secured.

What's your favorite hymn? Put this book down for a minute and sing it right now with all your heart.

_____

_____

_____

_____

honor your father and mother

If you surveyed one hundred teenagers about their parents, how many would respond, "My parents are precious, valuable people whom God has given to me for my good. I appreciate their guidance, life principles, correction, and rules"? Hah! Probably none. Sadly, parents are more likely seen as jailers or parole officers who arbitrarily limit children's freedom.

The God I know, however, thinks parents are worthy of praise and wants you to think so too. **"Honor your father and your mother, as the LORD your God has commanded you, so that you may live long and that it may go well with you in the land the LORD your God is giving you"** (Deuteronomy 5:16).

This is not just the right thing to do so God won't be angry with you and punish you. Honoring your parents triggers the release of a flood of benefits into your life. God has attached a double promise to parent-respecters:

- I will increase the *quantity* of your life.
- I will increase the *quality* of your life.

What does it mean to *honor* your parents? It means cultivating a spirit of gratitude, because they have done far more for you than you will ever know. Because they have made sacrifices you only partially understand to bring you benefit. If it is from them that you first heard about Jesus, it is they who gave you heaven.

----

alone again

Folk singer Joni Mitchell delivered a profound piece of philosophy in a song she recorded in 1970: "Don't it always seem to go, that you don't know what you've got till it's gone?" She was lamenting urban sprawl and pesticides, but you could say the same thing about family life.

It's so easy to grumble and complain about changing diapers on your babies, but then they grow so fast that soon they don't want to be held and kissed anymore. You wish you wouldn't always have to hire a sitter when you want to leave the house, and all of a sudden they're moody teenagers who don't seem to need you anymore. Your husband can be so irritating and hard to motivate . . . and then all of a sudden you're a widow.

Anna **"was a widow until she was eighty-four. . . . She gave thanks to God and spoke about the child** [the baby Jesus] **to all who were looking forward to the redemption of Jerusalem"** (Luke 2:37,38). Anna could have stayed home all the time with the windows closed, feeling sorry for herself, marinating in bitterness of spirit. Instead she spent her time with God and with people. She was in the right place at the right time when Mary and Joseph entered the temple with their precious baby Jesus.

Anna not only got a chance to see her Savior up close; she shared her faith with anyone who would listen. Alone again? Go where the people are.

_____

_____

_____

_____

me + God 4ever

We sling the word *forever* around pretty loosely most of the time. "Diamonds are forever," says a slick ad campaign. No, they aren't. "U + Me 4ever" is written in high school yearbooks every year. Forever? *Hmm*, no. "I will be forever grateful . . ." No again.

There is only one voice that you can believe whose "forever" is really forever. The voice is the Lord's. He has existed from all eternity backward in time; has experienced all decades, centuries, and millennia of human life; and will continue to exist going forward without end. He moves backward and forward in time effortlessly; in fact, it is all one gigantic present for God. When he makes a prophetic prediction, you know it will be true because he's already there watching it happen.

His great passion and great achievement is to bring you into his heaven and his eternity: **"I heard a loud voice from the throne saying, 'Now the dwelling of God is with men, and he will live with them. They will be his people, and God himself will be with them and be their God. He will wipe every tear from their eyes. There will be no more death or mourning or crying or pain, for the old order of things has passed away'"** (Revelation 21:3,4).

Safe. Immortal. Happy. Healed. Together. Forever.

July 31
he has a plan

You can bear almost any burden if you think that tomorrow has a chance of getting better. If you're laid off from work or have a major chronic illness, you dream about the next interview, the next operation. But when hopes are crushed, the light goes out in your eyes.

The stories of God's Old Testament people Israel will break your heart. The years 721 and 586 B.C. mark the disintegration and collapse of the two kingdoms. But God told his suffering and exiled people, **"'The days are coming,' declares the LORD, 'when [people] . . . will say, "As surely as the LORD lives, who brought the Israelites up out of the land of the north and out of all the countries where he had banished them." For I will restore them to the land I gave their forefathers'"** (Jeremiah 16:14,15).

And he did! After 70 years of captivity, God restored the nation to its land and at just the right time sent the Savior of the world to be born.

God knows your needs and your pain. You can give him your fears. He had a plan and a time for Israel, and he has a plan and a time for you too.

_____

_____

_____

_____

August

"Hope does not disappoint us, because
God has poured out his love into our hearts
by the Holy Spirit, whom he has given us."
(Romans 5:5)

August 1

they were minors then

Most parents don't need to be told that you treat children differently at different stages in their lives. Adult freedoms and privileges are denied to give children a chance to mature. Parents control their children's diets, bedtimes, and their access to cars and alcohol. These denials aren't from a lack of love, but precisely because parents love them so much. Minor children learn respect, patience, wisdom, self-control, and consideration for others when they are compelled to live under their parents' rules.

The key to understanding the differences between the Old and New Covenants is to realize that God chose to treat people before the time of Christ as though they were minor children. It's not that people today have evolved to be smarter and more responsible. It's people's sinful rebellion against God that caused them to lose their understanding of God and his ways. God decided to rebuild that understanding slowly, wrapping his gospel mercy in a context of laws and rules. St. Paul wrote to people who were used to this law experience: **"Before this faith came, we were held prisoners by the law, locked up until faith should be revealed. So the law was put in charge *to lead us to Christ* that we might be justified by faith"** (Galatians 3:23,24).

What this means for today is that we need to pick our way carefully through God's words in the Old Testament. Some of what is written there was for believers when they were considered minors. You're big now.

you are grown-ups now

If you read the first four books of the Bible that describe early Israelite life (Exodus through Deuteronomy), you will come away with several profound impressions. First, the God of Israel cared passionately about sustaining a faith relationship with those people and would stop at nothing to take care of them. Second, there was a streak of rebellion in the people that flared up constantly. Third, to help keep them together, keep them distinct from corrupting influences around them, and keep them focused on him, God established a detailed set of laws to regulate their personal, social, and religious lives.

This was no democracy. The people didn't vote on their laws. The laws were simply imposed from on high and got the basic job done. When Christ came to earth, he found people who were still faithful to God and ready for him. **"The law was put in charge to lead us to Christ that we might be justified by faith. Now that faith has come, we are no longer under the supervision of the law"** (Galatians 3:24,25).

Through Christ, God changed the style of his covenant relationship with people from law to faith-freedom. His basic moral commandments are timeless, of course, but the laws governing details of civic and religious life are no longer needed.

God treats you like a grown-up now. Act like it.

_____

_____

_____

_____

_____

leave an estate

More than half of all Americans will die intestate. Do you know that word? It means that they have no written Last Will and Testament. If you die intestate, the state will make all decisions regarding the disposition of your property and then charge your estate for its services.

Why on earth would people not make a will? Well, people do procrastinate, assuming that someday they will get around to it and never do. Or they reason that when they're dead, they won't care how their estate is carved up. Or they think they're immortal. Or they have a phobia about death and hate even thinking about it.

God loves it when people plan ahead with management of his stuff, and he absolutely loves it when people plan to take care of succeeding generations. **"A good man leaves an inheritance for his children's children"** (Proverbs 13:22). A bequest helps turn your children and grandchildren from renters into homeowners. It can help a grandchild go to college. It can relieve a crippling debt. It can help start a business.

It says thank you to the God who gave you such a great heritage from those who have gone before you.

_____

_____

_____

_____

_____

your work matters

As you grow from a young believer into a more mature believer, as you learn more and more of God's ways from the Bible, you become aware that God is sovereign over all human history. He causes the rise and fall of nations. He puts babies in our arms and calls people home. It is he who creates the very faith we need to trust in his Son and be saved.

But that doesn't mean that your own choices and deeds are irrelevant, like a toy steering wheel on a small child's car seat. Your work matters. Your bad choices can hurt yourself and other people.

But—your acts of love and mercy and service can change people's lives and bring God's light where there had only been darkness.

Can you do both things? Can you acknowledge the Lord God as the supreme Master of the universe, on top of every last detail, and at the same time believe that your words and actions are of vital importance to God's mission?

Let Moses, God's right-hand man, his personal agent in leading the great exodus from Egypt, encourage you: **"May the favor of the Lord our God rest upon us; establish the work of our hands for us—yes, establish the work of our hands"** (Psalm 90:17).

_____

_____

_____

_____

_____

You mean we're brothers?

Making friends into enemies is Satan's work. Making strangers into friends, antagonists into brothers, is God's work. The gospel of Christ has reconciled God to us and us to God, closing the great chasm of sin and judgment and death. And the gospel does that wonderful work between separated people groups.

Cornelius was an officer of the Italian regiment of the Roman legions that occupied Israel. He was proud of his Roman heritage in law, engineering, and war and was taught to despise the barbarian Jews and their backward religious obsessions. Peter was brought up an observant Jew, taught to avoid Gentiles and their unclean homes and food, taught to fear and resent this army of occupation.

To the surprise of both, the Spirit of the Lord taught them that they were brothers in Christ. **"As Peter entered the house, Cornelius met him and fell at his feet in reverence. But Peter made him get up. 'Stand up,' he said, 'I am only a man myself'"** (Acts 10:25,26).

The only reason that a Gentile like me is a believer is that some early Jewish Christians dared to share their faith with people not like them. Perhaps I can continue that holy process in my life. You?

_____

_____

_____

_____

_____

August 6

Naaman's servant girl

One of my heroes is a child. I hope she made it to heaven because I want to meet her. I don't even know her name.

"Now [raiding] bands from Aram had gone out and had taken captive a young girl from Israel, and she served Naaman's wife. She said to her mistress, 'If only my master would see the prophet who is in Samaria! He would cure him of his leprosy'" (2 Kings 5:2,3).

If I had been captured by raiders, taken from my family, and now forced to work as an unpaid slave for some foreigner, I would hate it. Worse—Naaman was a high-ranking military officer in the dreaded Aramean army, Israel's bitter foes on their troubled northern frontier.

I would work every day in a cold rage, burying my feelings under a bland mask and plotting either escape or revenge. Instead, this little girl showed kindness to her owner. She felt sorry for him because he had leprosy and urged him to see Elisha, Israel's great man of God.

Through her intercession, Naaman was not only healed, but he had a personal interaction with the true God's authorized agent on earth. He was led to exclaim, **"Now I know that there is no God in all the world except in Israel"** (2 Kings 5:15). A courageous little girl was the broker of God's grace to him.

_____

_____

_____

_____

_____

use your gifts

Years of TV watching have made most of us a passive audience of the performances of others—music, acting, sports, politics. How dreadful if God's army of royal priests prefers to watch a few "church professionals" while imagining that they have nothing to offer.

You may never play in the NBA or NFL, but you most certainly have a role in bringing blessings from God to the people in your life. Not only are you surrounded by opportunities for sharing God's love; you also have been given unique gifts that make you useful to God's agenda.

"*Each one* should use whatever gift he has received to serve others, faithfully administering God's grace in its various forms" (1 Peter 4:10). Let no Christian ever say, "I've got nothing." St. Peter states that all believers have gifts, gifts intended by God to be shared. Romans chapter 12 gives some examples to get you thinking.

Not sure what yours are? Do two things: ask a friend what he or she thinks you're good at, and then have a conference with yourself and determine what you're really passionate about that could help somebody else. That passion may be the Spirit's clue.

_____

_____

_____

_____

_____

think heaven

When you've been up all night with a sick child, washing bedclothes and mopping up the mess in the bathroom, think heaven. When someone you trusted turns on you, think heaven. When there never seems to be enough money to cover all the bills, think heaven.

Satan would like to beat you down and keep you looking down. Satan delusionally thinks he is a winner and you are a loser. Actually, the reverse is true. Your faith in Christ bonds you to him, and you can now identify with and participate in all of Christ's triumphs. **"Since you have been raised with Christ, set your hearts on things above, where Christ is seated at the right hand of God. For you died, and your life is now hidden with Christ in God. When Christ, who is your life, appears, then you also will appear with him in glory"** (Colossians 3:1,3,4).

On the outside you may not look like a prince or princess of the royal court of heaven, but the angels see you that way. Your name is written in the royal guest register. Your room is waiting for your check-in date. Though your true identity may seem hidden now, at just the right time the Lord Jesus will reveal all his family members. Everyone will know your heavenly identity.

He will shine in heavenly glory. You will too.

_____

_____

_____

_____

_____

there is no utopia

People of every century and every country have longed for heaven on earth. There have always been men and women who assumed that conditions on earth would improve steadily until we achieved utopia. War, poverty, famine, and sickness would slowly fade away as mankind marched toward a glorious future.

The hard reality is the opposite. People are just as violent as ever, and our constantly evolving technology means that individuals and armies can kill more people faster than ever before. One disease may be wiped out, only to be replaced by three others that are even more deadly.

People are also jumpy about the end of the world and its timing. Whether it's Year 2K or the Mayan calendar stone or mysterious Nostradamus prophecies, people assume that the end must be coming any day now. Jesus offers a word of patience and realism: **"You will hear of wars and rumors of wars, but see to it that you are not alarmed. Such things must happen, but the end is still to come"** (Matthew 24:6).

Such things must happen. A dreadful prediction, but a helpful one. The world we live in will be broken until Jesus returns. He will return exactly when his Father decides. In the meantime, we have work to do. Spread the Word. Love the people.

_____

_____

_____

_____

August 10
show respect

One of Jay Leno's regular features in his television shows is called "Jaywalking." He walks the streets of L.A. with a mike and cameraman and asks pedestrians simple questions about U.S. geography, politics, and history. The audience shrieks with laughter to hear the ignorant and crazy things in people's heads.

We shouldn't be surprised if people have crazy ideas about religion too. If you are trying to draw someone back into the truth, you won't get very far if you ridicule things people say, even if they sound nuttier than a fruitcake. **"Always be prepared to give an answer to everyone who asks you to give the reason for the hope that you have. But do this with gentleness and *respect***" (1 Peter 3:15).

That doesn't mean that you accept and agree with people's notions about religion and spirituality. What it does mean is that you show respect to a person and listen courteously. People will not give you a hearing if you have not first showed that you are listening to them.

People may respond to your invitation if they feel that you are real, caring, and honest. They will never respond if you have made fun of their unbiblical ideas.

_____

_____

_____

_____

_____

August 11
no, Jesus!

Aren't you glad that Jesus didn't listen to his disciples' advice on how to carry out his mission? It seems that every time he described his coming suffering, death, and resurrection, they protested. "No, Jesus!" they would say. "This shall never happen to you!"

They showed that they didn't understand the entire point of the ceremonial animal sacrifices that had been going on since the human race's beginning. **"He** [Jesus] **said to them, 'The Son of Man is going to be betrayed into the hands of men. They will kill him, and on the third day he will be raised to life.' And the disciples were filled with grief"** (Matthew 17:22,23). They should have been encouraging him. Instead, their protests were just that much more drag on his willpower, just that much more of an opportunity for Satan to try to deflect him from the cross.

Every one of the sin offerings of sacrificial animals was a stand-in for the Lamb of God who willingly went to his cross for us. Not a one of those slain animals would ever have done anyone a bit of good unless they were linked with the spilling of the blood of the Lamb. It was Christ who authenticated the priests' announcements of the cleansing of Old Testament believers. It is Christ who alone gives us the confidence of our forgiveness today.

Yes, Jesus!

_____

_____

_____

_____

_____

August 12
rainbow assurance

It's hard to imagine that there was once a time in earth's history when there were no rainbows. How could there not be? Did the sun not shine in the same way? Did water vapor not hang in the air after rain in the same way? Did God somehow alter the physical properties of light so that it would refract into its array of rainbow colors only after Noah's time?

I don't know the answers to any of these questions. If you really want to know, write them on your list for the day after judgment day. In the meantime, know this—the rainbow is not simply a meaningless phenomenon of nature. It is the miraculous design of God himself, and it appears in the sky just often enough to remind us of a promise he made, a promise that could be made only by the Maker and Preserver of heaven and earth.

God told Noah, **"As long as the earth endures, seedtime and harvest, cold and heat, summer and winter, day and night will never cease"** (Genesis 8:22). The seasonal, monthly, and daily rhythms of life on this earth will continue uninterrupted until he returns to remake all things. In the meantime, we have his promise that there will be no more planet-wide destructive judgments like the flood. But the rainbow also reminds us that God did indeed once destroy the face of the earth. We have important work to do before he returns to do it again.

_____

_____

_____

_____

August 13

my Savior is alive

Father, sometimes it looks as though Satan really has won after all. Christians are persecuted, children are abused, our streets aren't safe, good people lose their jobs, and families break up. Governments collapse; wars fester and consume staggering amounts of blood and treasure. Death is steadily stealing my friends and loved ones one at a time.

But Easter happened. The mighty prince of hell himself cannot change history. Your Son lived a holy life and lets me claim it as mine. Your Son died a horrible death and experienced hell for me so I won't have to. Your Son rose from his grave, changing everything, guaranteeing my forgiveness and my own immortality.

His words become my words: **"My heart is glad and my tongue rejoices; my body also will rest secure, because you will not abandon me to the grave, nor will you let your Holy One see decay. You have made known to me the path of life; you will fill me with joy in your presence, with eternal pleasures at your right hand"** (Psalm 16:9-11 and Acts 2:26-28).

I can overcome every hardship when I know that I win in the end no matter what. The grave could not contain my Savior. He is the first installment for the grand Easter yet to come. He's alive and will never die. I won't either.

_____

_____

_____

_____

but he's just a kid!

Long ago I taught middle school music for two semesters. One student's parents asked her how the class was going. "Well, he's okay, but he treats us like children," she replied. Her mom and dad had to look away as they suppressed their laughter.

Children need to be treated as though their opinions and thoughts matter, which, of course, they do. Even the prophet Samuel, as he was sent to anoint the next king, guessed wrong, very wrong, at which of Jesse's sons was God's choice. It was the kid, David. **"The Lord said to Samuel, '. . . The Lord does not look at the things man looks at. Man looks at the outward appearance, but the Lord looks at the heart'"** (1 Samuel 16:7).

It was a little servant girl who hooked up the Syrian military commander, Naaman, with the prophet Elisha. That girl's brave testimony brought Naaman healing from his leprosy. Jesus greatly preferred the children's hosannas on Palm Sunday to the Pharisees' sneering on Monday (Matthew 21:15).

Do you believe that children's praise matters to God as much as yours? . . . that God has given them insights that adults miss? . . . that the body of Christ needs them as much as you? . . . that they are important partners in carrying out God's rescue mission?

_____

_____

_____

_____

_____

remember to pray

Prayer isn't like fertilizing your lawn, which is indeed helpful but not absolutely necessary. Prayer is one of your soul's vital signs. It shows if your faith has a pulse.

Just as ungrateful children can get into the habit of just taking, taking, taking from generous parents, our prayer lives can suffer from neglect. We just forget. We put prayer off until later. We view it as a spiritual chore, like cleaning out the gutters, and defer it. We figure it can wait while we take care of important things. We mumble some religious clichés, get distracted by something else, and don't even finish.

Moses knew that his Israelites were susceptible to that same spiritual amnesia, forgetting who they were, forgetting how they were able to come so far, forgetting the One who was their very life. Shortly before he died, Moses urged them, **"Be careful that you do not forget the Lord, who brought you out of Egypt, out of the land of slavery"** (Deuteronomy 6:12).

Right now would be a great time to send a message to God to let him know how proud you are to be called his child.

_____

_____

_____

_____

_____

why, God?

Anyone who has ever read the Bible even casually resonates with the story of Job. Well-to-do and comfortable, he loses his wealth, servants, family members, and finally even his health. We generally remember Job for his courage and brilliant confession of confidence in his coming Redeemer.

But Job speaks for all of us when in his weaker moments he complained to God about the bitter unfairness of the way his life was turning out. Job cried out what we cry out when we are frustrated, hurting, and confused: "Why, God? Oh, that I had someone to hear me!"

We are creatures whose lives are fixed to one moment in time and one spot on earth. How amused, and probably also disappointed, God must be when we talk as though we see the big picture. How little we know! How little we have seen! God could have answered Job in many ways; he said this: **"Who is this that darkens my counsel with words without knowledge? Where were you when I laid the earth's foundation?"** (Job 38:2,4).

When Satan tempts us to doubt God's intelligence and management ability, let us recall that he designed the dazzling Northern Lights, arranged the Himalayas, froze water into glaciers, and built the oxygen-rich atmosphere without any advice from us. Job's life turned out okay. We'll be okay. God is good at what he does.

_____

_____

_____

_____

_____

fantasy

Pretending and fantasy are integral to the Disney World® experience. In fact, Disney coined the term "imagineering" to describe the way in which its writers and designers and artists construct wonderful imaginary realities on a grand scale.

Pretending makes Disney World work. Too much pretending in your day-to-day life, however, can make you spiritually sick. A woman who invites her boyfriend to move in with her might only be fantasizing that he is committed to her. She might imagine that having his baby will bond him to her forever. A man might fantasize that the models in his porn magazines really do desire him, and he comes to find more satisfaction in pretending with his virtual babes than in actually building a real relationship with a real woman.

A woman wants a loving home so badly that she puts up with verbal and physical abuse, redefining what "normal" is just to keep the illusion alive. **"He who chases fantasies lacks judgment"** (Proverbs 12:11).

How can you be set free from sinful fantasy? Listen. Listen to the Word of your God. His Word is always true and healthy, even though it is sometimes not fashionable or cool. Pray for wisdom and discernment. Listen to the advice of people who have earned the right to tell you things you may not want to hear.

_____

_____

_____

_____

_____

grace in action

Jesus' disciples were often an embarrassment to him during their three years of training. The four gospels report in painful detail when the Twelve exhibited confused priorities and uncaring people attitudes. Two of the four books, Matthew and John, were authored by men who had to describe their own spiritual immaturity in those years.

But after the outpouring of the Spirit on Pentecost, the disciples ("learners") became apostles ("sent ones"), and they grew mightily in wisdom and understanding. Their former confused utterings gave way to passionate and articulate proclamations about Christ and his wonderful work. They also learned how to love people: **"With great power the apostles continued to testify to the resurrection of the Lord Jesus, and much grace was upon them all. There were no needy persons among them"** (Acts 4:33,34).

God would like us to treat one another the way he treats us—with patience, forgiveness, hospitality, kindness, compassion, and generosity. The early church was concerned not only with teaching but with helping people with their physical needs as well.

It was true then and is even truer today that people who are strangers to the Christian faith will take our words much more seriously when accompanied by clear evidence of love and caring. You might call it "grace in action."

_____

_____

_____

_____

_____

it's congenital

Our church's gospel choir once played for a conference involving the hard of hearing. A woman told me through an interpreter that she had "heard" music for the first time in her life—we sing and play pretty loud, and by standing up and leaning on a wall, she could "feel" our songs through the wall's vibration.

Which do you suppose is worse—to be congenitally deaf or to lose your hearing later in life? Is it better to have known light and color at least for a little before blindness sets in, or is it better never to know what you're missing?

Here's the worst fear of all: to dread that a congenital disability is a punishment from God. But take heart! God's punishing was accomplished on the cross of Christ. **"There is now no condemnation for those who are in Christ Jesus, because through Christ Jesus the law of the Spirit of life set me free from the law of sin and death"** (Romans 8:1,2).

Our disabilities now become God's opportunities. What an honor it is to be a canvas on which our God can paint a beautiful picture! How much more joyful our lives can be when we are willing to let God use us as we are, broken and limping, blind and deaf, for his agenda of human spiritual rescue.

_____

_____

_____

_____

I'm afraid of God

It's all very well and good to hear beautiful promises about how good the believers have it and how their future will be even better. But what if you're not sure if you've ever been a believer? Or worse—what if you once were an active believer and churchgoer and then lost interest?

What if you've closed up your feelings about God for a long time? What if you're terrified of facing up to the fact that you have ignored and defied your Creator, Owner, and Judge? What if you are afraid that any religious talk now coming out of your mouth will just sound like pathetic, self-serving hypocrisy?

Let that fear become repentance. Let these words come out of your heart and mouth: **"O Lord, do not rebuke me in your anger or discipline me in your wrath. For your arrows have pierced me, and your hand has come down upon me"** (Psalm 38:1,2). The guilt and fear that you feel are not proof that you are condemned.

What they are is proof that the Lord is making you uncomfortable with your sinful choices. That's good news for you—before he can fill you with his goodness, he must first empty you of your pride.

_____

_____

_____

_____

_____

God controls death

When you're making a list of the things that make the world look out of control, surely *death* will be near the top. What is more terrifying than seeing someone you love in a coffin or watching your own life slip away? Are you afraid of death?

In Luke 7:11-17, the Bible tells the story of how Jesus interrupted a funeral procession leaving the little town of Nain. First he told the sobbing mother, **"Don't cry."** Then he did something even more arresting—he raised the corpse of her son back to life.

It is Jesus' intention to give each of *you* that same gift—resurrection of your body and life forever with him. Every coffin will be opened by our Lord—not in a ghoulish way as a grave robber, but as a grave liberator. Every person under the ground will hear the voice of the archangel and the trumpet call of God (1 Thessalonians 4:16).

Ever noticed how funeral directors make the casket look like a comfy bed where the deceased is just taking a little nap? I kind of like it that way. When it's a Christian in there, that's what it is. Don't cry.

_____

_____

_____

_____

love your singleness

Do you think it's strange that a pastor would endorse singleness? Aren't pastors all pushing marriage on everybody? Here's the point: You will probably not be able to build a happy marriage until you have learned to like and accept yourself as a single person.

In 1 Corinthians 7, St. Paul wrote, **"It is good for a man not to marry"** and **"I wish that all men were as I am** *[i.e., single]***"** (verses 1,7). Huh?? What on earth could he mean?

For one, God created you as a single person. He adopted you as a single person, drew you into his family, and developed a relationship with you all by yourself.

For another, it is a dangerous fantasy to think that if you are miserable as a single person, marriage in and of itself will make you happy. Misery is portable. If you are insecure and needy as a single person, you could become a permanent energy drain on your poor spouse.

But joy is portable too. So is contentment. Enjoy who you are—a masterpiece of God's design, dearly loved, redeemed by Christ, and immortal. It's much more fun to be married to someone who's secure and at peace.

_____

_____

_____

_____

_____

I'm anxious all the time

When something happens that you don't understand, does your mind leap immediately to the worst possible fear? When your husband is a half hour late, are you afraid that his car is in a ditch? When your teenagers aren't where they are supposed to be, does a little voice in your head fret that they might have been abducted?

Do you hate going to the doctor because you're afraid of what you might hear? Hear people laughing in a room and conclude that they must be laughing at you? Do you wake up three times during the night because of bad dreams?

Irrational fear and extreme anxiety are part of the human condition, broken ever since sin invaded our bodies and minds. For some, taking antidepressant medication can bring some relief and even out the mood swings.

Everyone can benefit from listening to the soothing voice of the Savior. Anxious people more than anyone will find calm and strength in his promise: **"Cast all your anxiety on him because he cares for you"** (1 Peter 5:7). If your stress is something over which you have control, it is your problem. If you can't control it, it doesn't belong to you. Cast it on Jesus and let go. He's up all night anyway, and he will work on it while you're sleeping.

_____

_____

_____

_____

remember what you were

There are some bad boys out there who have forgotten about their quadruple bypass operation and are eating fat-fried food again. There are some bad girls who have forgotten about their emphysema and have started smoking again. There are some reckless diabetics who are careless with their insulin injections. Such people apparently have lost their fear of—and respect for—their disease.

A real danger for people who have been Christians for a while is that they grow sleepy and careless in their security. They forget who they were and where they came from. They have lost their shock and awe at the fearful wrath of God on all evil. **"The Lord's curse is on the house of the wicked"** (Proverbs 3:33).

We all need to remember the terrible punishment that our Savior Jesus Christ absorbed for our sake on the cross. We all need to re-appreciate how expensive the forgiveness is that he bought for us there. We all need to respect and fear our enemy from hell. We all need to reaffirm our gratitude for Word and sacrament that bond us to Christ now and forever. Lord, wake us.

---

powered by God

Do God's principles of marriage sound hard? old fashioned? impossible? That's what Jesus' disciples thought too. **"The disciples said to him, 'If this is the situation between a husband and wife, it is better not to marry'"** (Matthew 19:10).

You know what they meant. They didn't think that they could fulfill those expectations. They didn't think that kind of marriage could last or would be any fun. They took comfort from rabbinic rules allowing no-fault divorce. All you had to do back in the day was provide a certificate.

To be sure, unless the Spirit of the Lord breathes in a home, God's rules may seem impossible. **"Jesus replied, 'Not everyone can accept this word, but only those to whom it is given'"** (Matthew 19:11). That is, if you haven't been given the gift of faith, if you aren't a believer, you don't have the desire or strength to stay faithful in a one-flesh relationship until death parts you.

But if you are connected by faith to the power source of the universe, it is indeed possible. And fulfilling. And satisfying. And beautiful. And fun. God's Spirit enables you both to will and to do what is pleasing to God.

_____

_____

_____

_____

_____

sky taxis

Have you ever been airborne before? You may have flown to another city on an airplane. You may have been swung aloft in a giant Ferris wheel at a state fair. You may have been whisked up to the top of the Arch in St. Louis or the Washington Monument in D.C. or the Statue of Liberty in New York harbor.

But I guarantee that you have never before experienced the ride that awaits you when Jesus Christ returns to judge and remake the world. When he and his holy angels burst onto the scene without warning someday soon, the angels will carry out the complete separation of believers and unbelievers.

All who recognize and rue their own sin and trust in Christ as their Savior will get to ride on angelic sky taxis: **"After that, we who are still alive and are left will be caught up together with them in the clouds to meet the Lord in the air. And so we will be with the Lord forever"** (1 Thessalonians 4:17). Imagine that! From the safety and security of our angelic embrace, we will get to watch the re-creation of earth into its new format, one that will integrate heaven into it.

Like Adam and Eve on their first day in Paradise, like Noah and his family when they stepped off the ark, we will step into a beautiful new world as the Grand Adventure begins.

_____

_____

_____

_____

_____

August 27

God and my family

"I can do this by myself!"

Parents generally are glad to hear that from their kids. We spend tremendous amounts of energy helping our children achieve independence in all phases of their lives, from potty training to getting dressed to homework to getting a driver's license to taking on their own college debt.

But certain projects are too big for a "do-it-yourself" mentality. **"Unless the LORD builds the house, its builders labor in vain. Unless the LORD watches over the city, the watchmen stand guard in vain"** (Psalm 127:1). Those sage words come from King Solomon, a man gifted with supernatural wisdom. He appears not to have put them into practice in his own life—his own family life was a mess— and thus illustrated the truth of his own words.

So how do you invite the Lord as co-builder of your family? Start with searching the Scriptures for his holy design for holy matrimony. God's will for marriage is ignored and trashed today, with devastating consequences for all of society. Commit yourself to God's design. Trust and wait for God's blessings. Let your home be a place where the Word is heard, where prayer and singing abound, and where the peace of Christ rules. Treat your spouse the way God treats you, with patience, humility, and forgiveness.

Love your family the way God loves you.

_____

_____

_____

_____

_____

pray boldly

"I am Oz, the great and terrible," the wizard face roared above the flames. "Who are you, whippersnapper?" "I am Dorothy, the small and meek," she replied. Is that how you visualize your interactions when you dare to speak with God?

God doesn't merely tolerate your "interruptions" in his daily business. He doesn't resent your requests. He welcomes them. He commands them. He tips his hand and lets you know that he is pre-inclined to say yes to you. Here is Jesus' challenge: **"Ask and it will be given to you; seek and you will find; knock and the door will be opened to you. For everyone who asks receives; he who seeks finds; and to him who knocks, the door will be opened"** (Matthew 7:7,8).

You are not a stranger in God's presence anymore. Through your faith in Christ you are now family. You belong there. Act like you belong there. Be bold when you pray. Claim your blood-bought identity. You are not irritating God with your chutzpah. You are honoring his invitation and promise.

What do you need right now? Is someone you know struggling? Ask! Seek! Knock!

_____

_____

_____

_____

_____

materialism

Is your life a success? Would you consider yourself a successful person? How do you think other people view you? How do you measure success? What are your life goals? Whose approval do you most crave?

Some people measure success in terms of acquiring material things. Gold jewelry, a big boat, and designer clothes proclaim "I made it; I'm somebody." And here's trap #1: If you lose your job or income source, you might feel destroyed as a person. Suddenly you think you're a nobody. Trap #2: If you enthrone money and possessions in your heart, you have set up an idol, a false god that neither loves you nor will help you.

"Keep your lives free from the love of money and be content with what you have, because God has said, 'Never will I leave you; never will I forsake you'" (Hebrews 13:5).

Christians in Egypt in the fourth century began the practice of going out to the desert to live as hermits, cutting off as much contact with the (sinful) world as possible. That option won't work for most of you. But what you can do is decide what you value most in your life. Practice with me and say, "I like my life right now. I don't need to acquire stuff to impress people. My relationships are more important than my stuff. I am somebody! My Savior is my most valuable treasure."

_____

_____

_____

_____

_____

August 30
who crucified Christ?

The list of people who are responsible for the crucifixion of Christ is a long one. His money-sick disciple Judas betrayed and sold him. The temple guards arrested him, and the Pharisees and priests in the high council falsely convicted him of blasphemy. The Roman governor Pilate weakly ordered his crucifixion, fearing the Jewish mob screaming "Crucify!" outside his praetorium. A detachment of Roman soldiers carried out the death sentence by pounding nails in his hands and feet. Your and my sins made his death journey necessary.

Does it surprise you to know that God the Father can be added to this list? **"It was the LORD's will to crush him and cause him to suffer, and though the LORD makes his life a guilt offering, he will see his offspring and prolong his days"** (Isaiah 53:10). Though every sinner along the way carries his own responsibility, the Father used their sins to carry out his great plan to offer his own Son as a sin offering for the world.

In that way alone could he have it both ways—he could punish human evil with the severity it deserved, but he could also pardon the guilty because the debt was paid. As you reflect on the horror of the scene on Mt. Calvary, your thoughts will dwell on the suffering of the Savior. Let your heart swell with gratitude also for the Father, who had to endure the ordeal of smiting his holy Son to death. For us.

blessed by your spiritual family

Can I make a confession? I need my church the way AA attenders need their meetings. God's primary relationship with people is with us as individuals, to be sure. But he has enormous blessings to give us through our spiritual family, and I crave 'em all.

Through our congregation we are taught, baptized, nourished with the Supper, counseled, encouraged, invited to serve, and held accountable. Through our church our circle of friends is multiplied greatly. Through our church Satan finds it much harder to confuse and manipulate us. Through our church we can reach out with the gospel much more effectively and on a much wider scale.

The best part is worship together. Listen to the plurals: **"Come, let us bow down in worship, let us kneel before the LORD our Maker; for he is our God and we are the people of his pasture, the flock under his care"** (Psalm 95:6,7). In a group setting, it almost seems as if faith is contagious. I am lifted up by the singers, heartened by the faith testimony of others, drawn into the prayers, glad for a sympathetic ear and hug in my troubles, and built up by gifted teachers of God's Word. On top of all that, God smiles as his name is lifted up in praise.

There is heavenly magic in God's house every week.

_____

_____

_____

_____

_____

September

"The LORD your God is with you,
he is mighty to save."
(Zephaniah 3:17)

work is a blessing

It seems to be people's dream to quit working just as soon as they can afford it, or as soon as their employment contract permits.

In God's view and design, work is not a painful, necessary evil that one puts up with for the least amount of time possible. Scrounging off other people is nothing he admires. In fact: **"When we were with you, we gave you this rule: 'If a man will not work, he shall not eat.' We hear that some among you are idle. They are not busy; they are busybodies. Such people we command and urge in the Lord Jesus Christ to settle down and earn the bread they eat"** (2 Thessalonians 3:10-12).

When you bend your intelligence, strength, and servant-spirit to your tasks, you are doing nothing less than continuing the divine work that God began in the six days of creation. He is exerting his intelligence and strength each day, sustaining all things and feeding the world. We honor his work when we work.

We do our country and our God a great service when we teach our children and grandchildren the dignity and satisfaction of labor.

_____

_____

_____

_____

he ain't heavy; he's my friend

Video gamers pay a lot of attention to POV. That stands for "point of view," and it refers to the viewpoint and angle at which you want to see the action in your game. Do you want to see things at ground level through the eyes of your character, or do you want to hover above and get the big picture?

You may be familiar with the amazing story of Jesus' healing of a totally paralyzed man who was lowered through the roof of a house where Jesus was teaching. Your POV in the story may be in the audience, watching the Son of God display his mastery over disease and injury. Or maybe you imagine yourself jumping with joy and running around as the ex-paralytic.

Here's my POV: **"Some men came carrying a paralytic on a mat and tried to take him into the house to lay him before Jesus"** (Luke 5:18). My heroes in this story are the friends who loved this man enough to carry him around, and, failing to get into the house where Jesus was, hauled him up to the flat roof. They actually made a hole in the roof big enough to drop a man through and lowered him with ropes. Their faith and determination were rewarded by seeing God in action and their friend healed. Would you have done that?

_____

_____

_____

_____

_____

September 3
back to school

Are you delighted or saddened when it's time for your kids to go back to school?

How can any parent not have two simultaneous and conflicting emotions? On the one hand, your home and work life will be greatly simplified now that someone else will have to tend them during the day. You won't have to put up with their sinful behaviors 15 hours a day.

On the other hand, as they step up one grade level, you are made aware of how rapidly they grow up. When I was a dad of young children, people would tell me to cherish every moment while they were young. Of course I didn't listen. Now I get it. I would give every dime I have to reverse the clock 15 years.

The schools that our children attend are precious resources and deserve our partnership in every way we can. Our goal is not to keep them young and dependent forever, but to help them become mature, responsible adult Christians. Mary and Joseph must have been so proud of their oldest son as they watched him grow: **"Jesus grew in wisdom and stature, and in favor with God and men"** (Luke 2:52).

May your children and grandchildren grow in favor with God and man.

_____

_____

_____

_____

whose fault, God?

When a badly needed job disappears through layoff, when a child is seriously ill, when the biopsy comes back positive, when your family income is so strained you miss another house payment, when your marriage breaks up, how can you not want an explanation of cause and effect?

It's one thing to take personal responsibility for personal sins and mistakes. It's another thing entirely to attempt to figure out if someone is getting punished by God. It's not our job to judge. If God seems to prefer to work quietly and behind the scenes, we should hold back on laying guilt on others or ourselves.

"As he [Jesus] went along, he saw a man blind from birth. His disciples asked him, 'Rabbi, who sinned, this man or his parents, that he was born blind?' 'Neither this man nor his parents sinned,' said Jesus, 'but this happened so that the work of God might be displayed in his life'" (John 9:1-3). It may well be that God sends a hardship as a rebuke for our hardheadedness. It may also be that he is allowing a grief, and then grieving with us, so that he can work in our weakness and bring about something great because of it.

Since we can't tell the difference, let's let God do his own business. Our job is to thank him for our blessings and pray to him for help in time of need so that the work of God might be displayed in our lives.

_____

_____

_____

_____

thank you, Lord, for forgiving me

I appreciate being given some slack. I love it when my friends overlook my bad behavior. I am relieved when my boss understands and gives me some extra time. I know I can be hard to live with sometimes and appreciate it when my spouse doesn't keep score. But I am grateful most of all when you, O Lord, choose not to hold my many sins against me.

I will never stop praising you for your gospel. If I had to earn your favor on the basis of my performance, I would stay an outsider for all eternity. Your Word assures my nervous heart that our good relationship rests on *your* work and *your* attitude and *your* choice, not mine: **"As high as the heavens are above the earth, so great is his love for those who fear him; as far as the east is from the west, so far has he removed our transgressions from us"** (Psalm 103:11,12).

Lord, remember what you said! East by definition never meets west. Don't let the evidence of my sins anywhere near you. Please, Father—when you think of me, think of Jesus your Son first. View me always through your Christ-lenses. Thank you for giving me a righteousness I could never accomplish or afford on my own. I love living in your love.

_____

_____

_____

_____

_____

September 6
God's lemonade

It's not too hard to see the blessings of God when he sends us financial prosperity, a good job, spouse and family, nice home, and good neighbors. It's more of a stretch to imagine that he blesses us through hardships and trouble.

Have you ever inhabited a prison cell? Worn cuffs or chains or leg irons? St. Paul did, first in Jerusalem, then Caesarea, and finally in Rome. What a disaster, right? His traveling ministry ceased, his freedom disappeared, and his ability to communicate with others was at the whim of his guards.

And yet those very limitations and frustrations became the platform that God used to make him even more useful in communicating the gospel of Christ. Many people who would never have met Paul the free man heard about their Savior from him when he was a prisoner. **"It has become clear throughout the whole palace guard and to everyone else that I am in chains for Christ. Because of my chains, most of the brothers in the Lord have been encouraged to speak the word of God more courageously and fearlessly"** (Philippians 1:13,14).

The restrictions on Paul's freedom of movement also compelled him to train and rely on a network of younger men who would carry on his ministry long after he was dead.

You can complain about the lemons in your life, or you could get a glass and have some of God's lemonade.

_____

_____

_____

_____

_____

I'm so ashamed

Does anybody feel ashamed about anything anymore? The immediate response might be no. Criticism like the phrase "you ought to be ashamed of yourself" doesn't seem to haul much freight anymore. Cohabitation and childbirth out of wedlock no longer carry much social stigma.

But I think people still feel shame. For one, their consciences are still basically tuned to God's unchanging moral standards. God wired consciences to make people uncomfortable when they sin. For another, even if society no longer imposes consequences for sin, God still does.

Unresolved guilt does not go away by itself. People can play denial games, distract themselves with staying busy, try to pay it off by doing charitable deeds, or rationalize it, but they can't make it go away. God's goal: bring people to confess, "Lord, have mercy on me, a sinner."

There's only one way to get rid of shame and guilt—by putting it on Jesus. It is his gift, his delight, to take that load off you. Let him give it to you today. **"The LORD redeems his servants; no one will be condemned who takes refuge in him"** (Psalm 34:22).

_____

_____

_____

_____

_____

grandchildren aren't just for spoiling

From what I hear, grandchildren are God's reward for making it through all the years of worry your children caused you. You can play with grandchildren—and give them back when it's time for diaper changes or bedtime routines. Having grandchildren is like a mulligan from God—you can make up for some of your parenting mistakes by doing it better with them.

While you now enjoy a break from the physical work, God still has important spiritual work for you. **"Only be careful, and watch yourselves closely so that you do not forget the things your eyes have seen or let them slip from your heart as long as you live. Teach them to your children and to their children after them"** (Deuteronomy 4:9).

Here's a special salute to all the grandparents who for whatever reason have to (get to) raise their grandchildren. What a gift of love! You rock!

This is also for everyone over 60—the world needs honorary gramps and grannies. With the stories you tell children, you have a fabulous opportunity to share the good news of God's forgiving love. The offerings and gifts you give keep the Word moving in the ministries you invest in. Even from your nursing home, your prayers can reach around the globe and change lives.

The seniors who gave you extra mentoring and love when you were little are eagerly awaiting your arrival in heaven. Well done, good and faithful servant!

_____

_____

_____

I don't feel very good about myself

Lord, you know that many days my smile and outward calm are only a mask. They are the mask I wear to hide what's really going on inside me. I wish I felt like more of a success. I wish I didn't spend so much time worrying about my looks and hating all my flaws. I wish I felt more self-confident. Here's my guilty secret—I don't like myself very much.

I have many dark feelings and moods. I am painfully aware of my failings and shortcomings. I try so hard to improve my appearance, but I fear it's a lost cause. I will never think of myself as good-looking.

Lord, you are my great hope. You are the great lover of the unlovely. You are the one who befriends the lonely and the losers; you give beauty for ashes. You make me feel wanted and precious. **"When anxiety was great within me, your consolation brought joy to my soul"** (Psalm 94:19). Help me stop obsessing about my looks and what people might think about me. What matters most is that you care for me. Thank you for your unconditional love for me. If you forgive me, I can forgive myself. If you like me, I can like myself. If you think I'm somebody, then I'm somebody indeed.

_____

_____

_____

_____

_____

September 10
God came to live with man

Adam and Eve's disastrous experiment with complete independence from God ended very, very badly. Among the worst of the consequences of their rebellion was the disconnecting of their daily personal interaction with their Creator. They were driven from their beautiful home in the Garden and blocked from returning by an angel with a flaming sword.

It was the mission of Jesus Christ, God's Son, to restore that broken relationship. He would bring back true "Sabbath" (the serenity and rest that characterized the seventh day of creation). He would come to earth to bring back the joy of God's personal presence: **"The Word became flesh and made his dwelling among us. We have seen his glory, the glory of the One and Only, who came from the Father, full of grace and truth"** (John 1:14).

He came not only to live for us, not only to die for us, but also to live again for us. And even though he withdrew his physical presence when he ascended to heaven, he promised to be with us in spirit, listening to our prayers, speaking through his Word, becoming one with us in the Holy Supper, and clothing us with himself through the washing of Baptism.

The end of the Bible promises that God will do it again, and this time permanently. When Christ returns, it will be Christmas all the time: **"Now the dwelling of God is with men, and he will live with them"** (Revelation 21:3).

_____

_____

_____

_____

September 11

9/11

That date is now burned forever as a national memory for every American. It is a "day of infamy" just like December 7, the day of the great attack on Pearl Harbor.

The attackers may have framed their actions as a high and noble service to their deity, but most of the world saw 9/11 for what it really was—cowardly murder of unarmed and innocent civilians. How can anyone feel safe anymore? Are the wheels and hinges coming off our civilization? Will evil triumph over good? Will Satan triumph over Christ?

Believers for centuries have cried out to the Lord God for wisdom and protection. We need help in making sense of a world gone crazy, and we need divine and angelic protection in a world gone violent. Have you ever feared that God's plans have failed and that the throne in heaven is empty? Let King David's shout of confidence be yours too: **"The kings of the earth take their stand and the rulers gather together against the LORD and against his Anointed One. The One enthroned in heaven laughs; the Lord scoffs at them. 'I have installed my King on Zion, on my holy hill'"** (Psalm 2:2,4,6).

The King is alive. He rules from his heavenly Zion and governs all things according to his plan. He will come back and bring us all to the new Zion. Soon. Don't be afraid. Soon.

_____

_____

_____

_____

_____

September 12
I feel so lonely

It's me, Lord. Here I am again.

We've had this conversation before. When I was single, I was so lonely—remember? I would ask you for a decent man to marry, and I waited a long time. Well, I'm married now—why do I still feel lonely?

I try to tell my husband all my feelings and emotions, but even though he tries to be polite, I can tell he doesn't really get it and doesn't see how important these conversations are to me. After a bit I think he just tunes me out. I wish he could get into the things I am trying to tell him, but he just sits there. I want to tell him all the stressful and happy things about my day, but he fidgets. At first I would get angry inside; now I am just sad. What's wrong with me?

I know you always listen to me, Lord. What a comfort it is to know that you understand me completely. Can you help me? **"Turn to me and be gracious to me, for I am lonely and afflicted. The troubles of my heart have multiplied; free me from my anguish"** (Psalm 25:16,17).

Help me continue to be a supportive and loving wife. Help me be attentive to him and meet his needs. Help me understand him better. Please help him notice my loneliness. Please.

_____

_____

_____

_____

_____

September 13
God is omniscient

Normally we don't like it when people think of themselves as smarter than we are. We call them know-it-alls, and that name is not meant as a compliment. Well, guess what? God is omniscient; he really does know it all. His mind is vast enough to track all the thoughts and actions of all the people on earth. His memory has enough RAM to remember all human history, small and great.

Psalm 139:1,2 says, **"O Lord, you have searched me and you know me. You know when I sit and when I rise; you perceive my thoughts from afar."** This has to be terrifying to an unbeliever. It means that you will never ever get away with anything.

But those who believe they are forgiven in Christ will find the concept of an omniscient God greatly comforting. It means that we are worshiping a great big God. It means he won't forget to take care of us, the way we forget to feed the fish and find them floating upside down. It means he remembers all his promises, keeps all his commitments, and won't ever lose track of a single one of us.

_____

_____

_____

_____

don't worry; be happy

It's not hard to spot new parents, is it? One look in their haggard, sleep-deprived eyes and you can see the physical toll a little seven-pound infant is taking on them. Babies turn their parents into slaves whose lives are turned upside down to keep that little bundle alive.

I don't know if raising older children is any less stressful. I think parents can lose just as much sleep worrying about their teenagers. How will we pay for school? Am I too strict or not strict enough? Where are the kids? Why don't they pick up when I call? I hope they're making good choices. Why are they so secretive? I'm not sure about their new friends. Why are they so moody all the time? And *why* must they dress like that and listen to *that* music?

Your almighty Father invites you to relax. His Son, Jesus, asks you, **"Who of you by worrying can add a single hour to his life?"** (Matthew 6:27). The unwritten corollary is "Who of you by worrying can add a single hour to your child's life?" Worry is fear, fear that you are losing control, fear that we lose in the end, fear that God has left the building.

God takes the long view about developing people, and we should too. Look at how he worked on and changed people like Jacob, Joseph, and Moses, all of whom were pieces of work early in life. If you have a heavy heart about a family member right now, how about putting that burden on God? Do it now. Exhale.

_____

_____

_____

_____

September 15

pray for Babylon

Some American Christians find it hard to love America out loud. They are so aware of our national shortcomings—whether the injustices, governmental intrusiveness, societal violence, level of taxation, wars, and foreign policy—that they bristle at the idea that Christians are supposed to obey their government.

Imagine the difficulties of living a Christian life in countries where Christians are a tiny minority or where the Christian faith is repressed and persecuted. How can you love your country when your country doesn't love you?

The prophet Jeremiah was not popular with the power structure of the rapidly shrinking kingdom of Judah in the late 600s B.C. He was allowed by God to foresee that Judah would collapse militarily and that going into exile was not a disaster but in fact the only way that people would survive. He counseled his fellow Jews to go along with the deportation, learn to like Babylonia, and even to pray for its well-being: **"Seek the peace and prosperity of the city to which I have carried you into exile. Pray to the LORD for it, because if it prospers, you too will prosper"** (Jeremiah 29:7).

Peter, Paul, and our Lord Jesus all were persecuted by the Roman government, and yet all three urged Christians to obey Caesar. It should be easier today. We can do that.

_____

_____

_____

_____

September 16

is gambling okay?

Gambling is a huge industry in America. Las Vegas no longer has a monopoly on it—it seems that every state now has a lottery, riverboats, and American Indian casinos. Americans willingly threw away $34 billion in gambling losses just in casinos last year.

Some Christian leaders denounce all gambling as sin. And yet you will search the Bible in vain for a prohibition of gambling. Although the ancient world was full of games of chance, dice, and horse racing, the word *gambling* is not even found in Scripture. So if God does not call it a sin in and of itself, we won't either. You aren't automatically going to hell if you play the slots.

But pay attention to the money you put into it. The iron rule of all gambling is that ultimately there is only one winner—the house. Can you truly afford what you lose? Are you stealing from your savings? your children? your God? Does the powerful lure of trying to get something for nothing make your day-to-day job seem sluggish and boring? Are you able to stop?

"Like a city whose walls are broken down is a man who lacks self-control" (Proverbs 25:28).

_____

_____

_____

_____

_____

September 17

we won already

Life is a struggle. There is no way around it. Life is hard, full of setbacks, and acquaints everyone on earth with pain. Take a walk through a nursing home, a prison pod, a neonatal intensive care unit, a homeless shelter, or a mental health wing. I can't blame you if some days it looks to you as if we are all just a collection of the walking wounded. Satan whispers that you are a loser.

Actually, you aren't. In fact, you have won already. Christ has overcome sin, Satan, death, grave, and hell. Through faith in him you have too. Yes—*now. Already.* **"You, dear children, are from God and have overcome them** [i.e., false prophets and evil spirits], **because the one who is in you is greater than the one who is in the world"** (1 John 4:4). You can rise above your pain and setbacks because they are temporary. They are part of life that is sliding by and will soon pass away.

Christ's cross changes the Father's "Guilty!" verdict upon you to "Not Guilty!" Christ's resurrection enables him to promise that whoever believes in him will never perish.

Christ indwells you. You are bonded to him—you are part of his body. And even if it drives Satan into a rage, you can start your victory dance now, so certain is the outcome. Since the One who is in you (Christ) is greater than the one who is in the world (Satan), you are too.

_____

_____

_____

_____

build up

I think I know why I am so stingy with compliments. Half the time I am so aware of my own failings and shortcomings that I can't waste any energy on lifting up anybody else. I convince myself that it will take all my strength to cope with my own troubles. I think maybe if I brag enough about myself I can talk other people (and myself) into thinking that I am important.

As usual in God's world, his reality is the exact opposite (you know, that "last shall be first" stuff). Here's another wonderful secret from God's vault: the best way to deal with your own insecurity is to praise somebody else. Seriously! **"An anxious heart weighs a man down, but a kind word cheers him up"** (Proverbs 12:25).

Are you ready to dare to be a servant (instead of trying to pretend you are a lord)? Do you believe that you can be God's voice, God's touch, God's hug in your world? All around you are broken and dispirited people who are running on fumes. A few words of appreciation and praise cost you even less than what you put into a parking meter.

_____

_____

_____

_____

_____

September 19

the gospel makes us optimists

"Why do you look for the living among the dead," the Easter angels inquired of some sad and fearful women who had come early to the mausoleum to embalm a corpse. **"He is not here; he has risen!"** (Luke 24:5,6).

Easter changes everything. It is the triumph of life over death, forgiveness over condemnation, heaven over hell, and Christ over Satan. It is unchangeable, irreversible, and forever beyond the reach of Satan to alter or sabotage. It is done! Satan is done! It is finished! Satan is finished!

That means that all things really do work together for the good of those who love God. That means that we win in the end, no matter what we have to go through now. That means all believers are essentially optimists, since the outcome of everything has already been determined to be victory.

So? **"Rejoice in the Lord always. I will say it again: Rejoice!"** (Philippians 4:4). What a great message and great vibe to bring to the world. Every Christian congregation every week can be a place of celebration, where through faith in Christ we can join his victory lap, arms raised up high in triumph. Every Christian congregation every week can be a place of healing, where sad and hurting and beaten-down mortals can find peace and love and hope. Rejoice always, fellow optimists!

_____

_____

_____

_____

_____

God and my worship

Of all the things that Satan is trying to steal from you, stealing the joy from your worship ranks right at the top. He will keep you out of the Bible if he can. If he can't, he'll try to make Bible reading a chore and a bore. He will keep you out of church if he can, but if he can't, he will try to make it all "hafta" and little "wanna." He will distract you and deflect you from praying, but if he can't stop your prayers, he will try to make your praying rote and perfunctory.

Let's bust loose from Satan's attempted mind drugging. Think! Think for two minutes what our God has done: created our vast, complex, beautiful world . . . sent his Son to a bloody death to make full payment for all human evil . . . sent his good Spirit to change our minds around and claim our new identity. What can you say to all that but Wow! Hallelujah!

"Shout for joy to the LORD, all the earth, burst into jubilant song with music; make music to the LORD with the harp, with the harp and the sound of singing, with trumpets and the blast of the ram's horn—shout for joy before the LORD, the King" (Psalm 98:4-6).

The word *worship* comes from an old Anglo-Saxon word essentially meaning "worthship," i.e., the central idea is that we proclaim to him and anybody listening that our God is *worthy*, worthy of all the praise, honor, and glory we can generate. Can I get an Amen from somebody?

_____

_____

_____

_____

_____

September 21
I can't take it anymore

Every boiler has a pressure gauge. That gauge is an extremely valuable indicator of the health of the system. The boiler engineer adjusts the pressure so that it stays within the limits for which it was designed. He knows that if the water level gets too low, the steam gets angry. He doesn't want it to blow open any joints or pipes on his watch.

When Christians suffer, and especially when they have it really bad, we're tempted to think that God isn't paying attention, or worse, doesn't care. Did you know that the opposite is true? Like a skilled boiler engineer, God watches each of us in our struggles, and he carefully sets limits to our pressures according to what he knows about our inner abilities.

The Bible says in 1 Corinthians 10:13, **"God is faithful; he will not let you be tempted beyond what you can bear. But when you are tempted, he will also provide a way out so that you can stand up under it."**

He made you. He loves you. He knows your limits.

_____

_____

_____

_____

the center of everything

People can do just fine living their lives without thinking much about gravity, the rotation of the earth, friction, the weak and strong forces in atoms, and electromagnetism. A great many people also seem to be doing just fine living their lives without Jesus. Perhaps you too had a long stretch in your life when you thought about him not at all.

And yet, whether people are thinking about him or not, believing in him or not, Jesus Christ is absolutely the central organizing principle of the entire universe. **"By him all things were created: things in heaven and on earth, visible and invisible. . . . All things were created by him and for him. He is before all things, and in him all things hold together"** (Colossians 1:16,17). The planets move, stars shine, rain falls, wheat grows, and babies are born because Jesus Christ says so.

Life is meaningless unless you are connected to the One who designed and created you. Life is purposeless unless you are connected with the One who helps you see the divine purpose and mission of your life. Life is hopeless unless you are connected with the immortal One who promises his immortality to all who believe in him.

What do you need to do today, right now, to realign your life with life's central Force?

_____

_____

_____

_____

_____

September 23
I'm so afraid

President and Mrs. Benjamin Harrison had electricity brought into the White House in 1889, but they were so terrified of it that they had the servants turn the light switches on and off. If the servants had already gone to bed, the Harrisons slept with lights blazing.

It's one thing to be cautious around things that are dangerous, like sharp knives, poisons, and electricity. But it's a whole other thing to allow your mind to be consumed by irrational fear. How's the fear level in your mind? Has basic caution ever morphed into dread in your mind? What is the stuff of your nightmares? Being alone? Business failure? Infertility?

Maybe it would help to name it right now. Is your fear something you can affect, or is it out of your control? If there is something you can do about it, form a plan and do what you need to do. If it is beyond your control, it is not your problem!

It might just be God's. He doesn't mind at all when you come to him with things that are bigger than you are. **"Surely, O Lord, you bless the righteous; you surround them with your favor as with a shield"** (Psalm 5:12).

_____

_____

_____

_____

_____

a paradox

Some teachings of the Bible are hard because we don't want to do them. "Love your enemies," Jesus said. "Turn the other cheek." "Forgive each other not seven times but seventy times seven times." "Love your wives as Christ loved the church and gave himself up for her." "Wives, submit to your husbands as to the Lord."

And then there are passages that are hard because they seem to contradict one another. They are paradoxes— revelations of God's identity and God's ways that are given to you more to believe than to understand. Here's a puzzle: has God condemned the world or saved the world? **"All have sinned and fall short of the glory of God, and are justified freely by his grace through the redemption that came by Christ Jesus"** (Romans 3:23,24).

The answer is (c) Both. Those two seeming contradictions come together in the cross of Christ. There God punished every sin by punishing his Son. There God forgave every sin by punishing his Son.

That wonderful forgiveness is yours through faith in Christ. That message is yours to believe, yours to treasure, yours to share. Do you know someone who needs to hear about this divine paradox?

Israel lived in a theocracy then

Throughout Israel's history God chose to lead directly. He spoke forcefully and often, directing their course of action. This is called theocracy, i.e., rule directly by God. God spoke through Moses, through Joshua, through his prophets, and through the judges. Israel's political, military, geographical, and economic high point was the time of King David and King Solomon.

The people of Israel would call the united monarchy their golden age. **"King Solomon was greater in riches and wisdom than all the other kings of the earth. . . . The king made silver as common in Jerusalem as stones"** (1 Kings 10:23,27).

You might think that getting instructions directly from God would have made decisions easy. Wrong. People could reject God's direct words as easily as his indirect words. Leadership by theocracy made it clear what God wanted, but it did not guarantee either obedience or God's blessings.

America's secular government has turned out to provide a far better environment for the church. It is better for leaders in the church not to carry swords or guns.

_____

_____

_____

_____

_____

September 26
Christ is our King now

All the prophets of the Old Testament were but forerunners of Christ. All the judges of the Old Testament were but forerunners of Christ. Moses and Joshua and all the kings were merely placeholders until Christ came.

Just before he ascended into heaven, Jesus told his disciples that all authority in heaven and on earth had been given to him. Here is our true leader—one who will never lie to us, abuse us, take advantage of us, or manipulate us. Here is our true leader—one who will protect us, lead us in the right direction, always speak the truth to us, always build us up, make our lives better, give us hope.

St. John shares with you and me his thrilling glimpse of Christ as he appears now: **"I saw heaven standing open and there before me was a white horse, whose rider is called Faithful and True. With justice he judges and makes war. His eyes are like blazing fire, and on his head are many crowns. He has a name written on him that no one knows but he himself. He is dressed in a robe dipped in blood, and his name is the Word of God. The armies of heaven were following him"** (Revelation 19:11-14).

Christ is our King now. Christ is our King forever. He is good to us. We are blessed.

_____

_____

_____

_____

_____

trust and wait

To love another human being means that you will hurt at some point, because love means that you let down your defenses. It is inevitable that other people will embarrass us, betray us, turn on us, reject us, put us down, or steal from us sooner or later. It is inevitable because of sin.

Among the worst hurts are those inflicted by children on their parents. How Eli, Samuel, and David must have grieved over their rebellious children. How could they not blame themselves? How could they not feel humiliated at the damage done to the family's reputation?

Perhaps you are old enough to have tasted rebellion from your own children, including the bitterest pill of all, seeming rejection of the Christian faith you tried to pass on to them. What a lead weight on your soul!

When they reach a certain age, you can no longer make choices for your children—they must now choose for themselves, and any attempt at control by you will make them go in the opposite direction just to teach you that you can't push them around any longer. Sometimes your only options are to trust and wait. To let go and pray.

And hold God to his promise: **"Train a child in the way he should go, and when he is old he will not turn from it"** (Proverbs 22:6).

_____

_____

_____

_____

_____

devoted to prayer together

The apostle Peter was once sprung out of prison by an angel who infiltrated perimeter security, cut the chains right off Peter's wrists, and led him out. Did he go home after that? No. Where, then, did he go? He immediately went to find his friends. They had been so worried about Peter that they were gathered together praying. Seeing him come through the doors was a stunning and direct answer to their group intercessions.

God loves when you pray not only *for* other people but *with* other people, because it helps you pay attention to other people's needs. He says, **"If two of you on earth agree about anything you ask for, it will be done for you by my Father in heaven. For where two or three come together in my name, there am I with them"** (Matthew 18:19,20).

God loves to hear your solo prayers, but he promises even greater things when you bind your individual heart with other believers' hearts. When you pray together, your burdens become only half as heavy. When you pray together, your joys are doubled.

Nurses will tell you that patients who feel loved and connected to other people get better faster.

_____

_____

_____

_____

_____

September 29
fear of failure

Fear of rejection is what keeps low-performing salespeople from becoming top producers for their company. Fear of rejection keeps a man from daring to ask a woman for a date. Fear of failure keeps a promising athlete from competing for a place on the team. Fear of mockery keeps a younger employee from applying for a higher-ranking job.

Fear of failure also keeps people mum about their faith in Christ. They don't want to risk criticism or risk bungling the message. It seems safer to keep still. Jesus has great compassion for our fears, for he felt them all, but he refuses to do our talking for us. He wants the gospel to touch every person on earth, but he waits for us to speak up.

And he doesn't leave us with a blank playbook and an empty toolbox. His Word brings us the thrilling content the world needs to hear. His Spirit gives the gifts we need to get the message out there, and he gives also the courage to stand up to those who think the gospel is foolishness: **"Make up your mind not to worry beforehand how you will defend yourselves. For I will give you words and wisdom that none of your adversaries will be able to resist or contradict"** (Luke 21:14,15).

Don't be afraid. Just open your mouth, tell the story in your own words, and let Jesus keep his promise to supply the extra words and wisdom.

_____

_____

_____

_____

_____

September 30

God controls nature

Sometimes the world we live in seems like a beautiful, peaceful place. But our environment can be nasty too — sometimes it seems as though nature itself is trying to destroy the people who live in it. Wildfires, hailstorms, typhoons, avalanches, hurricanes, tidal waves, and earthquakes can destroy property and people.

St. Paul explains why nature sometimes seems so broken. It's because it is. **"The creation was subjected to frustration . . . in hope that the creation itself will be liberated from its bondage to decay and brought into the glorious freedom of the children of God"** (Romans 8:20,21).

It comes as a great comfort to read in the Bible the stories of the miracles of Jesus and to watch him work. Everyone who as a child trembled during severe thunderstorms will be comforted by hearing how Jesus could still a violent storm with just a word.

The Christian faith is not merely an interesting philosophy. It is trust and confidence in the One who made the world and the One who still controls it.

_____

_____

_____

_____

_____

October

"Peace I leave with you; my peace I give you. I do not give to you as the world gives. Do not let your hearts be troubled and do not be afraid."

(John 14:27)

October 1

grace means second chances

I don't play golf competitively or for money, and that's a good thing. I'm just not that good. The duffers I play with will, after smirks and some appropriate remarks, occasionally give me a mulligan after a particularly horrible swing.

Jesus Christ has paid for the ultimate do-over. Even though we will be sinners till the day we die, his grace means that he has chosen to love us unconditionally. It means that every day we can start fresh, for his mercy is new every morning.

It means that his Father, like the father in his parable of the prodigal son, is a giver of second (and more) chances: **"While [the son] was still a long way off, his father saw him and was filled with compassion for him; he ran to his son, threw his arms around him and kissed him"** (Luke 15:20). Isn't it a great feeling to know with certainty that the forgiving Father's arms are around you right now, and will be tomorrow as well? When your heart is broken and repentant, can you believe that God actually *runs* to hug you?

P.S. People who know that they have been forgiven by grace are now invited to show that same mercy to the fools and sinners around them.

_____

_____

_____

_____

_____

cherish your independence

Marriage is a serious partnership. Once you are married, everything you do has to be in step with your partner. It's no longer my money. It's our money. It's no longer my vacation. It's our vacation. Our time off. Our apartment. Our car. Our TV. Our kitchen.

Before you commit to marriage, ask yourself, "Am I ready to give up my freedom?"

St. Paul, a lifelong bachelor, found that his choice of lifestyle had a lot going for it. **"I would like you to be free from concern. An unmarried man is concerned about the Lord's affairs—how he can please the Lord"** (1 Corinthians 7:32).

Did you notice the second advantage to singleness that Paul mentions? As a single person, you can volunteer much more time to serving the Lord than a spouse or parent can. You can make more unilateral decisions, travel more, and take more risks. Some of the greatest missionaries and most dedicated educators in Christian history chose the single life so that they could serve the Lord more effectively.

They had great lives too.

_____

_____

_____

_____

_____

October 3
the long view

I don't know if people who live in Western culture ever had a particularly long attention span, but I'm convinced it's getting worse by the week. The blazing speed of digital communication tools means that we never have to wait long for anything anymore. The devices in our hands—TV remote, game controller, smartphone—issue commands and expect instantaneous fulfillment.

God is not impressed. He too can move with blinding speed, but his plans also can take decades to unfurl and develop. He saw in the precocious, spoiled teenager Joseph gifts and talents that would be useful in his plans for the nations, but they needed long, slow cooking to develop. Joseph didn't know it at the time, but being sold into slavery by his brothers and being thrown into prison actually were woven into God's greater plans.

Later in his life (but certainly not at the time) Joseph realized that God takes the long view. He told his forgiven brothers, **"God sent me ahead of you to preserve for you a remnant on earth and save your lives by a great deliverance. So then, it was not you who sent me here, but God. He made me father to Pharaoh, lord of his entire household and ruler of all Egypt"** (Genesis 45:7,8).

Are you confused right now about God's plans for you? Relax. You'll know when it's time.

_____

_____

_____

_____

_____

old folks just might know something

"Never trust anybody over 30." That taunt came from a student radical in the 1960s, and it struck such a chord that it has been repeated a million times. Young adults have always viewed the generations above them as slow and stodgy, clueless and out of it. It is part of the arrogance of the young to overvalue their energy and creativity and to fail to learn from the hard-earned wisdom of those who have gone before them.

There are only two ways to learn: talk and pain. God invites all young people to utilize the former so they won't have to suffer the latter. **"Listen to your father, who gave you life, and do not despise your mother when she is old. Buy the truth and do not sell it"** (Proverbs 23:22,23). Some things are in constant change: communication technology, pharmacological research, medical technology and devices.

Some things are timeless: money management, personal growth and awareness, employment attitude, good manners, and understanding human nature. It costs nothing to listen to parents and grandparents. The older generation needs to make sure there is a tone of respect when they speak—no one listens well when being treated like a child—but the young hurt only themselves when they squander the life knowledge that could have been theirs.

Millennials who listen are young *and* smart.

———————————————

———————————————

———————————————

———————————————

———————————————

October 5
fear of disappointment

I have to admit that one thing that slows down my eagerness to pray is fear. I am afraid of being disappointed. Prayer, real prayer, honest prayer, involves opening up your heart, baring your feelings, taking a risk, exposing your tender side instead of the hardened armor we usually present to the world.

The prophet Elisha's intercession once brought a long-hoped-for son to an older woman. It was ecstasy to her soul; she had wanted so, so badly to be a mother. Then the boy grew sick and died in her arms. Mute with shock at first, she finally burst out in bitter distress, in "I knew it!" soul pain: **"Did I ask you for a son? . . . Didn't I tell you, 'Don't raise my hopes'?"** (2 Kings 4:28). It was Elisha's great privilege to channel God's life-giving power back into the boy, and he joyfully restored the boy to his mother.

But I know her fear, and you probably do too. Sometimes we may hesitate to ask God for something we desperately want or need because we assume we will be turned down.

Elisha's wonderful ministry helps us to trust that God always gets the last word, and his last word is always one of blessing, kindness, and victory. You don't have to be afraid to open your heart. Even if he lets you experience pain, the pain becomes the path to even greater joy.

_____

_____

_____

_____

_____

I'm afraid my money will run out

I put on a brave face for my family. I don't want any of my friends or coworkers to know. But, Lord, you know the heart, and you can read me like a large-print book. You know how anxious I am about our finances.

I'm afraid our money will run out. We've suffered some setbacks; we've made some bad decisions I would do anything to undo; some things I was counting on turned out to be a bust. I'm juggling bills right now and just can't seem to get ahead. I feel cursed sometimes—cursed to struggle with money issues my whole life.

You say that you will never leave or forsake me. You say that the believers will never beg bread. Your Word tells me, **"He raises the poor from the dust and lifts the needy from the ash heap; he seats them with princes, with the princes of their people"** (Psalm 113:7,8). Father, keep that promise. I ask you for daily bread and you have delivered every day, right on schedule. Help me trust you and believe your gracious promises. Take away my fear and replace it with joyful confidence.

After my time of financial stress, I know you will bring relief. Father, I don't need to sit with princes—could we start with just enough to pay the credit card bills? I am glad to be your child!

_____

_____

_____

_____

God owes me nothing

"Power corrupts," observed Lord Acton. Even minor clerks and municipal functionaries enjoy their petty ability to make people wait, to follow their official routines and procedures. They seem to enjoy the power to issue their summons and tickets and levy their fines.

Just as bad is the sense of entitlement that you find everywhere. People think the world owes them a living. People also think that God owes them a better life.

A military officer once approached Jesus to intercede for a valued member of his military staff who was suffering terribly and was paralyzed. But even though the officer was used to issuing orders, he came without attitude and without demands on Jesus' energy or time. **"The centurion replied, 'Lord, I do not deserve to have you come under my roof. But just say the word, and my servant will be healed'"** (Matthew 8:8).

I love this man's humble spirit, and I love his total confidence in Jesus' kindness and power. When I pray to the Lord, this is how I want to sound. Can your prayer life use some of this humility therapy?

_____

_____

_____

_____

_____

what's the answer? what's the question?

Every advertiser and marketing executive and salesperson in the world is focused on one overriding question: What do people want? They spend their energy and time and money trying to figure you out so that they can position their product or service under your nose and trigger a buy impulse. If they're any good, they will sell you not only a thing but an experience, a feeling, a promise that they say will satisfy you.

How many different toys and experiences have you chased in your life? Have you lived long enough to have discovered the truth in Isaiah's words: **"Why spend money on what is not bread, and your labor on what does not satisfy? Listen, listen to me, and eat what is good, and your soul will delight in the richest of fare. . . . I will make an everlasting covenant with you"** (Isaiah 55:2,3).

You were designed to relate to your Designer, invented to enjoy your Inventor. Unless you are being fed with his Word, your spirit will be restless and unfulfilled. Unless you are hearing from him and he from you, the things you chase will only leave you empty and depressed, perhaps because you couldn't get them or perhaps because you could.

When your covenant-relationship with the Father, Savior, and Counselor is your most important treasure, the joy comes back.

_____

_____

_____

_____

_____

stop the abuse

People don't dream of becoming alcoholics when they grow up, and I really doubt that they fantasize about how they will beat their wives and children someday. Where does abusive behavior come from?

It comes from insecurity. From a desire to control others. From a cheap desire to shift blame from me to you. From a failure to learn to control anger and temper. From an addiction to the adrenaline rush that comes with losing it. From intense selfishness. From fear. From a pathetic need to cover up one's own failures.

"Fathers, do not exasperate your children; instead, bring them up in the training and instruction of the Lord" (Ephesians 6:4). How can you be set free from the sickness of family violence?

Listen. Listen to the voice of your God, who accepts and loves you and encourages you to be at peace with yourself. You are forgiven and freed from the shame of your past. Listen to the voices of your spouse and children. Listen to the generation older than you. Listen to friends and neighbors. Fight the urge to control other people. Instead, by love and leadership, allow their God-given potential to blossom and flourish.

_____

_____

_____

_____

_____

God and my gifts

In a track meet or in a wrestling match, it would be grossly unethical for the judges and referees to intervene to help a player. The athletes are supposed to be completely on their own. Judges are not supposed to show favoritism or get involved in helping a competitor.

Is God your judge? Absolutely. The Bible leaves no doubt of that. But he is a judge who is committed to helping you succeed in your life (according to his standards of success). He not only gives you personal gifts and skills; he steps in to make you better than you are. Imagine that! God is not merely passively watching you. He actually intervenes in your life's history to do things for you to lift you up to greatness.

Listen to the shepherd/king/poet David: **"It is God who arms me with strength and makes my way perfect. He makes my feet like the feet of a deer; he enables me to stand on the heights. He trains my hands for battle; my arms can bend a bow of bronze. You give me your shield of victory, and your right hand sustains me; you stoop down to make me great"** (Psalm 18:32-35).

God needs and wants you in his kingdom-building work. God thinks you are a valuable part of his team. God thinks that you have an important role to play. God thinks you are worth investing in. God actually stoops down to make you great. Seriously!

_____

_____

_____

_____

October 11
I'm sick

Adam and Eve surely had no idea that their mad experiment would go so horribly wrong. They could not possibly have imagined that being disconnected from God would mean being connected to diabetes, HIV, strokes, and congestive heart failure.

We can't even see the viruses and bacteria that assault us. They invade silently, do their evil replication without a sound, and by the time we notice that something is wrong, they number in the millions. Has sickness or disease touched your home? Has it just been the usual childhood stuff—colds, flu, and chicken pox—or have you tasted some of the nastier illnesses, like lupus, autism, cerebral palsy, or cancer?

How's the benefit package in your health insurance? Do you have dental? optical? Jesus has by far the best health plan in the universe. **"Praise the Lord, O my soul, and forget not all his benefits—**[He] **forgives all your sins and heals all your diseases"** (Psalm 103:2,3).

Jesus' insurance plan has two main benefits: forgiveness of our sins, which takes away any reason whatsoever for us to see our illnesses as punishments from God, and healing.

Just remember this: healing comes only from God.

Are you sick? Relax. Jesus is going to heal you—either on earth or once and for all in heaven. You win either way.

_____

_____

_____

_____

_____

October 12
the fish

Where I live people love to advertise their life philosophies. Their three favorite "personal billboards" are their T-shirts, their tattoos, and the rear bumpers of their cars. You can read unbelievably frank expressions of their views on politics, religion, and gender.

Sometimes you can tell you're following a Christian driver because of a simple line drawing on a bumper sticker—a fish. In the original Greek of the New Testament, the first letters of "Jesus Christ, Son of God, Savior" spell out the Greek word for *fish (ICHTHYS)*. The "fish" was an insider logo that early Christians used to find each other in the big cities.

You may or may not wish to use fish imagery as you express yourself, but the Christian content behind it is not optional. Your one hope of a great relationship with God in the here and now is through Christ alone. Your one hope of a happy eternity on the other side of the grave is through Christ alone.

St. Peter, once a fisherman and later an apostle, knew doubt and fear, but he found this comfort and certainty: **"To those who through the righteousness of our God and Savior Jesus Christ have received a faith as precious as ours: Grace and peace be yours in abundance through the knowledge of God and of Jesus our Lord"** (2 Peter 1:1,2).

October 13
I worry all the time

What is it that transforms normal basic human prudence (good) into worry (bad)? I think it is this: the gut-level urge to assume the worst in every possible outcome. Did I just hear a noise downstairs? There must be a robber in my house. Did I get a bad grade in that class? I'm going to fail the semester. Are we invited to your parents' house? I will probably say or do something stupid and then they'll all think I'm a brainless twit.

The best Rx for worriers? The gospel. The more we marinate in the gospel of Christ, the more we become optimists and look for and expect good outcomes to the unknowns in our lives. This is the gospel: that God chooses to look past our sins and see good in us . . . that God chooses to get involved in our lives to make good things happen . . . that God actually makes our hardships become blessings for us . . . that God always has the last word in every situation.

What are the worries that are dragging down your heart right now? Money? Your job? Your marriage? Your lack of a marriage? Your health? The gospel helps you pray like this: **"In the day of trouble I will call to you, for you will answer me"** (Psalm 86:7).

_____

_____

_____

_____

_____

October 14
remember the power you have

One of Obi-Wan Kenobi's most difficult tasks in training Luke Skywalker to be a true Jedi Knight was to help him access *all* his resources. "Use the Force, Luke!" Obi-Wan would exhort him. We all know that this talk of "the Force" is just space mythology cooked up by George Lucas, right? You don't have a Force within you.

Or do you? George Lucas was perhaps closer than he realized to a powerful truth of authentic Christianity: the third person of the Trinity, God the Holy Spirit, comes to live within the hearts of all believers when they are baptized. Scripture promises that your baptism is a washing of rebirth and renewal by the Holy Spirit. The Spirit is *power* from God for thinking, saying, and doing things that are pleasing to God.

The Spirit brings you God's *wisdom* from heaven through his wonderful Word. The Spirit also brings you God's *power* to act on what you know. **"Trust in the Lord with all your heart and lean not on your own understanding . . . and he will make your paths straight"** (Proverbs 3:5,6).

Use the Force.

_____

_____

_____

_____

_____

serve your boss

It is a great temptation to keep your Christianity parked in church, where expressing your faith is safe and expected. It is a step up to live the Christ-life of joyful service in your home. It's a whole new level to live it at work.

Even if overt Christian talk and testimony is discouraged where you work, the way you treat your coworkers and customers says a lot about how real your faith is. Especially the way you treat your boss: **"Serve [your master] wholeheartedly, as if you were serving the Lord, not men, because you know that the Lord will reward everyone for whatever good he does, whether he is slave or free"** (Ephesians 6:7,8).

in•teg•ri•ty \in-'te-grə-tē\ *n.* 1. Adherence to a code or standard of values; 2. the quality of being whole or undivided; completeness. Joy in serving means that you are honest and work hard even when no one is watching. Joy in serving means that you trust that God will reward you in his own way at his own time.

_____

_____

_____

_____

he is in your future

My brother knows more about cars than I ever will. But even he sometimes met his match. He bought a 1950 Ford once that was in pretty rough shape. After working on it for many months, he just felt overwhelmed and gave up on it. The car sat in the driveway for a long time, its dull brown primer making it look like a candidate for the junkyard.

Do you ever feel as though your once-bright hopes will never come true? Has your optimism ground to a halt? Do you no longer believe that anything good is coming in your future?

I've got some good news for all you. God lives in your future. He likes you a lot and loves to get involved in making things happen for people he cares about.

God isn't just an observer, just watching as your hopes and dreams wither. He cares about you. He created you for a purpose, rescued you at the cost of his Son's life, and wants to spend eternity enjoying life with you. He gets no thrill from your misery. God says in Jeremiah 29:11, **"I know the plans I have for you . . . plans to prosper you and not to harm you, plans to give you hope and a future."**

There is hope in his Word. Let him talk to you today.

_____

_____

_____

_____

_____

I love to play with children

Lord, how did you know? Do you have any idea what a lift children bring to sad and weary adults? Of course you know—you invented children.

I love to play with children. They're too young to be cynical, evasive, and aloof. They let their feelings out immediately and blurt out whatever is on their minds. I love to teach them things (and, truth be told, love to let them teach me things). I love kissing their soft cheeks, giving them gifts to see their squeals of delight, and helping to shelter them from the many cruelties of life. I love making children feel safe, involved, and important.

Even men and women who aren't married have abundant opportunities to be with children. Our world will always need tender and compassionate childcare providers, teachers, coaches, and mentors. Lord, you have abundant ways to bring children into our lives: **"He settles the barren woman in her home as a happy mother of children"** (Psalm 113:9).

When I think back to my childhood, I see now and am amazed at how many wonderful adults you sent me. I was sheltered, entertained, educated, and loved by more people than I can count. Thank you! I am honored that you let me be part of that same loving support network for the children in my life.

_____

_____

_____

_____

_____

October 18

wait for it

I am convinced that one of people's greatest frustrations and hindrances to their faith and confidence in God is the dilemma of "unanswered prayer." When you have asked and pleaded for help during a season of stress and nothing seems to have happened, all you can conclude is that God is unable, or if able does not know what to do, or if he does know and doesn't act he must not love you anymore. If any one of those three conclusions is true, our faith is devastated.

We are earthbound. We are locked into the rigid grid of time, able to experience only one second at a time. God is unlimited in space and time. He is everywhere and "everytime" at once, managing the lives of the believers for good over both the short and long term.

Sometimes we have to wait because God's answer involves a complex set of occurrences that have to happen first. Sometimes we wait because God, knowing us better than we know ourselves, sees that we need to wait. Sometimes we wait because we are too immature for the gift that he *will* give.

What Scripture makes clear is that you can trust God's brain and his arm and his heart. **"I am still confident of this: I will see the goodness of the Lord in the land of the living. Wait for the Lord; be strong and take heart and wait for the Lord"** (Psalm 27:13,14).

_____

_____

_____

_____

giving money God's way

I was crushed. As I was greeting people after worship one Sunday, one of the members came by and said, "Gosh, Pastor, if I had known that this was going to be Stewardship Sunday, I would not have brought a friend." Ouch! Was I that bad? Had I made Jesus look bad that day? Had I turned one of a Christian's most joyful privileges into a joyless duty?

Giving is worship. Giving to God acknowledges him as Maker of all (remember—"The earth is the Lord's, and everything in it"), Giver of all (remember—"What do you have that you did not first receive?"), and worthy of our best (remember—"He made himself poor, so that we through his poverty might become rich").

Giving God's money back to him is a "wanna," not a "hafta." **"Honor the Lord with your wealth, with the firstfruits of all your crops; then your barns will be filled to overflowing, and your vats will brim over with new wine"** (Proverbs 3:9,10).

God is already living in your future, and he is capable of giving back to you faster than you can give to him. Feel the love. Feel the joy.

_____

_____

_____

_____

_____

October 20

itching to fight

When New York mobsters decided to retaliate against rival gang members in all-out war, they would "go to the mattresses," i.e., they left home and lived in secret locations to launch their attacks, hoping to avoid detection by their enemies. In Old Testament times, angry civilians who were ready to become warriors would "go to the tents."

The nation of Israel had north/south tensions as bad or worse than America in the 19th century. Even during the reign of such a great king as David, regional hatreds simmered and the people were just itching to fight. Only a spark was needed. **"A troublemaker named Sheba . . . sounded the trumpet and shouted, 'We have no share in David, no part in Jesse's son! Every man to his tent, O Israel!' So all the men of Israel deserted David to follow Sheba"** (2 Samuel 20:1,2).

Do you have a temper? Do old hatreds simmer inside your chest? Do you like to fight? Does the adrenaline rush of "going off" on somebody give you a buzz? Realize that you are working for Satan and his agenda whenever you start or further a fight.

Jesus came to earth as the Prince of peace. He ended the conflict between God and his creatures, and he pronounced his divine blessing on all peacemakers. True strength is demonstrated in self-control and restraint. Anyone can go to the mattresses.

_____

_____

_____

_____

sometimes church people aren't your friends

Now you will think I've popped some important screws in the brain. All pastors, including me, want people to love church life and attend worship and enjoy the fellowship and get involved in ministry and service.

But there's a dark side, and you need to be aware of it. People, including Christians, are still flawed and sinful, and the organizations they build are flawed and sinful too. You would expect to be hurt in situations where there is no Jesus. But Jesus himself gave his disciples a shocking warning: **"You must be on your guard. You will be handed over to the local councils and flogged in the synagogues"** (Mark 13:9).

Church people can be harsh, judgmental, fearful of change, and slow to welcome outsiders. Church people can be territorial, cliquish, political, and control obsessive. Did I mention rude and unfeeling?

In spite of his warning, Jesus didn't dismiss the value of church fellowship. The Word urges us not to forsake assembling ourselves together. Just be on your guard. Knowing that some people have been wounded or turned off by church people, you can be a healer both in and out of the church.

After all, on judgment day it will not matter so much on which congregational membership roster your name appears but whether or not you are connected to Christ in faith.

_____

_____

_____

_____

October 22

yielding to God's plan

If you want to see naked human ambition, just get inside a political campaign. The higher the office, the more desperate and hard-edged the game becomes. One of President Nixon's operatives said once, "You are measured in this town by the size of the people you have destroyed."

Imagine the pressure and longing in the heart of the crown prince in a monarchy. You won't have to run for election—supreme authority and wealth are guaranteed to be yours. King Saul's son Jonathan should have been king. But he knew that the prophet Samuel had anointed David as his father's successor.

Jonathan is a hero not only because he was such a true and loyal friend to David, but because he so cheerfully and generously gave up his hopes for the throne. He told David, **"May the Lord be with you as he has been with my father. But show me unfailing kindness like that of the Lord as long as I live, so that I may not be killed, and do not ever cut off your kindness from my family—not even when the Lord has cut off every one of David's enemies from the face of the earth. So Jonathan made a covenant with the house of David"** (1 Samuel 20:13-16).

Can you root for people who have a high position you think you deserve? Could you buck your own father when you know he's wrong? Can you accept a smaller role in life than you wanted or expected if you see that it is God's will? Have you learned how to find joy in sacrificing your wants so that someone else can benefit?

_____

_____

_____

October 23
God hates religious lethargy

One of the features of life in the 21st century is people's growing reluctance to commit to anything. People today know that they have a lot of choices, and they stall off deciding so that they can keep their options open till the last possible second. They job jump and delay engagement and marriage much more than previous generations.

Alas, that translates also into a lack of commitment to God and church and a Christian life. If people endlessly want to hang back, stay a spectator, stay just a fly on the wall, they will never have closeness and engagement and fellowship in the Word. They will stay small and weak and unproductive in their faith.

That attitude characterized a certain congregation in western Asia Minor. Jesus Christ gave everything for those people. His view of their lethargy: **"These are the words of the Amen, the faithful and true witness, the ruler of God's creation. I know your deeds, that you are neither cold nor hot. I wish you were either one or the other! So, because you are lukewarm—neither hot nor cold—I am about to spit you out of my mouth"** (Revelation 3:14-16).

Another feature of the times we live in is the fascination with extreme sports, of going crazy, all in, for something. Are you ready to go all in for Christ?

_____

_____

_____

_____

_____

October 24

getting old

Some of the people I admire most are those who age gracefully. You know what I mean. Anyone can complain about what age does to the human body—sight and hearing fade, memory fails, hair falls out, chin gets baggy, clothes shrink, blah, blah, blah.

Nobody wants to hear about your operation, and nobody really wants to hear how age has made your life more difficult. What we need are inspiring examples of how people use for God's glory the unique powers and insights that come with maturity. We need stories of how people have overcome physical limitations to do great things for other people.

We will leave it to the young to be beautiful and strong. We older folks just want to be useful. We would like to be respected for what we sacrificed for the next two generations. We would like our words of wisdom to be heard because we have earned the right to be listened to. And we would like to finish the most important work of all—passing on our faith.

Today I promise to stop whining about getting old. Will you join me? I have important work to do, and so do you. **"Even when I am old and gray, do not forsake me, O God, till I declare your power to the next generation"** (Psalm 71:18).

_____

_____

_____

_____

be merciful

"Lord, have mercy!" Do you ever say that? I hope you do, and when you say it, I hope you mean every word of it. We are utterly dependent on the Lord's mercy for our spiritual life and hope. Mercy means to be shown kindness that we do not deserve. Mercy comes from goodness in the heart of the giver, not merit on the part of the receiver.

You and I are bathed in mercy from God, and it is our privilege to be reflectors of it to other strugglers and stragglers. God would like us to treat others in their time of weakness in the same way that he has treated us. **"Be merciful to those who doubt; snatch others from the fire and save them; to others show mercy, mixed with fear"** (Jude 22,23).

What sin have you ever seen in other people that you yourself were not also once guilty of? Doubt? Rebelliousness? Meanness? Deceit? Cruelty? Adultery? Theft? Hypocrisy? Christ Jesus allowed himself to be blamed for all of your sin, and its guilt is attached to you no more.

A believer who is fully aware of being treated better than he or she deserves finds joy in being merciful to others.

_____

_____

_____

_____

_____

the Lord God dwelt in his temple then

It's hard to believe and not see. God knew that. As a gift to the nation of believers that he was raising up, his beloved Israel, God chose to make his presence visible and local. He appeared often as fire and smoke in various configurations — in a burning bush, in a pillar of cloud by day and fire by night, as a smoking firepot, and as a bright burning light that moved into the Most Holy Place of the tabernacle (and later the temple) and stayed there.

He let his Israel know that the One who filled the universe had chosen to localize his presence *right among them!* **"For the generations to come this burnt offering is to be made regularly at the entrance to the Tent of Meeting before the Lord. There I will meet you and speak to you; there also I will meet with the Israelites, and the place will be consecrated by my glory"** (Exodus 29:42,43).

What a comfort it was for Israel to have the Lord's presence right among them. What a comfort to see that blazing fire and know that the divine power was ready to go, that the divine eyes were on watch. What encouragement they could derive from the glory-cloud as they navigated all the hardships of their national existence. He's here! Right here!

_____

_____

_____

_____

_____

the Lord God now dwells in you

Do the stories of the visible glory of the Lord make you wistful and nostalgic for the good ol' days? Do you struggle with moving forward in faith but not sight? Do you long for more empirical evidence for God's existence and God's love? Do you resonate with Christian songs that plead, "Lord, show me your glory"?

As believers in the Lord Jesus, you have been honored by God to be designated as living temples for him. When you came to faith, the Holy Spirit came to live within you. You don't have to make a pilgrimage to the temple. You *are* God's temple. **"As you come to him, the living Stone—rejected by men but chosen by God and precious to him—you also, like living stones, are being built into a spiritual house to be a holy priesthood, offering spiritual sacrifices acceptable to God through Jesus Christ"** (1 Peter 2:4,5).

You don't have to envy Old Testament believers because they could see more. They had to live on promises. You are blessed to have heard the stories of the fulfilled promises and completed plans. God no longer needs a Jerusalem temple to live in. You are his temples—places of worship and places of spiritual strength, for you now carry the Spirit wherever you go.

It's both a terrifying responsibility and an awesome privilege: with our words and witness we may be the place where some people meet God for the first time.

Schadenfreude

There is no exact word for it in English, but the Germans have one: *Schadenfreude* (SHAH den froy deh). Schadenfreude is a spiritual sickness that leads you to enjoy other people's misery. So who tends to do that? People who feel cheated in life . . . people who resent other people's successes and secretly enjoy it when they later struggle . . . people who feel weak . . . people who feel miserable and want some company.

The divine Father who stooped low in mercy to lift us up cannot stand it when we show no mercy to the other fools and sinners around us. **"He who mocks the poor shows contempt for their Maker; whoever gloats over disaster will not go unpunished"** (Proverbs 17:5). God takes no joy in human pain or suffering, and he forbids Schadenfreude in us as well.

As faith in Christ more and more takes over our hearts, we will hurt when we see others hurting. We will weep with those who weep and comfort those who have to bear affliction. As we reflect on the Savior who bore our griefs and carried our sorrows, we will offer to be Jesus' hug and voice to people in their time of need.

An added plus of visible Christian compassion is that it authenticates what we say. As the old evangelism slogan goes, people don't care how much you know until they know how much you care.

_____

_____

_____

_____

_____

October 29

I'm tired of the drudgery

Have you ever wondered how much of your life is consumed by repetitive chores of cleaning and maintenance? How many times your knives, spoons, and forks have cycled from the drawer to the table to your mouth to the sink and back to the drawer? How many times you have picked up other people's clothes, vacuumed endless lint, cleaned the bathroom, attacked the dust layers, and pulled weeds?

What we call drudgery God calls humble and helpful service to others. Patient and steady toil, honoring God right where he put you, in some ways is just as worshipful as singing hymns in church. If you can do it without complaining, all the better.

How do you suppose Joseph felt about the grimy and gritty slave life in a dungeon? **"But while Joseph was there in the prison, the LORD was with him; he showed him kindness and granted him favor in the eyes of the prison warden. So the warden put Joseph in charge of all those held in the prison, and he was made responsible for all that was done there"** (Genesis 39:20-22).

Joseph's humble prison labor resulted ultimately in being elevated to assistant pharaoh. When you are scrubbing pots and pans, dedicate them to God and thank him for the dignity of work.

_____

_____

_____

_____

_____

I ache for my children

Dear kids,

Your mom and I want you to know how much we love you. We will always love you, always, no matter what. We have tried to be good parents, although we realize that we often fall short. We see you as God's gifts to us. Thank you for all the joy you've brought us.

You're grown up enough now that you are pretty much on your own. You don't ask us much anymore and sure don't tell us what's happening in your lives. That's okay, I suppose. You're big now. You want to show that you can handle things on your own. We want you to know, though, that we are always here for you. We may be able to help you work your way through something that we've already faced. We don't want you to have to struggle any more than you have to.

The most important heritage that we can leave you, more important than money, is our faith. We have done our best to help you get to know your Creator, Savior, and Counselor. We can't believe for you. Our greatest wish and prayer for you is that you will claim it as your own.

"My son, do not forget my teaching, but keep my commands in your heart, for they will prolong your life many years and bring you prosperity" (Proverbs 3:1,2).

Love, Mom and Dad

_____

_____

_____

_____

_____

God's treat has no tricks

During the month of October, two colors dominate offices and stores—orange and black. In every store you are bombarded by displays of candy and almost any type of costume that you can think of. Whether or not you will put out candy for the superheroes and goblins ringing your doorbell is a matter of personal opinion.

But October 31 is more than just candy and princess costumes; it is also Reformation Day, a day that celebrates the reformation movement that brought to light the authority of Scripture and salvation by God's grace alone, through faith alone. The Bible, the inspired Word of God, tells us: **"It is by grace you have been saved, through faith—and this not from yourselves, it is the gift of God—not by works, so that no one can boast"** (Ephesians 2:8,9).

For many centuries believers had been held in fear and guilt their whole lives because they had been taught that their relationship with God depended at least in part on their good works. The biblical truth that the reformation movement rediscovered and proclaimed centers on grace, the unbelievably good news that Jesus Christ has paid all our debts, forgiven all our sins, and even gives us to the Holy Spirit to help us believe it.

When the little ghosts and witches come to your door, their implied threat is "treat or trick." Because of Jesus Christ, you can enjoy the ultimate treat—forgiveness of your sins and eternal life. No tricks. It's his gift!

November

"Trust in the LORD with all your heart and lean not on your own understanding; in all your ways acknowledge him, and he will make your paths straight."
(Proverbs 3:5,6)

I love quiet time in the Word

You know, Lord, I have done enough complaining about the aches and pains of aging. But there are some terrific advantages to getting older.

I am far more patient than I used to be. I enjoy people more and accept them as they are. And I have grown to appreciate regular quiet time with your Word. I used to be too busy—or thought I was too busy—to read my chapter a day. Now it's the best time of my day. **"Oh, how I love your law! I meditate on it all day long. Your statutes are my heritage forever; they are the joy of my heart"** (Psalm 119:97,111). My joys are now twice as big because I know that you sent them. My troubles are only half as big because I know you are carrying them with me.

Your Word explains the riddle of human existence. Your Word tells me the truth, comforts my heart, and gives me hope. Your Word reveals that you are actively managing affairs behind the scenes to work all things together for the good of those who love you. Your Word assures me that you will never stop loving me, that I have great worth in your sight, and that you still have a use for me.

Tell me in today's reading how I may serve you best.

_____

_____

_____

_____

offerings make God happy

Did you know that three miracles happen whenever you gift a monetary gift to God? The first is that you make God smile. Seriously! The Bible says that your gifts, given freely for grace freely received, **"are a fragrant offering, an acceptable sacrifice, pleasing to God"** (Philippians 4:18)?

Second, you gain a deep sense of personal satisfaction. We are designed for worship, and worshiping with your wallet is perhaps the most sincere form of all. A generous spirit is a good personal indicator of whether or not your faith is real. Giving is actually fun!

Finally, gifts of money to the Lord are reinvested and make ministry happen—perhaps in your own congregation, or perhaps making outreach ministry happen far away. Your gifts of money make it possible that the Word of the Lord can touch the hearts and lives of people who live on the other side of the globe.

That too thrills the heart of the Lord.

_____

_____

_____

_____

_____

unity in the community

"Rugged individualism" is a phrase Herbert Hoover often used; it became a theme of his presidency. It refers to a feature of Americans that he cherished and wished to foster—that people work hard and take care of themselves, not dependent on others or begging for handouts.

That admirable quality can become *ragged* individualism, however, when people think only of themselves, when they look to their relationships only for what they can get. God himself loves a diversity of viewpoints—after all, he made us remarkably different from one another. But working out basic beliefs about God does not belong to individual options.

There is a core of revealed truth about God and his mighty acts in human history that is not negotiable. **"May the God who gives endurance and encouragement give you a spirit of unity among yourselves as you follow Christ Jesus"** (Romans 15:5). There is one God, not many. There is one source of revelation, not many. There is one faith, one Baptism, one Supper, one Savior, and one heaven.

Thus gatherings of Christians are not just a random collection of individuals, but a living organism. Good leaders work hard for unity in people's beliefs and unity of purpose and mission. Good followers help that unity take hold and grow.

_____

_____

_____

_____

_____

mentors

You've learned a lot of things from a lot of people, but some individuals stand out. You connected with them. Why? Whom has God sent into your life to lift you up, show you things, explain mysteries, model how to act, demonstrate how to succeed? Who released energy in your life, made you feel like a winner, raised the bar of your expectations?

More important, who have been your faith mentors? Who most vividly led you into the Word? Who modeled how to make God-pleasing decisions? Whose spiritual talk and actions do you find yourself imitating? Whom would you most want to be like? When confronted with a tough moral or ethical dilemma, whose name is in your thoughts at that moment: "What would _____ do?"

It is no accident that these mentors are in your life. Be more aware of them—they are God's gifts to you. **"Remember your leaders, who spoke the word of God to you. Consider the outcome of their way of life and imitate their faith"** (Hebrews 13:7). Mentors put flesh and blood on abstract principles. Mentors distill life learning and pass on little bottles of it. They are happy to share what they know, because all good mentors had mentors of their own.

Do you suppose that there's anybody trailing behind you that looks up to you?

_____

_____

_____

_____

_____

watch out for yourself

Here's a crazy feature of the Christian life—as you become more effective in helping other people to come back to the Lord, you become just that much bigger a target to the devil. Even as you become more proficient in understanding and explaining the Scriptures to people, you can succumb to pride, hypocrisy, or mental gymnastics and game playing to justify ignoring what you have told others.

St. Paul knew that he needed to guard his heart: **"I do not run like a man running aimlessly; I do not fight like a man beating the air. No, I beat my body and make it my slave so that after I have preached to others, I myself will not be disqualified for the prize"** (1 Corinthians 9:26,27).

Those who are talkers for Jesus must also be listeners for Jesus. Those who are proud to represent him must also humble themselves. Those who speak words of rebuke to those in rebellion should let those same words hit their own hearts. Those who urge others to cling to Jesus should also re-declare their own dependence on his saving mercy.

November 6
blessed to be a blessing

It is the lowest point on the face of the earth: 1,388 feet below sea level. Freshwater flows in, but nothing flows out, and so the salinity levels are off the charts. It is a small body of water eight times saltier than the oceans. No animal life is possible in it, and so it has been given the name Dead Sea.

The Dead Sea only takes. It gives nothing and only reluctantly surrenders its water to the steady evaporation of desert heat. *Dead* also describes the condition of a human soul that only takes and never wishes to give, where resources flow in and nothing flows out. **"If a man shuts his ears to the cry of the poor, he too will cry out and not be answered"** (Proverbs 21:13).

Everything we have is a gift, a loan, from the great Giver. Everything we have is because he is generous, not because we are so brilliant. Everything we have is a careful investment from heaven to see if we will choose willingly and joyfully to become part of God's agenda.

Every one of us has opportunities to relieve human suffering around us. We have been given mercy so that we might show mercy. We have been blessed in order to be a blessing. May the angels call you a "Living Sea."

_____

_____

_____

_____

am I dying?

Even tough guys are afraid to die. In the weeks following the September 11, 2001 terrorist attacks, what became instant hot sellers? You got it—gas masks and vaccines. Terrorism does indeed breed terror.

We cling to life and do everything we can to preserve it. We pour billions into medical research and care. In the 1950s and 1960s, we built bomb shelters in case of nuclear attack. We work out, huffing and puffing on treadmills. We look for heart-healthy menu items. We eat vitamins and tofu, yogurt, and bean curd.

And yet, no matter what we do, we will never be able to anticipate and defend ourselves and our loved ones against all the many ways that death could come upon us. There is only one way not to die—Jesus Christ. He alone holds the key to death. Jesus said in John 11:25,26, **"I am the resurrection and the life. He who believes in me will live, even though he dies; and whoever lives and believes in me will never die."**

If you allow yourself to believe that promise, your fear of dying evaporates.

_____

_____

_____

_____

_____

November 8

time for you to know what you believe

Every couple of years there's a hot new religious trend that comes along and gets a lot of media attention. Think of the Beatles with the Maharishi Mahesh Yogi or Madonna with her Kabbalah mysticism or John Travolta and Kirstie Alley with Scientology. Perhaps people in your family have been drawn to Zen or meditation—or maybe you yourself are fascinated with New Age spirituality.

There are not many truths. There is one. There are not many gods. There is One. God calls all competition idols and quietly promises to destroy them all, as well as all who worship them. This is serious business—Satan uses false gods to lure spiritually minded people away from the Lord to their deaths.

God loves you enough to give you his Word, and he gives you also teachers and pastors and mentors and Christian friends and family to keep you anchored in that Word. Here's how it benefits you: **"Then we will no longer be infants, tossed back and forth by the waves, and blown here and there by every wind of teaching and by the cunning and craftiness of men in their deceitful scheming"** (Ephesians 4:14).

November 9
God and my gratitude

Don't you hate it when people take from you and don't acknowledge you? Don't you hate it when you do things for people and they don't bother to say thank you? Can you imagine the hurt in God's heart when the Giver of everything good is ignored?

A thankful spirit is learned behavior. Parents have to work at it and work at it with their kids. A lot of grown-ups, me included, are still working on their own attitudes. Every so often I have to rediscover the transformational truth that absolutely everything good in my life can be traced back to heaven.

Take inventory of your treasures right now, like the abundant food all around you, so abundant that most Americans are desperately trying not to eat so much. Basic clothing has never been cheaper. Communication technology can keep you in touch with people all over the globe. Through Christ you are part of a spiritual family, and through him you have significance and meaning in your life.

"Give thanks to the LORD for he is good. His love endures forever. Give thanks to the God of gods. His love endures forever. Give thanks to the Lord of lords: His love endures forever" (Psalm 136:1-3). The greatest of all God's gifts are his love and forgiveness through your Savior Jesus. He really is good! His victory over Satan can't be undone. His love really does endure forever!

the Father wants you back

One of the aspects of God's ways that people have trouble understanding and accepting is his unconditional love.

It's because there is no parallel in human behavior. Our forgiveness toward each other is hesitant, grudging, fingers-crossed, partial, and often just part of a ploy to get something we want. Often it is not forgiveness at all, and we bring up old sins all over again to use for leverage with other sinners.

Guilt is a terrible slave master. It keeps us afraid, making excuses, bargaining frantically, and ultimately giving up in despair. But get this—God's love for you is based not on your performance or accumulated merit. It is based on his decision to love you no matter what. Jesus told a splendid story of a father with an aching heart to illustrate the way God forgives: **"But while he** [the prodigal son] **was still a long way off, his father saw him and was filled with compassion for him; he ran to his son, threw his arms around him and kissed him"** (Luke 15:20).

This is the message of the gospel—that God loves sinners for Jesus' sake and forgives them while still sinners, i.e., before they've been cleaned up. Let that unconditional love comfort your guilty heart. Let that unconditional love release worship from your heart and lips. Let that unconditional love fuel a new attitude and new life each day.

_____

_____

_____

_____

_____

well done!

Trained animals need immediate reward, don't they? Even the very best animal entertainers get their sardines right after their tricks. Kindergartners need immediate rewards too, but you shouldn't. Still—it is hard to be virtuous when it seems that no one's looking and no one is keeping track. God wants you to know that he sees and he remembers.

"After a long time the master of those servants returned and settled accounts with them. The man who had received the five talents brought the other five. 'Master,' he said, 'you entrusted me with five talents. See, I have gained five more.' His master replied, 'Well done, good and faithful servant! You have been faithful with a few things; I will put you in charge of many things. Come and share your master's happiness!'" (Matthew 25:19-21).

The "five talent" servant was ready to report. His business investments and hard work had paid off. His profit for his master far outran simple interest yield. How gratifying it was to stand in his master's presence and—

• realize that his integrity and hard work had counted for something;

• bask in the master's approval;

• hear that this was only the beginning—that there were new adventures yet to come and the master wanted to use his leadership for even bigger things.

Do you suppose that God is using earth as a training ground for new adventures in heaven and that he's building his leadership team for eternity?

_____

_____

_____

God's gift

Happy is the man who has learned to say, "I married above myself." I have heard this dozens of times from fellow pastors, who give huge credit to their wives for taking them through "finishing school."

Marriage is far more beneficial than just helping men find a way to express sexuality without sin. Wives help males understand the way the other 50% of the world thinks. Wives bring grace and beauty, fragrance and flowers into life. Wives bring intuition and sensitivity, attention to relationships and heart-emotion. It is to women that human reproduction has been granted, and only through them can babies be born into a lonely home.

The only way Adam could get his missing rib back was to be married. He was excited to meet Eve. Adam's sons still thrill to be given one of Eve's daughters. **"He who finds a wife finds what is *good* and receives favor from the LORD"** (Proverbs 18:22).

Husbands, are you listening? Say it with me: "Thank you, Lord, for your gift of my wife."

_____

_____

_____

_____

_____

sign in the sky

That ubiquitous arc of colors—red/orange/yellow/green/ blue/indigo/violet—is everywhere. Sometimes it announces a Chicago political organization. Sometimes it announces advocacy for gay rights. But its ultimate meaning was given by God himself.

Somehow in the world before the great flood there were no rainbows. After the waters went down, God tweaked something in the physics of light and atmospheric moisture and now on special occasions gives us that brief little dazzle-display of his art. Here is what God means to tell us when we see the seven colors in the sky: **"This is the sign of the covenant I am making between me and you and every living creature with you, a covenant for all generations to come: . . . Never again will the waters become a flood to destroy all life"** (Genesis 9:12,15).

The rainbow is more than a cute icon or natural wonder. It is first a solemn warning that human sin is a capital crime in God's court. The great flood was real; so were the deaths it caused. Second, those who listened to God escaped his violent judgment. Noah and his family believed God's Word and were saved. Finally, the bow God placed in the sky is his promise to be patient with the human race and give his precious gospel time to work.

Until he returns.

_____

_____

_____

_____

_____

remember who loved them first

"She acts just like you did at that age." "He's the spittin' image of his daddy." Proud parents love to hear such things about their children (assuming the children are being praised). Not only is our parenting being validated; *we ourselves* are being complimented, and who ever gets enough of that?

When we think of children strictly as "ours," however, we do well to remember that God loved them first and still loves them best. We hold them in solemn trust for him. One day a group of moms brought their little children to Jesus. As the children climbed all over him, the disciples tried to shoo the children away. Jesus was indignant. He said, **"Let the little children come to me, and *do not* hinder them, for the kingdom of heaven belongs to such as these"** (Matthew 19:14).

The sharpness in Jesus' tone was necessary, forcefully getting across two huge concepts: (1) These children need me. They are sinners too. (2) Word and sacrament can build faith in their little hearts too. They can believe in me. They are part of God's kingdom of faith, not someday but right now.

Here's the good part—if God claims them, then he obligates himself to help us. Forgiveness for our selfishness and negligence. Rescue for our parenting mistakes. Blueprints for decision making. And above all, joy—joy at being given the grandest work any human being could ever do.

_____

_____

_____

_____

Paul, a prayer hero

Paul is a prayer hero of mine because he models for me constantly how a good spiritual leader shows appreciation for the people he is serving. If you read his epistles, you will see how often he praises the believers in those places and how he calls on God's blessings on their lives.

One such example would be the Christians in the Macedonian city of Philippi: **"I thank my God every time I remember you. In all my prayers for you, I always pray with joy because of your partnership in the gospel"** (Philippians 1:3-5). What makes prayer so valuable is that it is not bound by distance, age, wealth, or physical strength. Communication was very slow back in those days—Paul was separated from most of his converts most of the time.

But through prayer he was close to them and close to the Lord. That joyful prayer bond was a first installment of the time in heaven coming soon when there will no longer be any separation. Paul encouraged his readers also to pray for him, and not just as a ploy for attention but because he really needed the spiritual boost.

Are you a spiritual leader? Would you pause right now and pray for the people you serve? Do you know missionaries who serve far away? Would you pause right now and pray for them?

_____

_____

_____

_____

_____

November 16
I like my life

It takes no brains to complain.

Have you ever noticed how people (you and me too) tend to look *up* the ladder, never *down?* Above us are people who have it better than we do: better jobs; better clothes; better jewelry; better homes; better cars; and a lake home, boat, and jet skis. Deep down inside us is a seething discontent that Satan loves to manipulate and provoke. *I* deserve those things. *I've* been cheated. I. I. I.

That kind of talk is not Spirit talk. Flush it out of your brain. Wash it out of your mouth. We have all been outrageously blessed by a kind and generous Father. We have more than we need. We can enjoy our lives and be content. **"Godliness with contentment is great gain. For we brought nothing into the world, and we can take nothing out of it. But if we have food and clothing, we will be content with that. People who want to get rich fall into temptation and a trap and into many foolish and harmful desires that plunge men into ruin and destruction"** (1 Timothy 6:6-9).

As if our material possessions weren't enough, Christ has made us his sisters and brothers, heirs of eternal life. We are immortal.

I like my life. I will like my eternity even better.

_____

_____

_____

_____

_____

I feel safe in you, Lord

As you know, Lord, our culture glorifies youth. Nobody welcomes the passing of time and the aging process. May I say, though, that you make aging more enjoyable? The older I get, the more I see how I was never alone, how you were always there watching me, ready to catch me, intervening at just the right time.

I panic less these days. I still can see only a few feet in front of me—the fog of life hasn't lifted much, but I have grown in my certainty that you are ahead of me and will watch my steps. You will reveal to me what to do when it is time. You will provide resources when I need them. **"Yet I am always with you; you hold me by my right hand. You guide me with your counsel, and afterward you will take me into glory"** (Psalm 73:23,24).

I feel safe in you, Lord. You are the One I can depend on. Your love for me is rock steady. Your purposes never waver. You have given me tastes of hardship and prosperity and benefitted me with both.

I am comforted by the absolute certainty you have given me that through your Son, Jesus, through his obedient life and innocent death and splendid resurrection, my life is already victorious. Through Jesus I am forgiven. Through Jesus I am immortal. I *know* you will take me to glory.

----

don't wait for harmony—create it

I feel no particular responsibility for the ambience, menu, waitstaff, and food at a restaurant that I visit. I come to consume and enjoy. Period. If the experience was great, I will be back. If not, I may never return. Not my problem.

I have no such luxury of disinterest in my personal relationships—at work, at church, at home. If there are dysfunctions in relationships, I own them. If there is tension in the air, I own it. If there are leadership problems, I own them.

God doesn't want me merely to be a consumer in my workplace, church, and home. I don't have the luxury of checking out if I don't like what I hear and see. It's as though God is telling me, "Don't just wait for a great vibe—create it!" **"All of you, live in harmony with one another; be sympathetic, love as brothers, be compassionate and humble. Do not repay evil with evil or insult with insult, but with blessing"** (1 Peter 3:8,9).

One of the great themes in the entire Scripture is the power of one. One person can change a relationship. One person can change the culture of a group. One person's leadership and example can bring the Spirit's power and affect the whole group.

God just needs me to go first. And you.

_____

_____

_____

_____

_____

God and my shame

A phrase you don't hear much anymore is "Shame on you!" But that doesn't mean that the concept of shame has disappeared.

I doubt if there are any people of retirement age who can't look back at parts of their lives with great embarrassment. I doubt if there are any families who haven't been shamed at some time or another by the actions of one or two in the clan. Everybody in prison has a family. Everyone expelled from school, fired from a job, or suffering bankruptcy feels shame, and those around them feel it too.

The worst part of shame is that it lasts. The memories just won't go away by themselves. Here is another great reason why the gospel of Christ is so important—it doesn't selectively delete memories from your mind, but it enables you to live peacefully and joyfully even *with* memories of past shame. **"O Israel, put your hope in the Lord, for with the Lord is unfailing love and with him is full redemption. He himself will redeem Israel from all their sins"** (Psalm 130:7,8).

The Lord's unfailing love means that he knows who you are and what you've done and loves you anyway. He knows your pile of regrets and assures you that his grace is even bigger. If he forgives you, you can forgive yourself. If he likes you, you can like yourself again. Your image before him has no shame, no regrets, only holiness. Forgiven fully, you shine like a star.

_____

_____

_____

November 20
I feel numb

Satan has many ways to attack you, but he will probably not waste his hellish energy on trying to persuade you today to curse Christ and throw your Bible in the trash. He seems to have had far better success with other people over the centuries in a slow and gradual seduction and distraction with other passions. The bigger danger to you is that your fire and love for Christ's gospel will just cool down a little more each day until one day you realize that you are spiritually numb. You don't care about anything. You feel nothing.

The New Testament epistle to the Hebrews has five powerful warnings. Here is the first: **"We must pay more careful attention, therefore, to what we have heard, so that we do not drift away. For if the message spoken by angels was binding, and every violation and disobedience received its just punishment, how shall we escape if we ignore such a great salvation?"** (2:1-3). Note the dangers: "Drift." "Ignore." You can kill your faith-relationship with God with neglect.

Forewarned is forearmed. Start by telling Satan to get lost. Rebuke him, and he will flee from you. Listen to the love letters in the Word that bring warmth and light and life. Let holy sap from Christ the Vine flow into your tired soul. Let the Spirit speak to your spirit. Smile again. You are loved.

I'm afraid of losing my health

I've talked to some pretty tough people who endured a lot of setbacks in their lives, but they could always say, "At least I have my health." What if you don't? A lot of older people are terrified of falling and breaking bones. What health issues scare you the most? Canes and walkers? Having to get around in a wheelchair? Having to drag around an oxygen tank all day?

Do you have to live with pain? Are you a cancer survivor? Have you had major surgery? Does a possible recurrence of those illnesses fill your heart with dread? Do you worry about the health of people close to you?

Job lost most of his material possessions, but at least he had his health. Then he lost that too. What do you suppose happened to his faith and trust in God? **"Satan went out from the presence of the LORD and afflicted Job with painful sores from the soles of his feet to the top of his head. Then Job took a piece of broken pottery and scraped himself with it as he sat among the ashes"** (Job 2:7,8).

Even in his physical misery Job found comfort in God's track record of steadfast love and steadfast purpose.

_____

_____

_____

_____

_____

do good for all people

Christians were persecuted as enemies of the state for almost all of the first three centuries of their existence. The irony is that Christianity can indeed flourish in a political climate of great freedom, but sometimes it does even better in times of great oppression.

In those early centuries, the Jewish and Roman states were missing a great resource. Christians actually make the best citizens. Our God commands us to care about our civic community, not just our church community. The God who loves us unconditionally trains us to love all the people around us, not just other Christians, unconditionally too. **"As we have opportunity, let us do good to all people, especially to those who belong to the family of believers"** (Galatians 6:10).

Of course, God wants us to take care of our church community. But sometimes we can worship God better on our own streets than in church. When Christians act like Christ in the world, they give honor to the One whose blood actually paid for the world's sins. When we love people as Christ did, with real and authentic caring, we destroy the caricature of Christians as hypocritical and judgmental snobs.

_____

_____

_____

_____

_____

energy drain

Are you sensitive to the moods and personalities of the people who surround you at work? Do the complainers and gripers and whiners suck energy out of your soul? Do you find it impossible to screen out people's criticisms and rants? Does negativity always find you somehow?

Jesus has given you powerful armor for negativity. His gospel makes us all optimists. Rise above. Here is the soundtrack and theme music to run through your head and heart when you feel the energy drain: **"Rejoice in the Lord always. I will say it again: Rejoice! Let your gentleness be evident to all. The Lord is near"** (Philippians 4:4,5).

You don't have to take the negativity personally. You have God's favor and Christ's love and the Spirit's indwelling with you wherever you go. You can recognize constant negativity for what it is—cries for help from a small person who feels overwhelmed, envious, bitter, and afraid. Your desk and phone and e-mails can be a steady source of positivity. People will notice. They may even ask why you are so cheerful all the time. You can tell them why your spirit rejoices.

Rise above. Perhaps you have been sent on a divine mission from God to that very office to make a difference.

_____

_____

_____

_____

_____

his mercy, not my virtue

People like to be in control of their relationships. They also like to control the relationship with God. They don't want to feel any sense of obligation; they don't want to feel powerless or needy; they hate to beg; and they want to accumulate heavenly capital so they can relax and actually count on God to perform for them when needed.

People think they can gain that sense of security by observing religious rituals, making appropriate financial donations, and striving to obey the rules. And while all those things are good, they are useless in solving the first and greatest problem—and that is that our sinful hearts make us unfit for heaven. All our good deeds can't erase even one of our bad deeds.

St. Paul thought he was a model citizen. It came as a massive shock that the good relationship with God that he craved came from God's mercy, not his own virtue. **"I thank Christ Jesus our Lord, who has given me strength, that he considered me faithful, appointing me to his service. Even though I was once a blasphemer and a persecutor and a violent man, I was shown mercy"** (1 Timothy 1:12,13).

Where does peace with God come from? Don't look at your works. Look at Christ's. Your heavenly capital was earned through his suffering, death, and resurrection. Let him give it to you.

_____

_____

_____

_____

family feud

One of the best parts of family life is the vulnerability. You can let down your guard in a safe place. You don't have to pretend to be strong, unemotional, and together 24 hours a day. There are understanding people who will like you anyway, even when you are confused, weak, and doubting.

One of the worst parts of family life is the vulnerability. Paradoxically some of the worst hurts in life come from those who profess to love us the most. How easy it is to take out our own frustrations on the other poor victims trapped in the house with us. How sad when children bear the brunt of the anger and dysfunctions of the adults who are supposed to be protecting them.

Happy, healthy families don't just happen. The leaders need to model the behaviors that they benefit from through Christ. More learned behaviors: **"Be kind and compassionate to one another, forgiving each other, just as in Christ God forgave you"** (Ephesians 4:32).

You can't change the past. You can't undo the hurts given to you by family, nor can you unspeak your own abusive words or undo your own past cruelties. What you can do is believe in Christ's forgiveness for your own wrongs and extend forgiveness in Christ's name to those who hurt you. The gospel heals.

_____

_____

_____

_____

_____

time to know the gospel

There is a double basic message in the Bible. God's first message demands your holiness and obedience and announces his judgment on disobeyers. Even people who've never cracked the Book know something about that, thanks to their consciences.

You have a lot of that negative message in your head already, don't you? It's the voice that tells you you're worthless, a failure, a loser, and ugly and fat and friendless besides.

What we do not know by nature is the gospel. We do not know there's hope. Someone needs to tell us that. Someone needs to tell us there's love for the loveless, beauty for the homely, and truth for liars. There's forgiveness for sinners, wisdom for fools, and kindness for crabby jerks. Paul tells you what the gospel is in Romans 5:8: **"God demonstrates his own love for us in this: While we were still sinners, Christ died for us."**

Did you know that? If so, it's not because you've figured it out by yourself. It's because God revealed it to you in his Word. Forgiveness of your many sins, comfort for your troubled heart, hope for your exhausted spirit, and immortality for your dying body are all his gifts. Who do you know that needs to hear this comforting message?

_____

_____

_____

_____

whatever happened to discipline?

Why is it that we notice other people's kids' disobedience so much quicker than our own? Maybe it's because parents of small children have to grow partially and temporarily deaf to survive. You just can't hear all the crying or you will go insane.

If you want to appreciate God's huge job in training you, just listen to other parents attempting to teach their children self-control and some degree of restraint. "No, Billy. Stop it, Billy. I mean it, Billy. Stop that right now! Or else!" Aagghh!

Some of the greatest work on earth is done by parents who teach their children that *no* means *no*. Who insist on obedience the first time. Who teach kids to wait. Who teach kids to defer gratification. Who teach the value and dignity of work. Who will impose painful consequences, not because they hate their children but because they love them so.

Incidentally, that may explain some features of how God treats you. Like me, you are a work in progress. **"My son, do not make light of the Lord's discipline, and do not lose heart when he rebukes you, because the Lord disciplines those he loves, and he punishes everyone he accepts as a son"** (Hebrews 12:5,6).

Not all pain is bad. Not every no is bad. It's because God loves us. It's because he accepts us as his children.

_____

_____

_____

_____

_____

God thundered from Sinai then

God's minor children needed to know that God's demands for holiness were serious, dead serious. The Ten Commandments were not suggestions, hints, or general principles. They were commandments of iron, carved into stone tablets. They expressed the holy will of God, binding upon all. The setting for the giving of the law: Mt. Sinai, dreadful and dark, loud and terrifying.

"You have not come to a mountain that can be touched and that is burning with fire; to darkness, gloom and storm; to a trumpet blast or to such a voice speaking words that those who heard it begged that no further word be spoken to them. . . . The sight was so terrifying that Moses said, 'I am trembling with fear'" (Hebrews 12:18-21).

That experience was necessary to teach the Israelites humility before the greatness of God and trembling before the holiness of God. The commandments cannot help you gain God's favor. They demand more than you can perform, and they condemn what little you attempt. If Mt. Sinai brought God's last words, you would be sunk. You would tremble with fear too.

But that's not the mountain to which you are coming. Jesus Christ obeyed all the commandments for you and took on himself the punishment earned by your disobedience. A different mountain awaits.

_____

_____

_____

_____

_____

God smiles from Zion now

When you meet God, you will not have to relive Mt. Sinai. No more thundering. No more terror. The biblical terms *New Jerusalem* and *Mt. Zion* are metaphors for *heaven*. This is what awaits you. Soon you will see for yourself.

"But you have come to Mount Zion, to the heavenly Jerusalem, the city of the living God. You have come to thousands upon thousands of angels in joyful assembly, to the church of the firstborn, whose names are written in heaven" (Hebrews 12:22,23). The commandments have been fulfilled. The sacrifice has been made. The law has been satisfied. The anger is gone. There is now no condemnation for those who are in Christ Jesus. His love drives out all fear.

You will meet the angels, who will come not to punish you or drive you into hell. They will be your limos, lifting you up so that you can watch heaven and earth remade into paradise for you. You will join them in worship of Father, Son, and Spirit. You will meet all the other believers who have gone before you.

These are called the "firstborn," probably a reference to the fact that they, like firstborn in Israelite history, were those who had the right to inherit the family estate. Their place in heaven and yours is guaranteed by the reservations in their names written by Christ himself in his great book. God will smile at you then. You can smile now.

_____

_____

_____

_____

_____

lepers' banquet

The Northern Kingdom's capital, Samaria, was under a ruthless and relentless siege by the invading Syrian army. The people were starving. Animal heads and seedpods were fetching a high price from people who were desperate to eat something. Anything. The prophet Elisha was calm, assuring people the famine would soon be over. Sure enough, just before dusk the Lord caused the invaders to hear the imaginary sounds of an even greater army from Egypt. They fled for their lives, leaving their clothes, money, and food.

People with leprosy have nothing and, therefore, nothing to lose. A small band of them from Samaria slipped outside the walls and discovered the vacant camp. They ate their fill and made several plunder trips before a generous thought occurred to them and gave them pause: **"We're not doing right. This is a day of good news and we are keeping it to ourselves"** (2 Kings 7:9).

We Christians are only lucky lepers who have discovered that the siege of death has been lifted and have had the chance to eat our fill of the gospel. We are forgiven and immortal through faith in our Savior Jesus! This is a day of good news. We must not keep it to ourselves.

_____

_____

_____

_____

_____

December

"The Lord himself will give you a sign:
The virgin will be with child and will give
birth to a son, and will call him Immanuel."
(Isaiah 7:14)

December 1

alien in a manger?

Nonhuman, extraterrestrial species (a.k.a. "aliens") taking on human form and mingling around in the midst of us—normally, that's kind of creepy, isn't it? I mean, Hollywood has made some pretty famous and pretty scary movies and TV shows about aliens who are disguised as people.

And yet, this very concept is the way in which God set about to rescue you and me from our worst nightmare—the dread of death, destruction, and damnation. Except this—God's plan did not include the coming of some alien to be feared. Jesus came to earth not as a fake human, nor as an android. He is not an alien posing as a human. Jesus *became* human to be like us, for us, with us.

Marvel with me at the meaning and miracle of the incarnation of Jesus: **"Since the children have flesh and blood, he too shared in their humanity"** (Hebrews 2:14). He came to this world not merely to be *like* us. He came *to be* us, fully, in every way. In this marvelous way, he came to bring about a rescue in person, one that only he could do. He came to obey the laws of God and man as a man. He became human to die for the human race.

If you believe this, you are going to have a very merry Christmas.

_____

_____

_____

_____

_____

December 2

it's not the quantity

Have you ever had to attend the funeral of a child? It is surely one of the most miserable experiences in life. Parents are not supposed to have to bury their children. According to the generally accepted script of the human race, we are all supposed to live into our 90s and then have a sweet, slow decline and die peacefully in our sleep. Well, nice thought, but the human story hardly ever turns out like that.

People's time is cut short regularly. Think of all the young men who have perished on the battlefields of the centuries. Think of SIDS and childhood cancer and street violence. Realize, though, that God is still in ultimate control and that it is he who assigns meaning and mission to our lives. He is the one who assesses if we have lived long enough to fulfill the purpose for which we were created. Think of Jesus himself, whose ministry lasted only three super-short years.

Or think of his herald, John the Baptist, whose ministry was even shorter. After about 18 months, he was imprisoned. Perhaps he was waiting for a miraculous angelic jailbreak. Here's what actually happened: **"The king** [Herod Antipas] **was greatly distressed, but because of his oaths and his dinner guests, he did not want to refuse her. So he immediately sent an executioner with orders to bring John's head. The man went** [and] **beheaded John in the prison"** (Mark 6:26,27).

Welcome home, John. Mission accomplished.

_____

_____

_____

_____

I love laughing with friends

Lord, have I thanked you lately for my friends?

How you have blessed me with the circle of people who keep me sane. Honestly, I think I would go crazy if I didn't have people to bounce ideas off of, talk me off the ledge, point out my foolishness, encourage me when I'm right but too timid, make me feel like I belong, help me out in a pinch, explain things to me, give me advice, and generally magnify my good times into great times.

As I think about the dear people you have brought into my life, I get what the psalm writer was talking about when he expressed his joys not just by himself but with people he loved: **"Our mouths were filled with laughter, our tongues with songs of joy"** (Psalm 126:2). Lord, you designed laughter as an amazingly healing human activity. My friends help me lighten up and not take myself so seriously. They give me perspective on my struggles, they share things they've learned, and they help me when I am in trouble.

I don't want to be just a taker. How can I show people how much they mean to me? Please let me give as much of a lift to other people as they give to me. How can I show you how much I appreciate the gift of loving people in my life?

_____

_____

_____

_____

December 4

the beast within

TV shows and movies about werewolves and vampires are popular, but really people have always had a fascination with monster stories. Partly it's because we are scared about what evil creatures may do to us, and I think partly it's because we know there is an evil creature within us as well. There is a beast within, raging to get out. Like werewolves, we can tear and destroy; like vampires, we have felt the sick thrill of wanting to use other people for our own desires.

Jesus made this sad observation about the human condition: **"Out of the heart come evil thoughts, murder, adultery, sexual immorality, theft, false testimony, slander. These are what make a man 'unclean'"** (Matthew 15:19,20).

What to do? Go back to Christ and his cross every day to be washed of yesterday's guilt and be refreshed for today. What to do? How about meaning it every time you pray, "Lead us not into temptation, but deliver us from evil"? Pray that the Spirit who also lives within you will restrain the beast. What to do? How about choosing to model your words and actions after Christ's own, seeing people as he did, treating them as he did, talking as patiently and gently as he did.

Christ's forgiveness is greater than your sin. His Spirit is greater than the beast within you.

----

today

The shortness and unpredictability of life is a lesson that people just can't seem to learn for long. Every time people die "before their time," the community goes into shock—tornado devastation, highway collisions, gun violence, deadly accidents, fire, childhood disease. It appears a fact of human nature that we need regular jolts and reminders not to put off personal repentance and personal confession of faith in our Savior. It is imperative that the day of our death does not catch us unprepared. God's personal judgment on us at that time is irrevocable and our destiny is final.

There has never been an era when people didn't need that regular wake-up call. They certainly did during the Old Testament era: **"So, as the Holy Spirit says: 'Today, if you hear his voice, do not harden your hearts as you did in the rebellion, during the time of testing in the desert'"** (Hebrews 3:7,8). The frequent disasters and punishments that the nation of Israel experienced are a dreadful example and warning for us about growing careless and dead in our faith life. The 40 years the nation spent in the desert would not have been necessary if they had been listening to and believing the Word.

Now is the time. Today is the day, your day. Are you and your family ready?

December 6
I feel like giving up

Not long ago a man driving on the Hoan Bridge high over Milwaukee's harbor watched in horror as a woman got out of a parked car on the bridge deck, climbed over the railing, and jumped to certain death hundreds of feet below.

A great many people can identify with the despair the woman must have been feeling. Who among us can deny wanting our lives to be over during a period of misery? In America alone, over 35,000 people killed themselves last year, and at least ten times that number attempted it. Ten times *that* number probably thought seriously about doing it.

Do you know anybody on the ledge right now? Speak up. Encourage people not to jump to their deaths but to jump into the arms of the Lord Jesus.

Jesus Christ has everything we really need on this earth. He promises to strengthen and sustain us in all hardships, and he promises on his sacred honor to come back and take us to live forever in heaven. Here is his promise: **"Cast your cares on the LORD and he will sustain you; he will never let the righteous fall"** (Psalm 55:22).

December 7
the enemy

On December 7, 1941, the naval aviators of the Empire of Japan achieved total surprise in their early morning attack on Pearl Harbor. Absolutely nobody in a U.S. uniform saw it coming. In fact, even when the bombers, torpedo planes, and Zeros with their "rising sun" insignia flew directly overhead, many U.S. personnel thought it was just a training exercise.

We have an enemy brooding in hell who is more dangerous than the Empire of Japan or any earthly threat or evil all rolled into one. Satan, the prince of darkness, has committed himself to destroying the relationship that exists between believers and their Savior Jesus and fully plans to enjoy all the suffering that he can inflict on them. All too often people don't see his nasty work and are caught by surprise at the destruction he causes.

St. Paul wrote, **"Our struggle is not against flesh and blood, but against the rulers, against the authorities, against the powers of this dark world and against the spiritual forces of evil in the heavenly realms"** (Ephesians 6:12).

One of the great tragedies of Pearl Harbor is that U.S. radar operators were tracking the Japanese planes when they were still hundreds of miles north of Oahu. But the operators said little, and what they did report wasn't believed. You'd better listen to St. Paul. He's telling you the truth.

_____

_____

_____

_____

_____

December 8

waiting for the Lord

How many days are left until Christmas? Are you counting? Do you need more time to get ready, or are you young enough to be itching with impatience?

It's hard to wait, isn't it? Sometimes I'm a very impatient person—I don't like sitting around in doctors' offices, standing in long lines, or crawling in traffic.

How hard it must have been for the people of Israel to wait for the promised Messiah. As the centuries dragged on and their national fortunes sank, they must have been tempted to think that God had given up on his plan, or worse—given up on them. As the "B.C." years came to an end, they had no king, no armies, and no independence. But—**"When the time had fully come, God sent his Son, born of a woman, born under law, to redeem those under law, that we might receive the full rights of sons"** (Galatians 4:4,5).

Our God is an on-time God. He showed that his Word could be trusted about the coming of the Messiah. Through faith in him, you receive the full rights of adoption into the royal family. You can trust his promises to love, help, and forgive you too.

_____

_____

_____

_____

_____

less me, me, me

I'll tell you what. I can certainly spot selfishness in other people a lot faster than I will admit it in myself. This should come as no surprise though. What is sin but being bent inward on MeMeMe? We are all born with a brain and spirit disease that is intensely interested in *my* comfort, *my* pleasure, *my* wishes, *my* agenda, *my* feelings, *my* appetites.

"Do nothing out of selfish ambition or vain conceit, but in humility consider others better than yourselves. Each of you should look not only to your own interests, but also to the interests of others" (Philippians 2:3,4). I am convicted by those words. How far I have fallen short! How my own ego has kept me from fulfilling my calling as a servant working for his Master.

But my Master does not despise me, punish me, or throw me away. He patiently forgives me, puts me back on my feet, and calls me to selfless service over and over. Refreshed by his gospel love and thrilled by his personal example, I am inspired to find satisfaction in lifting up the people around me.

Does that sound like pious pie in the sky? Maybe. But I'm here to tell you that the times in my life when I am the happiest are not when I am getting stuff or bossing other people around. I have found that I am happiest when I am acting like Jesus, spending myself on behalf of someone else.

_____

_____

_____

_____

_____

December 10
scattered sheep

I don't do well at coping with rejection. Do you? I can still remember every rebuff I got from girls 40 years ago in high school. I can still remember insults and mockery from grade school playgrounds.

It would be completely reasonable to assume that God stops caring about people who have stopped caring about him. It would be completely reasonable to suppose that God would just dismiss with a divine shrug those who fall away: "You want to experience life without me? All right then—go to hell. See if I care." Reasonable, but not true.

Here is how God truly thinks: **"This is what the Sovereign LORD says: I myself will search for my sheep and look after them. As a shepherd looks after his scattered flock when he is with them, so will I look after my sheep. I will rescue them from all the places where they were scattered on a day of clouds and darkness"** (Ezekiel 34:11,12).

Shepherds take the well-being of their sheep personally. Jesus, the Good Shepherd, died and rose again for the good sheep *and* the bad ones, *and he does not want to lose a single one. Not even one!*

December 11

what if we're fighting all the time?

Sometimes people lament that they fight all the time, but the truth is that they like arguing. There's a kind of sick thrill in push backs, zingers, and always getting in the last word. You can deflect shame and guilt for your own sins if you can tilt the floodlights on your partner's transgressions, right?

The reverse is just as bad—holding all that anger in, saving it up for a bigger explosion later. If you can't or won't forgive it and let it go, then speak softly about what's on your mind as soon as possible. St. Paul writes, **"'In your anger do not sin': Do not let the sun go down while you are still angry, and do not give the devil a foothold"** (Ephesians 4:26,27).

The same person who coined the foolish cliché forgive and forget also gave birth to time heals all wounds. Time does nothing of the sort. It only stores up and ferments anger. Only the gospel love of Christ heals wounds. Only you can decide to let Christ calm your spirit and speak gently about what is hurting you.

_____

_____

_____

_____

celebrating Christmas, not just surviving it

The holiday letter, coming during what was supposed to be a universal happy time, was a cry of pain. "I want to celebrate Christmas, not just survive it. Help!"

Could that voice have been yours? What is it that turns a time of magic and beauty and love into an ordeal to be dreaded? Without a doubt, it's the tyranny of the "hafta." We allow other people to pile up expectations on us, and we make it worse, because of our own feelings of insecurity, by imposing even more pressure on ourselves.

If we don't get control of our month, Christmas can become a performance for which we feel judged—judged by our kids, our mothers-in-law, our coworkers, and worst of all, our own weak self-confidence. The only way out is to refocus each day on the fact that Christmas is a birthday celebration. Whose? **"When they had seen him, they spread the word concerning what had been told them about this child, and all who heard it were amazed at what the shepherds said to them. But Mary treasured up all these things and pondered them in her heart"** (Luke 2:17-19).

Before you agree to the demands of others this month, do what those early believers did. *Marvel* at the message. *Treasure* God's gift. *Ponder* the love and commitment that Christ has for you.

_____

_____

_____

_____

_____

forgive your parents

I love saying "Father, forgive me," because he always answers that prayer right away. There is no bottom, no end, no limit to Jesus' forgiveness.

But then comes the hard part—"as we forgive those who sin against us." God says he wants me to be equally as generous in forgiving other people. **"As God's chosen people, holy and dearly loved, clothe yourselves with compassion, kindness, humility, gentleness and patience. Bear with each other and forgive whatever grievances you may have against one another. Forgive as the Lord forgave you"** (Colossians 3:12,13).

It is important to appreciate all that your parents have done for you. But let's get real—they have hurt you too. They are sinners and have sinned against you. Millions of Americans have grown up in homes with parents who are alcoholics, who have sexually abused or permitted the sexual abuse of their own children, or whose adultery and betrayal broke up the household. What hurts do you still carry with you? Where do you go with that anger?

The past cannot be changed. What can be changed is how you choose to remember it. As the Lord has helped you by forgiving your sins, he can help you also to let go of your anger so it will not punish, torment, poison, or imprison you any longer. Let it go.

_____

_____

_____

_____

_____

God loves it when you worship him all by yourself—reading his Word, humming and singing hymn stanzas and Christian songs, and showing appreciation and thankfulness when you see good things happening. But he likes it as much or more when you worship him with a group of fellow believers. It shows that you are proud of him, greatly increases your chances of learning things from the wisdom and testimonies of others, and builds up your courage and self-confidence through a living fellowship.

It's the same with your prayer life. God loves to hear from you one-on-one. But he takes such delight in group prayer that he attaches special promises to the experience: **"I tell you that if two of you on earth agree on anything you ask for, it will be done for you by my Father in heaven. For where two or three come together in my name, there am I with them"** (Matthew 18:19,20).

There are many ways to do this: interceding for one another in your worship services, small-group prayer gatherings, online prayer teams, phone prayers, family time, or school groups. The beauty of it is that not only does God show special favor to that kind of praying, but you also end up with deeper friendships as a result. As Solomon wrote in Ecclesiastes 4:9,10, **"Two are better than one. . . . If one falls down, his friend can help him up."**

Do you have prayer partners?

_____

_____

_____

_____

Christ-mas is Christ-time

Are you ready for Christmas? Please don't imitate me in your shopping habits. I'm absolutely dreadful. I am a procrastinating slug who waits until the 23rd or 24th before doing everything all at once in a frenzy.

I know some of you are ready because I received Christmas cards from you before Thanksgiving. My first thought when I got the first card was, "This is a sick woman." Then, my second thought was, "This is an awesome woman to be that well organized. She is totally into it. She's not afraid of the demands of the season because she is *so* ready!"

Whether you are an early-bird shopper or a last-minute panic buyer is not all that important. What does matter is how highly you value the birth of the Son of God as a human being. John the Baptist could be blunt and to the point: **"Prepare the way for the Lord; make straight paths for him"** (Matthew 3:3).

What does that "prepare the way" metaphor actually mean? Just this—that you reflect on your sinful condition, taking responsibility for all your rebellious thoughts, words, and deeds . . . that you welcome the Word that tells you of the miracle birth . . . and that you believe with all your heart that Christ Jesus loves you personally.

_____

_____

_____

_____

_____

December 16

generosity grows, not diminishes, wealth

Fearful children who grow up in needy circumstances may develop a scarcity mind-set. The pie is always small and fixed in size—if one kid's slice is a little bigger, yours will have to be smaller. Waste nothing; fight for everything; hold on tight to what's yours.

One of the divine secrets of the universe is that our God is a God not of scarcity but of abundance. God can easily expand the pie when people are aligned with his agenda. And a big part of his resource distribution agenda is to invest freely in us so that we find joy in helping others.

Here is his promise: **"A generous man will himself be blessed"** (Proverbs 22:9); **"A generous man will prosper; he who refreshes others will himself be refreshed"** (Proverbs 11:25).

Isn't that counterintuitive? If you give money and things away, you will have less, right? No! Wrong! It will flow back into your life faster than you give it away. After all, we are all just brokers, not owners, of God's resources. Whether you invest it in ministries of the Word or in ministries of mercy, you will invite the God of abundance to keep his generosity promises.

You will like God's pie.

December 17

Mary, wife of Joseph

When the angel Gabriel came to a woman named Mary with the world's most unusual birth announcement, it may have sounded a little glamorous. "Son of the Most High God, throne of his father David, reign over the house of Jacob forever . . ." Whew! Mary must have been giddy at first.

But her role was going to cost her. Bearing the label of unwed mother was no treat in a small town. Neither was deciding to go with Joseph to register in Bethlehem for the imperial census. **"Joseph also went up from the town of Nazareth in Galilee to Judea, to Bethlehem the town of David, because he belonged to the house and line of David. He went there to register with Mary, who was pledged to be married to him and was expecting a child"** (Luke 2:4,5).

Would you like to walk or donkey ride 80 miles over some very hilly dirt roads while very pregnant? No? I didn't think so. I don't know if Mary mistimed her due date or simply decided that she couldn't bear to stay alone in Nazareth, but she made the trek nine months pregnant.

What about the trauma of going into labor in a barn, in the dark, with your carpenter/fiancé as your midwife? This woman is a hero. All generations indeed shall call her blessed.

_____

_____

_____

_____

guard your heart

Time for a little personal inventory. What is your passion? What are you chasing? What are you thinking about just before you fall asleep? What is your most valuable possession? What would you dread most to lose? What do you have the burn for?

You probably have quite a bit of sales resistance. You need to or you would go crazy in our materialistic and marketing-mad world. You know not to believe the pitch for every product and service that comes at you.

Realize that Satan is going to look for any opening or crack in your armor to push or pull you away from Christ. Use your sales resistance on Satan. **"Above all else, guard your heart, for it is the wellspring of life"** (Proverbs 4:23). Learn to distinguish his tempting voice. See his promises as lies; see his threats as empty; see his pleasures as what they really are—bribes to induce you to commit spiritual suicide.

Guard your heart by filling it with the gospel. Claim and celebrate and prize God's unconditional love. Think often of Christ's full and free forgiveness of your sins. Fuel up with the Spirit's fire. When the wellspring of your heart is healthy, all your relationships and possessions will be in the right place. More God, less Satan.

_____

_____

_____

_____

_____

mood queen

God designed men with generally bigger bodies and greater muscle mass. But he certainly didn't leave women defenseless. Most women, along with their beauty, come equipped with a tongue that can cut like a stiletto. That oral fillet knife, coupled with an unhappy heart and mood swings, can do a lot of damage to a relationship.

"Better to live in a desert than with a quarrelsome and ill-tempered wife," Solomon wrote (Proverbs 21:19). **"A quarrelsome wife is like a constant dripping"** (Proverbs 19:13). Memo to wives: be careful of your tongue. Bitter words once set free can't be sucked back down. You have the power to use words to chop a man down, but you afterward might find that he doesn't stand quite as tall anymore.

Don't nag either. You cannot change your husband. Only he can change himself, and if you make him feel small, he will resist you out of spite. If you persistently make him feel small, he will live down to your expectations. Build him up, and he may just grow up into your high praise. Just as Christ has treated you better than you deserve, soften that tongue and speak to your husband better than he deserves.

_____

_____

_____

_____

_____

the Word. nothing more. nothing less.

Every writer, er, every *good* writer, that is, knows that his or her writing will be improved by submitting the copy to an editor before it sees print. Good editors notice discrepancies, gaps in logic, misspellings, and overused words and expressions. Good editors prune, because they know that less is more. Tight writing is usually better writing.

People are eager to offer their editing services to God. They are sure that they can improve the relevance and marketability of the Bible. They like to edit out the parts they don't like, lighten up on the commandments, and call "myth" or "fiction" the parts that seem to conflict with modern scientific thought. They are fascinated by other sources of religious information and enjoy picking and choosing new stories to add to the biblical narrative.

God's Word needs no editors. God wants no editors: **"I warn everyone who hears the words of the prophecy of this book: If anyone adds anything to them, God will add to him the plagues described in this book. And if anyone takes words away from this book of prophecy, God will take from him his share in the tree of life"** (Revelation 22:18,19).

The Bible gives you straight talk straight from God. It is best taken unadulterated. In its pure state it is nothing less than the power of God for the salvation of all who believe it.

_____

_____

_____

_____

_____

I doubt that God could love me

We all sing the blues sometimes. What's in your blues song this week? Dumped? Betrayed? Broke? Hung over? Robbed? Hopeless?

It's hard to lift yourself out of the blues. Satan wants to keep you down, whispering "Loser!" in your ears. That's why God sends us friends whose words of praise or comfort can help us back on our feet.

The ultimate comforting friend is God the Holy Spirit. When I am plagued by doubts, and especially the worst of all doubts—doubts that God loves me—the Spirit reminds me of the Calvary love of Christ our Savior. He helps me believe that such a great treasure can actually be mine, that heaven can actually be my destination too.

The Bible says, **"The Spirit himself testifies with our spirit that we are God's children. Now if we are children, then we are heirs—heirs of God and co-heirs with Christ"** (Romans 8:16,17). In the Spirit you've got a friend. In your God you've got a Father.

_____

_____

_____

_____

December 22
light show

Have you ever seen the aurora borealis (or aurora australis in the Southern Hemisphere)? Sometimes called the Northern Lights, they are a spectacular light show that tends to occur around the time of the equinoxes. Highly charged particles blown around in space by solar winds are occasionally strongly attracted to the earth's magnetic pole (near to but not identical with the North Pole). The collisions between these particles and the oxygen and nitrogen atoms of the upper atmosphere cause the atoms to be "excited," and they emit energy in the form of greenish light as they calm down. Paler than the sun, they show up best at night, ghostly streaks and swirls of mysterious phosphorescence.

An even greater light show took place on Christmas Eve. It pleased God to announce the arrival of his Son on earth. But that announcement was made not to priests or princes, but to some shocked shepherds working yet another dreary third shift. Suddenly heaven opened above their dropped jaws and a multitude of the heavenly host was diverted from other duties that night to utter praise and glory in the highest.

The very best light show comes from the smile on the Baby's face in the manger. He is smiling because he likes you and has come to rescue you. **"I am the light of the world. Whoever follows me will never walk in darkness, but will have the light of life"** (John 8:12).

December 23
school of hardship

We love hero stories. We love sports and romance and war stories of talent and leadership and brilliance and beauty and charm. What are not so compelling are the stories of the training and hardship and early failures that went before.

Moses is one of God's greatest champions—leader of the exodus from Egyptian slavery, receiver of the Old Covenant on Mt. Sinai, author of five Bible books. But all that came from the last third of his life. The middle third consisted of four decades of working as a shepherd boy for a bedouin in the Sinai Desert. But God knew that he would never have grown into a great leader if he had not first attended the school of hardship.

Moses grew up a pampered prince in the royal Egyptian court. He could have averted his eyes from the cruelty of Egyptian enslavement of the Israelites. He could have enjoyed an easy life and stayed in the palace. Instead, **"by faith Moses, when he had grown up, refused to be known as the son of Pharaoh's daughter. He chose to be mistreated along with the people of God rather than to enjoy the pleasures of sin for a short time. He regarded disgrace for the sake of Christ as of greater value than the treasures of Egypt, because he was looking ahead to his reward"** (Hebrews 11:24-26).

Don't be afraid of God's school of hardship. He may have a special mission planned for you.

_____

_____

_____

_____

God's perfect timing

"O little town of Bethlehem, how still we see thee lie!
Above thy deep and dreamless sleep the silent stars go by.
Yet in thy dark streets shineth the everlasting light.
The hopes and fears of all the years are met in thee tonight."

God did some amazing things in that particular little place on the face of the earth. What happened in that Bethlehem stable was nothing less than the personal arrival of the One who will keep you and me out of hell. For millennia men and women had lived and died, waiting and hoping that this day would come.

God had told his people about what would happen in little Bethlehem centuries earlier through the prophet Micah: **"But you, Bethlehem Ephrathah, though you are small among the clans of Judah, out of you will come for me one who will be ruler over Israel, whose origins are from of old, from ancient times"** (Micah 5:2).

Isn't it just like God to do his world-changing work in a little town, in the middle of the night, in an animal shelter? May the light streaming from the stable touch your face this Christmas and make you smile.

_____

_____

_____

_____

_____

December 25, Christmas Day
with childlike awe

It really helps to be a kid at Christmastime, doesn't it? You don't have to nag or persuade kids to be pumped about Christmas. In fact, if anything, you have to rein them in a little bit. When you're a grown-up, getting excited about anything gets harder year after year, doesn't it? Each year we get a little more cynical, a little more blasé. Dare I say it—sometimes even the Christmas message doesn't seem quite so fresh and stirring as it used to be.

Let's not let Satan, the ultimate Grinch, steal our joy. I'll tell you what—let's listen to the Christmas story this year as though we are small children, hearing it for the first time. Let's let the outrageousness and beauty and love of that holy night give us the shivers all over again: **"Do not be afraid. I bring you good news of great joy that will be for all the people. Today in the town of David a Savior has been born to you; he is Christ the Lord"** (Luke 2:10,11).

Kids love Christmas because they figure they are going to get something they like. Kids love Christmas because they feel important and love to be spoiled by adults who love them. Think for just a minute of what Jesus came to give you—forgiveness for your sins, love to drown out the hate, the supreme honor of being called a child of God, and immortality to lift you out of your grave.

All this was wrapped in humble strips of cloth. Amazing!

_____

_____

_____

_____

_____

December 26
humble and ambitious?

Can you be ambitious in church life, especially in making career plans? The first and quickest answer is no, of course not. Ambition belongs in the business world. The church world prizes humility. You should be on your knees, confessing your unworthiness and averting your eyes. Wait around for someone higher up to notice you and ask you to do something.

Actually not. The truth is, God doesn't mind if believers with talents and ambition aspire to leadership. He even encourages it: **"Here is a trustworthy saying: If anyone sets his heart on being an overseer, he desires a noble task. Now the overseer must be above reproach"** (1 Timothy 3:1,2). The Greek word for *overseer* could also be translated *bishop*. It means someone who exercises a supervisory role in carrying out the mission of the church.

You better be ready. The rest of 1 Timothy chapter 3 outlines the lofty standards and requirements in Christian character and ability that the church should insist on in its leaders. But Paul's basic message is one of encouragement for younger people to dream big, be ambitious for the kingdom, and seek to use gifts that God himself gave. The church is always desperately in need of good leaders, and you may be one of God's answers. Go for it!

But still be humble.

_____

_____

_____

_____

act like the royal priests you are

One of the words about life in America that I have come to dislike is *consumer*. I wouldn't like that word applied to me, as though my principal function on earth is just to *consume,* use up resources. It seems to define me as just another potential customer to someone who wants to sell me something, just a user of goods and services, just a me-oriented materialist.

God doesn't want you to settle for being just a consumer of religion either. He has bigger dreams for you than simply to be a pew sitter, just a passive consumer of religious experiences, critiquing a Sunday service the way you and your friends might critique a movie. When you were brought to faith in Christ, you were drafted into God's ministry organization with the title "royal priest."

"To him who loves us and has freed us from our sins by his own blood, and has made us to be a kingdom and priests to serve his God and Father—to him be glory and power for ever and ever!" (Revelation 1:5,6).

Make it a priority to find out what being a royal priest means. Act like one.

_____

_____

_____

_____

_____

December 28

live within your means

My late father-in-law is my hero for a number of reasons. I remember him especially for his self-control. He used to sigh about wanting a boat. After his children were grown, people would urge him to get the boat he'd been dreaming of. "No," he'd say. "Why not?" "Because then I'd just want something else." For him, the boat was the edge where he knew he needed to stop in order to live within his means.

Way too many people feel terrific pressure to pretend to be somebody who they're not. They drive themselves into debt to maintain their image. God isn't fooled: **"Better to be a nobody and yet have a servant than pretend to be somebody and have no food"** (Proverbs 12:9).

Practice some phrases with me: "I can't afford it." "Maybe someday." "I don't need to impress her." "It'll have to wait."

Jesus Christ accepted you as you are. You can accept yourself as you are. People will accept you as you are. My father-in-law lived a very happy life without ever owning a boat. Are you possibly overspending so that you can pretend to be bigger than you are?

_____

_____

_____

_____

_____

December 29

be patient

For a society that claims to reject organized crime, we Americans sure like gangster movies and television, don't we? From Al Capone to Tony Soprano, we lap up the stories of revenge, violence, and naked power.

What is it about those stories that we find so attractive? Well, for one thing, we all groan at the many injustices that the small and weak and unconnected must suffer. The judicial system often seems to work too slowly and inefficiently, and too many criminals get away with their crimes. It would go so much faster if we just took matters into our own hands (or so we fantasize).

It takes no brains to seek revenge. It takes strength and character to forgive another. **"A man's wisdom gives him patience; it is to his glory to overlook an offense"** (Proverbs 19:11).

Need help to think like this? Reflect on how God has forgiven you. The greatness of God is shown in his creative and sustaining power, but it shines even more brightly in the way in which his love triumphed over condemnation. You can choose to forgive, as the Lord has chosen to forgive you. Which sinful fool in your life needs some mercy from you? Give it today.

my son despises me

Every parent would love to be able to freeze time.

There are some moments when your kids are little that you wish you could make last forever. They need you. They adore you. They play with you, giggle for you, pose for pictures with you, and more or less listen to you.

But we are not given these little treasures to own and control forever. We are entrusted with them to teach them, train them, raise them right, and then let go. But sometimes the nightmare ensues—they grow up and then reject us and our values and our faith. Do you know anyone who feels King David's gloom? **"A messenger came and told David, 'The hearts of the men of Israel are with Absalom.' Then David said to all his officials who were with him in Jerusalem, 'Come! We must flee, or none of us will escape from Absalom'"** (2 Samuel 15:13,14).

God himself knows what it is like to have rebellious and disobedient children. All we can do is do what he does: love unconditionally, keep communication open, hold to our faith and principles, and wait.

Everyone, rebellious children included, has a conscience that gives no peace without Christ. The words of the gospel once implanted in a heart can be remembered. Prodigal sons sometimes do return.

Lord, you made me a winner

I have to admit I was worried, Lord. It was such a big challenge! I wasn't sure if I was up to it. Remember all those prayers? Of course you do. Nothing escapes your notice or memory. It took such a long time. I admit also that I was worried. I thought maybe I was on my own. But you taught me a lot through this whole thing—you taught me patience, tenacity, and toughness. You made me wait, but you came through for me.

I know some of my friends think I did this, but you and I know the truth. **"Not to us, O Lord, not to us but to your name be the glory, because of your love and faithfulness"** (Psalm 115:1). This experience will stay with me and fortify me for the next challenge. Please help me remember these days when I am tempted to panic later in my life.

Lord, I am thrilled to be useful to you in all your kingdom work. I can't always figure out what you're up to, but in hindsight everything seems to fall into place. The older I get, the more I see that you can be trusted to manage everything. Thank you for developing me, growing me, maturing me. Perhaps there is a struggling soul nearby that I can encourage for you?

_____

_____

_____

_____

Devotions for Special Days

Good Friday

it is finished

One of the two most important days in human history seemed pretty ordinary to some Roman soldiers. It was their grim duty to perform three public executions in Jerusalem the day before the Passover Sabbath. They carried out their assignment with macabre and practiced efficiency, hammering the nails into their victims' hands and feet.

Two screamed their pain and hatred. The One in the middle bore his suffering mainly in silence, once speaking to ask his Father for forgiveness for his tormentors. As Jesus was dying, it began to dawn on the noncom who was in charge of the crucifixion detail just who it was who hung before him: **"When the centurion, who stood there in front of Jesus, heard his cry and saw how he died, he said, 'Surely this man was the Son of God!'"** (Mark 15:39).

That centurion went back to his barracks that day carrying three things: his share of the clothes the soldiers had taken from the executed men, the terrible guilt that they had crucified not only an innocent man but the very Son of God, and a gospel message of forgiveness that extended even to murderers like him.

There are many takeaways for you and me from this incredible scene, but two matter more than all the rest. First, the crucifixion of Christ shows us how bad our sins really are. Second, his crucifixion shows us that his purchase of forgiveness for all was successful. It is finished. Satan is finished. Christ has made you free.

_____

_____

_____

you are immortal

It's human nature to take important things for granted, is it not? When you're sailing along in your car and suddenly see bright red taillights just ahead, you don't even think, "I wonder if the laws of friction will apply today?" You just slam on the brakes. Or when you get up in the morning, you don't wonder, "Might this be the day that the gravitational pull of the earth lets go and I just slowly drift off into space?" You just step out on the sidewalk and assume that your feet will stick to the ground. We tend not to pay much attention to the universal principles that hold our lives together. But what if Easter hadn't happened?

If Christ has not been raised, everything you think you know about Christianity begins to crack and crumble, like a building with no foundation in a windstorm. If Christ has not been raised, here's the scariest part of all: Your sins remain unforgiven and you will be judged for them. Those who have fallen asleep in Christ are lost. If only for this life we have hope in Christ, we are to be pitied more than all men, Paul said.

But get this: The Bible says, **"But Christ has indeed been raised from the dead, the firstfruits of those who have fallen asleep"** (1 Corinthians 15:20). Christ Jesus is the first installment of the resurrection. Because he burst out of his grave in soul and body, you and I are immortal. His resurrection guarantees your forgiveness. His resurrection guarantees yours.

_____

_____

_____

_____

Jesus had a mom too

I know for a fact that Jesus never gave his mom a box of chocolates for Mother's Day.

Both the cacao bean and a national day of maternal recognition were still many centuries in the future when Jesus lived. But he loved his mom dearly, even to the point of thinking of her needs while he was suffering in agony on the cross. It is a beautiful feature of God's plan of salvation for us that our Savior was both fully human and fully divine. Jesus had a birth, childhood, and adolescence just like everyone else. He knew all about growing up with siblings. It was his heavenly Father's plan that the Son should have a human mother and be as dependent on her as any other baby.

During Jesus' lifetime, his very ordinary-looking background was a stumbling block for people expecting more pizzazz from their hoped-for Messiah. **"'Isn't this Mary's son and the brother of James, Joseph, Judas and Simon? Aren't his sisters here with us?' And they took offense at him"** (Mark 6:3).

I hope you don't. Jesus' earthly humility and ordinary upbringing qualify him to be our Substitute, stepping in for us to provide perfect obedience to his Father and receive our condemnation from his Father.

As you thank God for your mom on this special Sunday in May, send a little prayer of thanks to God also for providing such a wonderful mother for our Savior.

_____

_____

_____

_____

Father's Day
fathers are important

You can forgive us fathers for feeling a little second-class if we compare the national mini-hubbub over Father's Day to the huge emotional outpouring given to mothers in the second week of May. Hallmark sales in mid-June are a small fraction of the previous month.

Much of that is our fault. Families are sick when children disrespect their fathers or when fathers are abusive, neglectful, or absent. Entire societies get sick when this happens on a large scale.

The nation of Israel was no exception; dysfunctional fatherhood was a blight. God promised to send a second Elijah (that was John the Baptist) whose prophetic ministry brought about repentance and new energy for family renewal. **"See, I will send you the prophet Elijah before that great and dreadful day of the LORD comes. He will turn the hearts of the fathers to their children, and the hearts of the children to their fathers"** (Malachi 4:5,6).

Our society badly needs the witness of God's Word to regain a sense of appreciation for his designs for marriage and the raising of children. Fathers, don't sit around sulking, waiting for the cards and gifts. Commit to your woman and lift her up in honor. Support, mentor, and lead your children. Malachi wants you to know that you will have God's mighty Spirit to help you.

Thanksgiving Day
backward and forward

This week our nation pauses. Most businesses and schools close. Kids come home from school with Pilgrim artwork, black buckled hats, and stories of Squanto. There will be much turkey, pumpkin pie, and football. There may even be some giving of thanks.

I don't mean just being "thankful," i.e., a generic, warm and fuzzy, slightly guilty awareness that we live pretty well. This day provides a great opportunity to ponder a direct object for the transitive verb *to thank*. Thanking *Somebody* who makes good things happen is learned behavior, like telling the truth, like honoring a promise, like staying faithful to a flawed spouse even when it's hard, like sticking to a job and finishing it.

The Bible helps us with deep insights into cause and effect in our lives. Are our treasures the result of our hard labor? . . . of blind, random luck? . . . of destiny or kismet or karma? No, actually not. Everything good in our lives comes as a result of direct intervention by a loving Creator and by a Redeemer who loves to do good things for his children. **"Every good and perfect gift is from above, coming down from the Father of the heavenly lights** [i.e., the stars]**"** (James 1:17).

Do you have time this week to take inventory of the treasures in your life? As you look backward and thank your Benefactor, has it occurred to you that you can look forward with the same gratitude and joyful anticipation? The One who made your past better is already planting gifts in your future.

_____

_____

_____

_____

About Mark Jeske

Mark Jeske brings the good news of Christ to viewers of *Time of Grace* in weekly 30-minute programs broadcast across the U.S. and around the world. Mark is senior pastor at St. Marcus Lutheran Church, a thriving multicultural congregation in Milwaukee, Wisconsin. Mark has also written one volume of the People's Bible Commentary series, *Time of Grace: A Devotional Companion, Messiah Is Coming, Straight Talk: Answers from God's Word,* and dozens of devotional booklets on various topics. He and his wife, Carol, have four adult children.

About Time of Grace

STRAIGHT TALK. REAL HOPE.

Time of Grace is an international Christian outreach media ministry that is dedicated to sharing the good news of Jesus Christ with as many people as possible. The ministry uses television, print, and the Internet to share the gospel with people across the country and around the world. On the television program *Time of Grace,* Pastor Mark Jeske presents Bible studies in terms that people can relate to and apply to their lives. (For a complete broadcast schedule, visit timeofgrace.org.) Watch *Time of Grace* or visit timeofgrace.org, where you will find the program via streaming video and audio podcasts, as well as study guides, daily devotions, a prayer wall, and additional resources. You can also call 800.661.3311 for more information.

TIME OF GRACE®
WITH PASTOR MARK JESKE

P.O. BOX 301
MILWAUKEE, WI 53201
800.661.3311 | 414.562.8463
info@timeofgrace.org
timeofgrace.org

5473031R00211

Made in the USA
San Bernardino, CA
08 November 2013